1987

Telemarketing Campaigns That Work!

Telemarketing Campaigns That Work!

Murray Roman

McGraw-Hill Book Company

New York   St. Louis   San Francisco   Auckland
Bogotá   Hamburg   Johannesburg   London   Madrid
Mexico   Montreal   New Delhi   Panama   Paris
São Paulo   Singapore   Sydney   Tokyo   Toronto

Library of Congress Cataloging in Publication Data

Roman, Murray, date.
  Telemarketing campaigns that work!

  Includes index.
  1. Telephone selling. I. Title.
HF5438.3.R637 1983   658.8'5   82-20385
ISBN 0-07-053598-1

  345678910 VBVB 09876

ISBN 0-07-053598-1

The editors for this book were William R. Newton and Esther Gelatt,
the designer was Jules Perlmutter, and the production
supervisor was Teresa F. Leaden. It was set in Electra
by Bi-Comp, Incorporated.

To Eva,

a loving partner who brings
very special insight, soul, and inspiration
to a people business

About the Author

MURRAY ROMAN, the leading innovator and world-renowned authority in the exploding field of tele-marketing, is chairman of Campaign Communications Institute, Inc. (CCI), headquartered in New York City. His company has franchise operations in France and Australia and is responsible for telemarketing campaigns in Europe, Asia, and Latin America. He is also the author of the classic work in the field, *Telephone Marketing: How to Build Your Business by Telephone*, already translated into German, Japanese, and French.

Contents

Preface

This is a book of case histories, examples, and ideas about how you can utilize the telephone to increase sales, recognition, or acceptance of your products or services. In order to make it more readable and to avoid "I" strain, it is often written in the third person. All the examples are true; all the quotations are accurate; all the stories are documented.

In the beginning, there was only an idea, a concept. It became reality for me in 1962 when, under the direction of a driving Lee Iacocca, Ford supported a 20-million-call program to produce a controlled flow of qualified leads (two per day for each salesperson!) for its 23,000-dealer sales force to beef up its sales, profits, and share of the automotive market.

The "how to's" of strategic and market-planning assembly lines, list segmentation, and creative scripting all came later; first off it was "how to" recruit, train, control, and invent accountability systems to manage the army of thousands of unskilled "communicators" spread across the United States to fit the needs of such a huge, demanding sales campaign. With no previous experience to go by, and with a total rejection of the telephone "boiler room" practices of the period, we created a standardized script that allowed us to measure call responses accurately and to project a favorable corporate image.

We developed production control systems and report forms for daily data feedback and validation. We also developed a duplicatable training format to fit varied market situations, recruiting people with the ability to "smile as you dial" as the only criterion for employment. Accountability for every lead was immediate! With a 24-hour delivery turnaround system, salespeople wasted no time in expressing their enthusiasm for quick sales or decrying every rejection by the prospect! As a program by-product, what we observed then as a unique learning experience is common knowledge today: that is, the deterioration and lack of motivation of the American salesforce. A good lead in the hands of a poor salesperson was just as self-defeating and real in 1962 as it is today. This factor alone may be the motivating spur to the growth of telemarketing today.

After Ford's pioneering efforts, any other call program seemed small by comparison. In introducing *The New York Times* to 11 Western states (500,000 calls in 1963), we learned about list segmentation and that "though the medicine is great, the patient sometimes dies": the phone produced the highly selected subscribers, but the shortage of advertisers buried the new venture. Too many leads can also kill a program: early on we learned that the hard way, from the now-defunct Railway Express Agency (REA). We then went on the phones to do it right for Pacific Intermountain Express (PIE)! More and more programs aimed at consumers at home: Dr. Suess children's books for Grolier; election and fund-raising campaigns for local, regional, and national political candidates; mail-order merchandise for the Amsterdam Company and Spiegels; insurance conservation for National Liberty Life Insurance; sales appointments for Encyclopaedia Britannica; and our "one and only" try at land sales with a low-key consumerist approach for General Development Corp.—all this became part of our experience in those early, difficult years. Reader's Digest, Silver Burdett, Time-Life Books, McGraw-Hill, and Xerox's University Microfilm introduced us to the educational and institutional marketplace in the late 60s. We pioneered the sale of textbooks to colleges for American Books, Van Nostrand division, during the period. The economic crunch of the 70s allowed us to merchandise the American Management Associations' seminars and multimedia materials aimed at business decision makers. Then, as now, AMA's many tools for management education spur our creative juices, because they always advocate multiple testing of any viable idea—and have the courage to back it! Then, with U.S. Steel, Bell & Howell, Motorola, and Pitney Bowes, came a new emphasis on targeting leads for industrial marketers. Finally, it was Norman Cousins and publishing history. Because of his generosity as a client and public fame as a personality, "telemarketing" was suddenly socially acceptable! It had lost its pariah image for intellectuals and had proved its ability to generate profit as an alternative marketing medium for *Saturday Review* and other publishers.

Since 1970, when Pete Hoke, publisher of *Direct Marketing* magazine gave us our first platform before a business audience at Direct Marketing Day in New York City, telephone as a marketing tool has come full circle. From the early, tottering steps of babyhood and childhood, past puberty and the teens, in our personal experience, it's been an organized practice for less than 30 years. Today it's hailed as the "booming medium for the 80s," the "fastest growing and exploding communications tool," and the "key to the knowledge business" by business executives everywhere, including the multi-million-dollar advertising campaigns of AT&T! Our own organization, CCI, serviced more than 50 of the "Fortune 500" companies, as their interest in probing marketing alternatives became necessary for further growth in the 70s.

Since Bob Stone had already promulgated his "Bible" (the Old Testament!) for the direct-marketing industry, we were left with creating the Eleven Commandments for telemarketers in our book *Telephone Marketing*,[1] published in 1976. That book motivates readers to believe in the benefits of a phone campaign and sets out the step-by-step procedures to follow for successful management. This new work, then, represents the next step in our biblical analogy; it hopefully provides the parables, teaching some of the subtleties of the subject through the particular cases and the lessons that can be drawn from them.

The casebook approach allows us to fill in some of the elements that could not be covered in our introductory book. *Telephone Marketing* provides the basic facts and an organizational structure for decision making within the context of the reader's own business. By demonstrating how these decisions have been made in the past by others, we can clarify the weighing and balancing process that is required on the management level. A major theme in our earlier work is that the telephone communicator must have the decisions on calling procedures fully predetermined for him or her. The executive contemplating telephone marketing, though, is the one who must make the judgment calls in setting up or determining the nature of the operation.

There is a good deal more information and illustration we've offered the reader here via the case history lessons we've learned. For instance:

■ How to decide whether to go into a telemarketing program at all. Is it right for your products or services? For each case presented, the specifics of why the business in question adopted the campaign will provide a framework of consideration for the reader's own needs.

■ Can I do it myself, or do I need help? Case histories of some homegrown operations, some with consultants involved and some in which the entire project was essentially handed over to my organization, CCI, will allow comparative evaluations of the options open to the reader. A checklist of considerations you will be able to determine for yourself (for example, Who will run the program? How much can I invest in this effort? Do I have the physical facilities to set up a similar phone operation in-

---

[1] Murray Roman, *Telephone Marketing: How to Build Your Business by Telephone*, McGraw-Hill, New York, 1976.

house? Is proper personnel available?) will help crystallize the case study learning experience.

■ What are the specific parameters for testing procedures and script development? The reader might reasonably ask how much testing to do—when are the results good enough? And what should the script say? How can the presentation be organized to convey the necessary information at an effective pace, maintaining comprehensibility and building up to the sale?

There is a good deal of straightforward advice on scripts in the first book. By presenting one or two successful scripts in their entirety, so that the reader can analyze program scripts that didn't work compared with effective versions, we hope to give the reader a sense of what the choices are and what script devices tend to get results.

■ Further points with regard to communicator personnel are also included. The fairly thorough lessons of the first book are recapped, although with some additional fine points with appropriate examples. For instance, what about the effect of regional accents, particularly if you are calling from a central facility far from the intended customer? Does the sex of the communicator affect sales, based on the traditional biases of the consumer? Does a young, college-student-type voice make the offer seem less serious to the listener?

Our successful case histories provide a visible and obvious response to all these questions, since our calls are placed from central workshops using young students—men and women interchangeably.

■ Specific points on getting through to the right person once you have the right list. For business customers, how do I get past the secretary to speak to the executive who will buy my product or seminar program? Will the use of a tape message fit my needs? For consumers at home, do I want the man or the woman of the house as the audience for subscription sales or funds solicitations—or doesn't it matter?

I see this casebook as a companion volume to *Telephone Marketing*, covering the same areas and making many of the same points, but coming at the subject from a decidedly different angle. The first book focuses on delineating the merits of telemarketing and organizing the reader's further inquiries. This casebook is a response to those inquiries, presenting pertinent past experience to demonstrate and elucidate the theoretical framework of the first book.

Our casebook gives us the opportunity to give more of the texture of phone marketing. The reader will get a feel for the enterprise through the "war stories" of previous campaigns. The first book was, of necessity, relatively dry. Now we can take more of a storyteller's approach, introducing specific situations with real people and products and deriving the morals and lessons to be learned from the evidence presented.

This can have several advantages. For one, it may be more interesting. In addition, businesspeople like to hear about how other companies spent their money and how it turned out. Each case offers you the opportunity to ask, "Is that what I would have done?" and to test your knowledge against that of the user or agency. Furthermore, many companies conduct aggressive marketing campaigns and offer high-powered or at least interesting goods or services (to name a few: home computers and word processors; special insurance policies and even diapers for incontinent senior citizens; exotic tours or ski lodge vacations or costly collectibles and art folios). Clearly political candidates, Planned Parenthood, and Norman Cousins each have their own individual charm. Now the seed company owner in Dubuque gets the opportunity to apply to his or her sales needs the methods used by the "big companies."

By concentrating on our firsthand insights into the problems that have been tackled in the past, with some quotes from customers describing campaigns from their viewpoint, we attempt a more personal rapport with the reader. We start with a brief introduction and overview, give one case in detail in all its aspects, and then focus on the major distinctive elements in each of the other cases. Exhibits and illustrations in the form of the actual numbers achieved and materials employed provide important hard data for analysis. We've also included supporting charts, multimedia support materials, telephone information, FCC decisions, consumer surveys, and recent ethical guidelines to add to the continuing learning experience CCI and I share with you.

In a study undertaken for us in 1980, the Arthur D. Little Company concluded that "Pots," plain ole telephone service, would still be our marketing tool for at least 10 years, through 1990. They emphasized the interest in ADRMP, or automatic dialer recorded message players (a lively media target in the late 70s!), the potential for computerized voice recognition equipment, and the emergence of AT&T as the major competitor to all telemarketers. To us, these developments represent the "right church, wrong pew!"

So far, the automatic dialers haven't boomed—and are mostly a bust. Consumers and the marketplace turned them off—but this is the era for "voice mail"—witness the marketing by American Express and Exxon of automatic circuitry that practically eliminates the need for the "old-fashioned" telephone answering service. Or AT&T's promotion of the "900" direct-response taped message system that will one day soon challenge the volatile, labor-intensive "800" response phone centers, because of AT&T's ability to control and manipulate central electronic switch systems. Voice recognition has come a long way, though the vocabulary is still inadequate and the equipment too costly. In the 1980s the Bell System has certainly emerged from its isolated, cocoonlike emphasis on "hardware and equipment" to underwrite a total, worldwide concentration on "telemarketing as the key medium for the knowledge business." Their unregulated subsidiary "American Bell" will be pushing the sale of "enhanced services," all tied to phone lines, reaching into 96 percent of America's homes and offices. This huge revolution in how the world's largest company does business guarantees the continuing explosion of the telephone as a business medium and our dependence on it as the critical tool for business-to-home and business-to-business communication. Whether by cable, microwave, or satellite—laser beam, "glass wires," or sound waves—the ubiquitous, familiar handset or hot-selling, computerized "Look Ma, no wires" instrument will be with us. We hope this book will help you to make better use of it—while there's still plenty of time to profit by the experiences we've detailed for your reading and study.

A work such as this casebook of telemarketing experiences over the last 25 years would, of necessity, represent the hard work, trial and sacrifice, knowledge, expertise, insight, and skills of countless people who have shared in the development "histories" with us. I was fortunate to be there at the right time to "put it all together" and speak out for them—so that you, the reader, might share in our learning process and then add your own to the future growth of the phone medium.

Telemarketing as we've practiced it certainly proved that "assembly and production lines" can work with machinelike efficiency—but we've also emphasized that people communicate personally! We still find that a CCI communicator with a good, bright personality produces more positive responses by phone than an archaic, tightly controlling, "blinders only" system! Production lines do produce automations—and machines aren't built to provide tender loving care! The telephone in the hands of a skilled, smiling "communicator" will still outproduce anyone simply "reading" a preset script! A warm personality over the phone projects *caring*— and that's the quality we've tried most to bring to these case histories. We hope future telemarketers will carry on with our number-one priority: TLC as the key to using the phone as a tool for business.

This book is for those who believe in TLC, or tender loving care too, and is dedicated to the telephone communicator who practices it.

Murray Roman

Acknowledgments

We acknowledge our debt to the loyal and devoted clients and the direct-marketing agencies that have brought them to us, thus making these case histories possible. Our deep gratitude to Norman Cousins, Dick Cremer of Montgomery Ward/Signature agency, Woody Manzer of New York Telephone, Jim Hayes and John Budlong of the American Management Associations. Bob Blair of IBM, John Schlactenhaufen formerly of Xerox, Richard J. Mahoney of Monsanto, Vern Anderson of A. B. Dick, Jim Corsey of ABA, Tom Wickersham of ITT, Frank Loscalzo of Citibank, and Jerry Turk for the Louisiana National Bank. Also Bob Perkins, Wyatt Stewart, and Rod Smith of the national Republican Senatorial campaign committees, Larry Grossman of PBS, and Donald David of the Ford Foundation—all of whose support and cooperation guaranteed the successful telemarketing campaigns this book describes.

We express our appreciation for the advice and counsel of Dr. George Brown, formerly with Ford, now with the National Conference Board; Dr. Blaine Cook, formerly with Ford and TWA, now professor of communications at the University of Minnesota; Herbert L. Golden of Bankers Trust Company; Lee Epstein of Mailman, Inc., a leading direct marketer and confidant; and our advisers, Maurice Austin, Solomon Berkowitz, and Ralph Perlberger, for their friendship and guidance every step of the way.

We specifically acknowledge the scholarship, determination, and writing skills of Steve Morgenstern, Fred Borden, Garry Mitchell, Aldyn McKean, and all the CCI* staff—communicators, account supervisors, and managers; most certainly our management team led by Jim Trager, who often met the pressures of my diversion of resources and people, under the urgency of writing deadlines, with utmost patience and under-

* Campaign Communications Institute of America, Inc., the telemarketing agency of which the author is founder and chairman.

standing. A very special thanks to Barry Levine, who organized the manuscript, and Karen Hamilton, who typed and "word processed" every word in this book, and to Carl Johnson and Rosemary Greenaway, who finally "put it to bed." Also Bill Sabin and Bill Newton of McGraw-Hill, who produced and nurtured it!

Our son, Ernan, devoted much creative time and energy to the final product before you—his "introduction" launches this work with an insightful and challenging overview. I hope he's as proud of the final case histories that he and Rosemary Bolgar, CCI's vice president of Health services, Michael Violanti, vice president of development and consulting services, Devin Scott, vice president of financial services, and many others brought into being as I am of their achievement in making it all happen for so many memorable programs, products, services, and people.

Keys to the Management of Telemarketing Programs

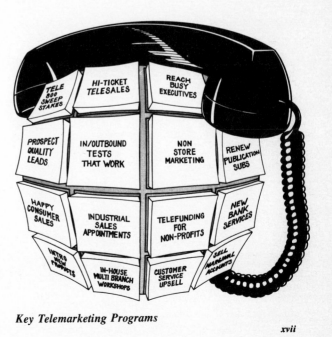

Key Telemarketing Programs

Introduction

Ernan Roman

Even if you weren't a business executive, you'd know that direct-response marketing has boomed in the past decade. As a consumer, you've been deluged by colorful pieces of mail trying to sell you everything from magazine subscriptions to garden plants to commemorative coins. Charities and political candidates have probably contacted you to solicit contributions. You're also being reached at your place of business by direct-response marketers eager to supply your needs for equipment and services.

According to the Direct Marketing Association, the direct-response business was at or over $100 billion in 1980. That's a lot of mail, and it's also an enormous number of telephone calls. We project that each United States household that can be reached by telephone will receive an average of 25 phone solicitation calls in 1983 and that the number will continue to climb upward from the 19-per-household figure that applied in 1978.

Why has direct-response marketing grown so dramatically? Just look at the costs of doing business by more traditional methods for the answer. The cost of having an industrial salesperson out on the road is astronomical—over $200 per sales call at this writing and jumping upward with each new rise in travel and salary expenses. Costs at retail establishments are skyrocketing also, as salaries, rents, and other operating expenses go through the roof.

Like any other business function, sales must now be handled with maximum efficiency. In the same way that automation has kept manufacturing costs down, nonhuman "salespeople"—in the form of direct-marketing vehicles—are helping to keep sales costs under control. And the buying public, responding to the lower prices and greater shopping convenience offered by direct marketing, has for the most part accepted this development enthusiastically.

The use of electronic media in direct-response marketing is where the action is today, particularly through the electronic wizardry of the telephone system. We tend to take the telephone's capabilities for granted. But stop to consider that this familiar device can reach nearly everyone in the consumer or business market, anywhere in the world, in a matter of seconds. From such a perspective, the omnipresent telephone receiver becomes more than an appliance—it is a powerful marketing tool. And this vast electronic network is already in place, tried and tested and ready to aid a wide variety of businesses to distribute their goods and services.

In this book we will focus on reaching out and into people's homes and businesses by telephone, presenting an offer or request to them directly, and motivating an immediate response. This approach has proven an effective strategy for such major corporations as IBM, Xerox, Montgomery Ward, Citicorp, and dozens of others, as well as nonprofit institutions including the Republican National Committee and the Public Broadcasting System.

It is worth reviewing some of the factors that have led marketers like these to "discover" telephone during the past few years. Certainly the most important factor is costs. Continuing inflation over the past five years has forced astronomical cost increases for all traditional selling and marketing media.

- Direct mail
    Bulk rates—up 70 percent
    First-class—up 55 percent
- Sales force (as noted)—up between 75 and 80 percent

Overall telephone costs, which had been fairly stable, increased 25 percent in June 1981 as the result of phone company tariffs, and they continue upward.

Another prime factor in direct marketers' added use of telephone has been intensifying competition. As a result of economic pressures, the fight to expand or even maintain market share is becoming more intense. And competitors are not limited to the traditional companies in a given industry. The players now include foreign companies and domestic corporations that have expanded their scope beyond historical boundaries. In the search for new markets, companies such as Mobil, Sears, Roebuck, AT&T, Merrill Lynch, Citicorp, and American Express have all expanded their definitions of "What business are we in?" The line between their traditional marketing stance and today's financial conglomerate becomes blurred and disappears!

These factors have driven marketers to seek new ways to reach their prospects. There are five special characteristics that have made the telephone one of the most important alternatives in today's business climate. Let's look at each of them in turn.

1. Person-to-Person Communication   Next to a live salesperson, telephone is truly the most direct and personal direct-response medium available today. Telephone provides the most vital quality of the personal sales call—two human beings in a "one-to-one" dialogue—normally on a cost-effective basis! Our decision maker (business or consumer) demands personalized attention. In fact, for many industries, as the lines differentiating one company from another begin to blur, the customer-service orientation of the telephone contact may become the major difference stimulating a prospect to do business with one firm as opposed to another. People will respond if given the opportunity. "When the phone rings, you answer it." Structure the use of the medium to encourage "involvement," and results will improve dramatically.

2. Immediacy and Flexibility   In an interactive conversation, there is always "feedback" from the person being called. This basic characteristic offers two benefits that are fundamental yet often overlooked.

Immediacy. The response from telephone prospects is immediate—though sometimes unnerving—allowing quick management changes in strategy, price, and product. Alert managers can take advantage of the constant information flow. Market research information is an incremental by-product of the telephone conversation. Specific market research questions can and should be woven into the communicator script.

Flexibility. Telephone provides marketers with flexibility to test different offers and creative strategies. Changes can also be immediate and inexpensive. There are no printing or production costs involved in testing different approaches on an ongoing basis. For example, communicator scripts for a high-volume telemarketer such as *TV Guide* are revised on a monthly basis to reflect seasonality, the economy, price advantages, new rates, and so on. This flexibility also creates the opportunity to structure the multiple product offerings you will find in these case histories.

3. Complementary and Incremental Effect   Telephone works best in combination with other media. Telephone follow-up to a direct mailing will generate an incremental response $2\frac{1}{2}$ to 10 times the response achieved by mail alone. For example:

Direct-mail response:	2%
Telephone response:	12 to 15%
Combined response:	20 to 30%

This lift in response is *incremental* and not the result of cannibalizing responses normally achieved by mail.

However, phone does more than generate an initial incremental response. It also lifts mail response after the call! Marketers have found that of the prospects contacted by phone who said they were not interested in the offer at the time of the call, a percentage subsequently order by mail. Clearly, this is related to the customer-service orientation of the call, which provides valuable product information and creates a positive impression even though the prospects did not order at the time of the call.

4. Economic   Costs for telemarketing are very reasonable, when you consider the costs for the next most personal selling medium, the face-to-face salesperson. Telephone-cost ranges, at this writing, based on a cost per conversation with the decision maker, are:

- $6 to $10 for business-market calls
- $3 to $5 for consumer-market calls

Because of the speed of response, telephone is also the most immediately cost-accountable direct-response medium. For every conversation you have a response that is easily quantified and measured against the expense of the telephone program.

5. Productivity   A well-managed and structured telephone operation can achieve a high level of productivity. One trained communicator:

- Speaks with 3.5 to 7 business decision makers per hour
- Speaks with 8 to 15 consumer decision makers per hour

Response will vary as a result of the complexity of the product offered and the category of decision maker, as shown in the following table:

Conversations per Hour with Different Decision Makers

Decision maker	Conversations per hour
Physicians	2.5–3.5
Middle managers	5.0–6.0
CEO/president	2.5–3.5
Small retail store managers	5.0–7.0
School principals	2.5–3.5

Here also are our definitions of the 9 considerations marketers must take into account to maximize returns from their telemarketing investment:

1. Market Planning   Marketers dare not launch a new product or campaign without a detailed plan outlining how they will market it (see Appendix A). Yet a formal telemarketing plan is often the exception rather than the rule for many companies. The perception and understanding of the telephone as a vehicle for distribution is still relatively new. Once the telephone is positioned as a valuable marketing channel, it is obvious that a marketing plan must also apply to this medium. The success of such a plan might be structured into the following operational procedures:

- Analysis of the current situation
- Goals
- Objectives
- Threats/opportunities
- Tactics
- Budget
- Measurement and analysis

These considerations can help ensure a successful marketing campaign.

2. List Segmentation   List segmentation is probably the most important requirement for successful telemarketing. Since phone is not a medium that lends itself to broad-based, scattershot use, cost-efficient results can only be achieved through pinpoint targeting of list segments for calling:

- While phone is considerably less expensive than a sales visit, it is by no means cheap. At an average cost of $4 (consumer) to $8 (business) per completed call, nonselective calling can quickly wipe out profits from a given campaign.
- The subject of the call, whether a product or a service, must have relevance to the person contacted. Nonselective, random calls do not fit the requirement for "personally relating" over the phone that we preach and practice. Unsolicited, random, "cold" calls have generated consumer negativism—and rightly so, in our judgment.

In segmenting lists it is important to consider some guidelines:

- The in-house list is most often the best list. Your previous buyer is a better prospect than a nonbuyer. This is especially important for telephone because the preexisting relationship with a customer helps justify the telephone call. The internal in-house-list guidelines presented by Bob Stone for direct-mail segmentation also hold true for telephone.[1]

Weighting for House-List Variables	
Recency	55%
Frequency	35%
Dollar amount	10%

---

[1] Bob Stone, *Successful Direct Marketing Methods*, Crain Books, Chicago, 1979.

■ Outside lists are those that are rented. There are currently in excess of 200,000 lists available for rent or exchange in the United States.[2] Many are available to telemarketers. Sophisticated segmentation, such as zip-code neighborhood and census block clustering by demographic criteria such as income, family size, type of dwelling, and life-style, can be done by services such as Claritas.[3] Such a service enables a marketer to profile the characteristics of a house list against a total prospect universe, thereby grouping total prospects into high-response-probability pockets, based on their similarity to the house list.

A final important factor that applies to both house and outside lists is source coding. Decision makers who have previously bought by telephone have indicated a predisposition to transact business by telephone. Previous "800" number buyers or out-WATS buyers within each of the recency-, frequency-, and dollar-amount categories are among your *best prospects*. Call them!

3. *List Utility* Once the best lists have been selected for calling, the marketer must consider how such lists can be most effectively utilized. These names are a limited and valuable resource.

On average, out of 1,000 gross consumer names, accounting for a 65 percent phone number look-up rate and an 85 percent completion rate, we net only 551 completed calls. The manual telephone number look-up procedures—searching through a directory or calling information assistance—still tend to be most practical and expedient for small lists of names.

Another approach is to use a computer to match your list against a larger phone data bank.[4] However the computer look-up rate is in the slightly better than 50 percent range. So the name balance still require manual look-up.

4. *The Crucial Service Orientation* Before we begin our case-by-case study, we stress the most crucial aspect of any telemarketing effort—*service*. In the best of all possible sales situations, the seller is performing a valuable service for the buyer by offering goods and services that the buyer wants or needs. The telephone allows us to make those products

[2] Direct Marketing Association.

[3] Claritas is a computer-based list-development service located in New York City.

[4] R. H. Donnelley, Metro-Mail, R. L. Polk Co., as well as other list services. In some areas the phone company will provide its computer tapes for a fee.

and services available to potential customers with unparalleled con- venience—one orders simply by saying "yes." Whether incoming or outgoing, telemarketing boils down to a convenient, "at your elbow" buy- ing service. Outbound phone calls are a *proactive* marketing tool: they reach directly into specific people's homes to invite them to buy. Inbound calls are *reactive*: respondents you don't know must call you. But the factor that makes the call welcome and an invitation, rather than an annoying interruption, is the emphasis and orientation on *service*.

As shown in the case histories that follow, the basic premise behind successful telemarketing is letting the prospect know what is being offered quickly, concisely, and accurately, and acting swiftly to fulfill the prospect's desires regarding the offer. Of course, persuasion may be necessary, but it is strictly through a gentle, logical, truthful, "soft-sell" presentation—the accent is always on convenience and the "person-to-person" interaction.

5. Scripts Another key element in successful telemarketing is *scripting*. Many companies traditionally attempt to develop the sales skills of indi- vidual telephone representatives to use their own style and approaches, filling the role of a field salesperson but without the travel cost and face- to-face contact. For example, advertising space in the Yellow Pages, steel tubing, cattle, stocks, and insurance have been sold successfully for many years by teams of professional telephone sales representatives. These reps are given training in the nature of the product they are selling. They call within a fairly loose control structure and attempt to sell their customers or prospects to close a sale. If commissions are good, they often con- tinue in telephone sales as a career, becoming experts on the product or service offered.

Our experience as a telemarketing agency servicing many different clients, varied products and services, and select *or* mass markets dictates that we must follow a substantially different route.

The communicators in programs we organize follow a carefully pre- pared, scripted text. Everything they are to say, from their first words when the prospect answers the phone to the "Thank you" at the end of the call, is structured. Scripts include detailed, pretested responses to the questions and objections they're likely to hear, and these responses are an integral part of the script from which the communicator works. Even with this disciplined call approach, each communicator's personality and character distinguish his or her phone presentation. Within the bound- aries of this human variation, management controls and directs what the communicators are saying on the phone.

Why is this systematized approach so important? We believe the following advantages are gained through this strategy:

■ *Confidence*. Management must have confidence that the person
called is being dealt with in a manner consistent with the company's own
high standards. These assurances come from careful scripting and ongoing call monitoring to ensure the quality presentation of a labor intensified
telemarketing center.

■ *Predictability*. In order to make a reasonable business decision
about marketing costs versus expected return, you must be able to predict
the effects of the program. Telephone has proven over the years to offer a
consistent pattern of results *when handled with a repeatable, standardized
presentation*. The scripted approach allows you to test the effectiveness of
your calls and derive statistically valid projections for an ongoing program.
It is also possible to test many script refinements and alternatives economically and quickly.

■ *Efficient labor utilization*. It takes a certain amount of talent to
follow a telephone script and make it sound natural, but it is a skill that
can be learned by a wide range of people. The ability to sell is a rare
commodity. Our companion volume, *Telephone Marketing: How to Build
Your Business by Telephone*, Chapters 5 and 6 particularly, will aid your
preparation of scripts and training systems.

6. Training Efficiencies   The skills required to be a successful telephone
communicator are substantially different from those of a salesperson
making face-to-face calls.

Key elements required in an effective telemarketing training program
will include the following:

- Familiarity with script and script procedures
- *Listening* abilities
- Voice clarity and diction
- Courtesy and customer-service orientation
- Productivity

The costs of telephone contact make efficient and precisely targeted use
of the medium an essential factor in maintaining a profitable operation. If
there is something wrong with the script or program as it is structured or
implemented, the difficulty will become apparent almost immediately.
The data measurement and analysis system passes this information to
management, providing the necessary base for decision making.

7. Management Supervision The role of management in the controlled telemarketing environment is usually more active and intimately involved in the day-to-day operations and results of the program. A nonscripted operation places strict emphasis on "commissionable sales." Unfortunately for the consumer, too many such operations show little concern for how those sales are achieved—or the high-pressure methods utilized by some unstructured sales reps.

Management should assume responsibility for all the initial steps involved in establishing the program—setting specific goals, objectives, and ethical standards for the telemarketing effort; continuing supervision of the preparation of the communicator script; monitoring and critiquing of the ongoing calling effort; testing through roll-out, with periodic reviews of the results of the program as it continues.

8. Consumer Responsiveness A scripted telephone workshop is a controlled, disciplined, ethical communications business, acceptable to the consumer.

Because industry has not been alone in focusing attention on telemarketing, the rapid growth of the medium has drawn the attention of legislators and the federal government, who have begun to restructure the legal requirements for telemarketing on a state-by-state basis.

Automatic dialer recorded message players (ADRMPs) had been around for over a decade, but they weren't cost-efficient and proved unacceptable to marketers and consumers. Suddenly, in 1977, automatic dialers caught the interest of the media. Exaggerated reports of their potential as invaders of privacy aroused the interest of lawmakers and regulators. Though "boiler rooms" and telephone "bucket shops" had been cut back over the years, many still preyed on the unsuspecting consumer with shady offers and unfilled orders for merchandise.

In 1978 the FCC issued a Notice of Inquiry into telemarketing, and bills were introduced in Congress that would have severely restricted marketing by telephone. The outcry by businesses, such as Hertz, Avis, Citicorp, GE, Greyhound, Sears, Roebuck, Time, Inc., Montgomery Ward, and CCI, to name a few, and industry associations led by the CCTU— Committee of Corporate Telephone Users, including the Direct Marketing Association (DMA)—was such that the FCC, citing its own independent studies, decided in 1980 that no further federal regulations were needed. (See Appendix B.)

State legislation has, however, set new conditions and guidelines on the use of the telephone for sales campaigns. No ethical marketer need fear their impact unduly, though many regulations are misguided and unwarranted. They have not and will not stop the consumer from buying ethical products or services via the phone.

9. Back-End Support Systems   A structured telemarketing script is consumerist in orientation and must be supported by swift delivery of the product or service offered and accepted. With telephone the "medium is the message," so to enhance the phone contact, speedy service is essential. If the order is not quickly processed and fulfilled, though, the benefit evaporates. The promptness and accuracy with which marketers handle telephone accounts not only impacts the current transaction but has far-reaching implications for that customer's value over the buying lifetime.

Disappointing a mail-order or retail customer with news that an item is "out of stock" will produce a negative reaction, but given the personal nature of telephone contact, the admission that the merchandise offered is not in fact available has a far more damaging psychological impact. A personal relationship, albeit brief, is established in the course of the telephone call. If the caller turns out to be unable to deliver on his or her offer, the customer feels betrayed in a very real sense.

Promptness of delivery, quality of goods sold, adequate response to customer complaints, strictly ethical business standards—all are goals for *any* reputable business.

Our case histories stress the importance of maintaining customer satisfaction in all telemarketing programs. We are in the midst of an exciting growth cycle. As readers of this book, you are hopefully interested in taking part in this boom. We urge you to set and support the highest ethical standards and to go beyond the levels of strict requirement when it comes to customer service, courtesy, reliability, and quality. Each satisfied telephone customer becomes a "believer," and that helps all of us engaged in a challenging, changing, but immensely rewarding industry. (See appendixes D and E.)

Telemarketing Campaigns That Work!

chapter one

Publishing

Case History: Building a New World

One of the most widespread and accepted uses of telemarketing has been in subscription sales. *Time*, *Playboy*, or *TV Guide* magazine, for instance, will call subscribers who have not renewed their subscriptions after receiving different mail reminders and offer to take their renewal order over the phone. In these long-running programs, there is no question that the people being called are familiar with the product offered, since they have bought it in the past. Even a phone program soliciting first-time subscribers for established magazines or newspapers doesn't have to work too hard to acquaint the respondents with the product, since most people have at least thumbed through a wide sampling of the periodicals on the market.

However, in the case we'll discuss in this chapter, the magazine being offered was brand-new. In fact, to be more accurate, it didn't exist yet! There was no staff, no mock-up advance issue shown to advertisers, no newsstand availability—the magazine actually didn't even have a name, but thousands of people bought full-price subscriptions anyway, directly over the phone, and by doing so launched a magazine whose success was a milestone in publishing as well as marketing history.

This nameless magazine had one powerful asset in the person of Norman Cousins, one of the most extraordinary creative individuals in the history of publishing. The story of his dramatic break with *Saturday Review*, the magazine he had nurtured as editor in chief for over 30 years, to found an entirely new publication and the eventual vindication of the idealistic stand that led to his departure are testimony to the strength of one man's dream. And as a direct-sales effort to a consumer audience, the case study illustrates several important lessons about the marketing vehicle that made Cousins' dream a reality—the telephone. The campaign by CCI that launched *World* magazine used the power of this innovative marketing medium to reach a very select group of prospects, to grab their attention, tell them, sell them, and listen to them as they reacted to the sales presentation, and in doing so, set the direction for the enormous growth of telemarketing expertise in the decade that followed.

In the November 21, 1971, issue of *Saturday Review*, a surprising editorial appeared. Written as always by Norman Cousins, *Saturday Review*'s editor in chief for 31 years, this editorial represented his farewell to his loyal readers, marking the end of a major era in American publishing. In his tenure at the magazine, Norman Cousins had achieved high visibility and had garnered enormous respect as a major American literary figure. Under his leadership, *Saturday Review* had grown into an editorially and financially sound publication. Through the pages of the magazine, Cousins had been an outspoken champion of several important charitable and philanthropic causes over the years. His articulate stands in defense of human dignity and the preservation of the planet's delicate ecological balance had made him a leading intellectual figure on the national scene.

Norman Cousins' sudden departure from *Saturday Review* was not brought on by a desire to retire or waning interest in the magazine—far from it. In fact, it was his commitment to the integrity of the magazine that forced him to leave it.

Five months before the fateful editorial appeared, *Saturday Review* had been sold by its parent company, Norton Simon, Inc., to the Boise Cascade Corporation. This meant a change from dealing with Norton Simon, who was himself a great admirer of Cousins, to heeding the management of Nicholas H. Charney and John J. Veronis, whose previous publishing experience had been with the trendier magazine *Psychology Today*. Charney and Veronis wanted to change the editorial focus on *Saturday Review*, converting it from a single, wide-ranging weekly into four separate monthlies, individually covering science, education, the arts, and society. They also planned to start the Saturday Review Book Club and other commercial ventures.

Cousins objected strenuously to the idea of carving up *Saturday Review* into separate, specialized publications, and especially to the proposed "exploitation" of the magazine's fine reputation, but he was unable to convince the new owners. He chose to resign.

In the weeks that followed, Cousins was approached with several attractive offers—three college presidencies, a television show, a syndicated newspaper column, and, of course, many book projects. But what he really wanted was to continue as editor of a magazine, one that would encompass the arts and sciences, the political and philosophical issues of the day, and appeal to the cultured, well-educated readership that had made up his distinctive following at *Saturday Review*. To accomplish this, he would have to start a brand-new magazine, an undertaking that most right-thinking businesspeople would quail at.

Marketing Objectives Introducing any new product requires a carefully planned marketing strategy and involves substantial financial risks. When that new product is a magazine, the process is complicated by the fact that there are two separate and distinct markets that must be reached—the consumers and the advertisers, with the advertisers representing the real source of profit. In order to begin selling ad space, though, magazine publishers must guarantee a specific circulation. As a result, most prospective publishers concentrate first on wooing large numbers of subscribers by offering cut-rate trial offers in hopes of quickly building circulation figures substantial enough to make advertisers sit up and take notice.

This tactic has frequently been successful, but it presents distinct hazards for the long-range health of the project. The readers gained in this way have given no real indication of their *continuing* interest in the new publication. By taking a six-month trial subscription at a rock-bottom price, the reader can afford to satisfy his or her casual curiosity about the new venture. While this can lead to impressive new-subscriber figures, these numbers have been known to plummet perilously when renewal time rolls around. With this in mind, banks and other sources of capital rightly see a new magazine with few long-term commitments as a risky investment.

Short-term subscriptions are also expensive in terms of marketing costs. It becomes necessary to start renewal attempts almost as soon as you've processed the initial order, and each reminder and plea costs money. If you lock a subscriber into a long-term commitment, you avoid that expense for a longer period.

Above and beyond these financial considerations, Cousins had to assess the amount of personal time and energy he was willing to devote to establishing a new magazine. He was not at all convinced that his new publication would excite enough interest in the reading public to justify the substantial efforts required in the start-up process—what he catalogs as "the inevitable fatigue, the financial hazards, the psychological wear and tear. So this was nothing I wanted to jump into without careful consideration."

This, then, was the scenario faced by Norman Cousins as he considered launching a new magazine. Working with very limited capital, he needed to determine whether he could draw sufficient support for his new publication before he made heavy investments of time and money in the project. He needed to generate continuing subscriber commitments, indications that the circulation figures did not represent people simply sampling a new magazine at a bargain rate but included individuals sincerely interested in becoming long-term, loyal subscribers. These expressions of reader enthusiasm had to be strong enough to serve as ammunition when confronting potential investors and trying to convince them that the new magazine was a viable publishing venture. At this time, Cousins himself still needed some convincing on that point.

The marketing effort had to get under way quickly in order to keep the momentum of the project. Norman Cousins was news in November, but two or three months out of the public eye would inevitably lessen the response to his next undertaking. And for a man very much in demand, a fast answer was essential to justify channeling his personal efforts into this risky undertaking, as opposed to accepting a more secure position in another field.

Test-marketing the magazine with direct mail with perhaps some space advertising support would be the traditional road to travel, but this route presented several drawbacks. First, the creative, printing, and mailing expenses involved in developing and sending out sales materials would be high. Direct mail tends to be cost-effective when there is a large, relatively homogeneous target audience, allowing the marketer to send out a mass mailing of identical pieces in quantity. If the segment of the population likely to respond to your offer is relatively small or specialized, it becomes more difficult to locate these individuals economically and to produce a mailing piece that fits their well-defined interests.

For a new, intellectually oriented magazine edited by Norman Cousins, the target market was too select to justify the cost of mass mailing. Discrete lists of highly qualified market segments would have to be isolated for an effective sales effort, and that required a willingness to conduct extensive testing. In addition, the approach to presenting this unique magazine clearly and convincingly had to be arrived at through trial and error, and that meant still further testing. Given these conditions, mail would be prohibitively expensive as a first step.

Expense was not the only barrier to beginning the marketing effort with a mail approach. Time was also a key consideration. All that testing, and the direct-mail effort itself, would be a slow-moving process, given the time needed to prepare a mailing piece and wait for the replies to trickle in. At this stage of the game, Cousins felt he needed an immediate positive response before he took preliminary steps toward publication.

Telemarketing held the potential for fulfilling all Cousins' requirements. It could be used to contact sample names from a variety of lists available from different sources and to identify those worth pursuing. Thanks to the immediate response produced by a phone call, each prospective list could be tested in a matter of hours, rather than the weeks of testing required for a mail effort.

The script approach to be taken in selling the new magazine could be tested and refined with similar speed. With an entirely new product, it is difficult to determine off the cuff just what the public will find most appealing about it. By highlighting different features and coming at the presentation from different angles, the telemarketer can try out several variations quickly and economically and, through testing, develop the script that strikes the most responsive chord.

The budgetary considerations of using phone as the medium for introducing the new magazine to the public were also favorable. Once the initial start-up costs have been covered in a telephone campaign, the process of making the actual sales calls can be controlled with great precision. Instead of pumping large amounts of up-front capital into a one-shot, big-budget broadcast, print, or mail campaign, you can begin your telephone program on a modest scale. This allows you to be sure that your campaign is making money before sinking your entire budget into the effort. It also lets you expand your campaign in response to favorable indications and finance the larger efforts at least in part with the revenues you have already produced, instead of footing the entire bill up front in a lump sum out of working capital.

The level of initial investment is especially low when dealing with a reputable telemarketing agency, since the agency bears the costs of the physical setup, the phone lines, and the hiring, training, and salaries of the communicators, supervisory staff, and creative people and divides these expenses among a number of clients who use its services simultaneously. Whether you are paying by the hour spent on the phone on your behalf or by the order produced, you can increase or decrease the intensity of your marketing effort as your budget dictates.

Most important of all, though, especially in introducing a new product, is the two-way communication that, of all the mass-marketing media, is offered only by telephone. With a mail offer, a "no" response is *no response*—you get the message because you never hear from your prospects. Even those who *do* respond favorably have only answered a simple yes-or-no question; they have not offered any hint of the reasons for their decision. On the phone, people respond with "yes" or "no" and, frequently, tell you *why* they are taking you up on your offer or turning you down. This feedback can be critically important in evaluating the product you are offering. Is there something in the design that is turning people off? Is the price too high? Are they having difficulty understanding the features that make your offer distinctive and appealing? When you contact people by phone, they will let you know.

It was this feature that particularly intrigued Norman Cousins. He was introduced to telemarketing by Ed Miller of Berlitz Language Schools, who had been extremely satisfied with the results of a phone campaign to turn up prospective students. When Cousins learned that, in addition to a healthy track record in sales, telephone had been used extensively in voter survey and public opinion research work on behalf of political candidates, he thought this combination of marketing skills might provide some of the unique decision-making information he was looking for.

In his own words, "When we were contemplating the possibility of establishing the magazine, we decided to find out beforehand whether there was an audience for what we were trying to do. I wanted something more than just scratching the surface of what readers wanted. I felt I had to know if enough people had a real *commitment* to what I was trying to do—and the extent of that commitment.

"I'd heard that a man named Murray Roman had done this sort of thing for political candidates. It had been important for these office seekers not only to know if a voter was for or against them but whether that person's attitude could be translated into real energy. The *kind* of answer was more important than just a simple yes or no. And that was precisely the sort of evaluation I needed.

"I guess I first heard Murray's name in casual conversation. I'm certainly glad I did. It seemed that the sort of thing he'd done in politics would be ideal for us. And that's the way it worked out."

In summary, then, the specific objectives for the Cousins telephone program were:

- Generate qualitative information regarding consumer reactions to the concept of the new publication.
- Measure responsiveness of a variety of test lists.
- Generate telephone subscriptions at a cost-effective rate.

List Segmentation The first key challenge lay in ferreting out those individuals who were likely to be interested in a new Norman Cousins magazine. Lists of individuals segmented by demographic criteria—age, sex, annual income, educational level, geographic location, and so on— were readily available. However, these simple census-based classifications did not hold much promise for this campaign. The appeal of the new magazine depended not on where the prospect lived or how much money he or she made but on intellectual interests and even philosophical outlook. Locating people who fit this sort of categorization requires list selection by *psychographic* distinctions.

Psychographic analysis of a population provides classifications according to attitudes, interests, and opinions. The data needed to categorize individuals along these lines may be derived in an academic setting through testing procedures—questionnaires that seek to determine personality factors. To locate the most promising prospect for a product or service, the marketer can employ survey research or make use of the psychographic categorization that individuals have exhibited on their own through their personal life-style choices. An individual's choices in organization memberships, charitable contributions, forms of entertainment, reading matter, and similar personal-preference items are strong indicators of that person's "psychographic profile," and lists based on each of these life-style items are readily available to direct marketers.

The perfect list of prospects in this case would have been *Saturday Review*'s own subscriber list, but this was clearly, irrevocably unavailable. It was necessary, then, to develop a list of prospects with psychographic profiles corresponding as closely as possible to those of *Saturday Review*'s readership.

One special source for this type of prospect was at hand through the membership list of the Center for the Study of Democratic Institutions (CSDI). This nonprofit liberal research and public interest group had solicited memberships and contributions, sponsored seminars, and published books and audio tapes. They also had a substantial file of 100,000 members who fit in one fell swoop the seven criteria deemed necessary for Norman Cousins prospects:

- Interest in literary affairs
- Interest in cultural affairs
- Interest in ecology and environment
- Concern with social action
- Higher income levels
- Higher educational levels
- Selected book buyers

The center could also offer a valuable distinction between the individuals on the membership roster. In order to solicit new members, the center regularly rented mailing lists from several sources, including lists of contributors to Common Cause and SANE and subscribers to *Smithsonian*, the *New York Review of Books*, and *Saturday Review*. When membership contributions came in, they were coded according to the list source from which the response was produced. This meant that the center's computer could provide CCI with separate list segments (called "panels" in market research) for each of these sources. This would allow separate testing of each panel to ascertain particularly promising sources of further prospects and possibly to allow dropping any segment of the center list that was not productive. In addition to the five panels mentioned above, a sixth list segment consisting of contributors of $25 or more to the center was also compiled for testing purposes.

Another very promising list was available through Norman Cousins himself, who in his personal correspondence over the years had amassed several thousand names of people who had written to him directly to comment on material in *Saturday Review* or other Cousins' projects.

Telemarketing Strategy   The prospect of launching a new magazine through telephone solicitation presented a series of tactical challenges in designing a marketing strategy. First there was the difficulty of selling what amounted to a "pig in a poke"—making phone sales efforts on behalf of new and unfamiliar products. The appeal of a new magazine, though, is so thoroughly tied to the print medium and the complex idiosyncrasies of editorial content and graphics that explaining the appeal of the new publication in a brief telephone contact loomed as a major obstacle.

However, a new magazine with Norman Cousins at the helm did have certain distinct marketing advantages that could be capitalized on. First, there was the strong identification of Cousins with *Saturday Review*. Unlike the readers of most magazines, a *Saturday Review* reader knew just who the editor of the magazine was—Cousins' personal presence was critically important and fully evident in every issue.

The circumstances of his departure from *Saturday Review* only served to heighten the public's awareness of him. The battles over policy and content at the magazine had attracted widespread media attention, particularly among the people whose special interests were served by the magazine. Cousins was depicted as a man of quality and integrity who was victimized by corporate politics. His next project would naturally attract substantial positive attention from the popular press as well as literary and cultural publications and the broadcast media.

On the other hand, while Cousins certainly had the editorial resources at his disposal to produce a magazine that would appeal to his former readership, the new publication would not be earth-shatteringly different from *Saturday Review* on the conceptual level. The primary distinction between the new magazine and the old would be that the still-nameless new publication would have a worldwide orientation, concerning itself with the arts, ecology, and other issues on a global scale, far broader than the distinctly American viewpoint of *Saturday Review*.

An additional obstacle was the fact that there was no introductory edition available for prospective subscribers to review and, given the enormous expense of putting together high-quality sample materials, there would not be any in the foreseeable future.

The key, then, would be to sell not the printed product itself but the man behind it—to sell Norman Cousins to prospective subscribers. The telephone presentation would be built around a creative strategy of highlighting the reader's trust in Cousins' ability to put together a magazine worth reading.

This put far more weight on a public personality's individual drawing power than the standard testimonial advertisement ever does, but the hopefully special relationship between Norman Cousins and his audience made the approach seem logical and, in fact, essential. He was the publication's only asset.

The subscriptions would not be offered at a cut rate. In fact, the pricing structure required a fairly hefty financial commitment on the part of the subscriber, with one-year subscriptions to the twice-a-month magazine going for $12, two years for $20, and three years for $25. There was also a special lifetime subscription offer at a one-time price of $200. At a time when *Time* magazine was selling for 50 cents on the newsstand and competitive *Saturday Review* subscription ads were offering 34 issues for $3.93, it could be expected that only prospects with a very substantial interest, those likely to remain with the magazine as long-term subscribers, would respond to Cousins' offer. The relatively high price served as a screening factor to isolate those individuals who had a strong commitment to the new project, fulfilling a major goal of the program. The higher price was also needed to justify the marketing and production expense of starting up the magazine.

The initial test marketing plan submitted for Cousins' approval proposed making completed telephone calls to 1,000 prospects chosen from a number of promising list segments. The primary stated goal of this initial phase of the program was to determine the viability and feasibility of marketing a new Norman Cousins publication, while at the same time measuring the response levels achieved from the selected lists and projecting from these results the likely outcome should he wish to proceed with a larger phone marketing effort.

The estimated cost of this test program would be approximately $2,500, based on projections of approximately 100 communicator hours of telephone calling to complete calls to 1,000 individuals. A daily data report would be transmitted to Mr. Cousins as the program progressed, so that patterns could be assessed as they appeared and adjustments to the program made immediately if needed.

Creative Strategy   Since the impact of Cousins' personal philosophy and integrity was to be the essential element in stimulating subscription commitments, an unusual creative strategy—one that had been started by Murray Roman in political fund raising—was proposed: playing a taped message over the phone to the prospect. Cousins would record a brief message explaining his project and his hopes and expectations for it. Trained telephone communicators would introduce the tape, play it, and then come back on the line to solicit reactions and, whenever possible, take subscription orders.

As Mr. Cousins says, "Murray suggested that I do a tape recording. I had 90 seconds to 2 minutes to ask people if they'd be willing to take a chance on us. After Murray and his people had made several hundred telephone calls, he asked me to listen to the replies. Somewhat astoundingly, the majority of the people who were called were willing to pay $25 for a three-year subscription to a publication nobody had ever seen. Nothing like that had ever happened before in the history of U.S. magazines.

"It was only then that I decided to proceed. CCI's survey had proved that there *was* an audience out there—not just curious people but a large group who were highly supportive."

As can be seen in the following transcript, the tape used in the test calls was carefully constructed not only to supply the basic information about the new magazine but to emphasize the personal nature of the appeal— including the editor's allusion to his own uneasiness about interrupting people at home, which he added in the second line of the script.

HELLO, THIS IS NORMAN COUSINS. I HOPE YOU WILL FORGIVE THE IN- TRUSION, BUT THIS IS THE MOST DIRECT WAY AVAILABLE TO ME TO TELL YOU THAT MY COLLEAGUES AND I HAVE DECIDED TO START A NEW MAGAZINE. EVER SINCE I RESIGNED AS EDITOR OF *SATURDAY REVIEW*, FOR REASONS WHICH I THINK YOU MAY KNOW ABOUT, I HAVE BEEN THINKING AND DREAMING OF PUTTING OUT ANOTHER MAGAZINE. I HAVE BEEN ENCOURAGED IN THIS BY LETTERS FROM MANY READERS. THESE LETTERS HAVE BEEN MOST HEARTENING AND, INDEED, NOURISHING. BUT STARTING A NEW MAGAZINE, AS I'M SURE I DON'T HAVE TO TELL YOU, IS A PRECARIOUS AND EXPENSIVE UNDER- TAKING. THERE IS, HOWEVER, ONE WAY IT CAN BE DONE. IT CAN BE DONE IF ENOUGH READERS ARE WILLING TO TAKE A CHANCE ON US AND COMMIT THEMSELVES TO LONG/TERM SUBSCRIPTIONS. FOR EX- AMPLE, IF WE CAN OBTAIN ENOUGH THREE-YEAR SUBSCRIPTIONS AT THE SPECIAL CHARTER RATE OF $25, WE CAN AVOID THE COSTLY AND PERILOUS BURDENS OF STARTING UP WITH SHORT-TERM INTRODUC- TORY OFFERS. IN THIS WAY THE MAGAZINE WILL BE OWNED, QUITE LITERALLY, BY ITS READERS AND EDITORS. READERS WHO SUBSCRIBE NOW NEED NOT PAY AT ONCE. THEY CAN PAY LATER. WHAT IS IMPOR- TANT IS THAT WE KNOW NOW THAT PEOPLE ARE WILLING TO STAND BEHIND US. INCIDENTALLY, THERE IS A LIFETIME SUBSCRIPTION RATE OF $200.

WE INTEND TO PUBLISH EVERY TWO WEEKS. OUR AIM IS TO PUT OUT WHAT WE HOPE YOU WILL BELIEVE IS THE FINEST MAGAZINE IN THE WORLD. WE WANT TO WRITE ABOUT THE THINGS THAT EXCITE THE HUMAN MIND. ABOUT THE GREAT ISSUES AND IDEAS. ABOUT WORTH- WHILE BOOKS AND FILMS, PLAYS, MUSIC, AND ART. BUT WE WANT TO DO THIS NOT ON A NATIONAL SCALE ALONE—WE WANT TO REPORT AND REVIEW ON A WORLD SCALE.

WELL, WHETHER FOR ONE YEAR OR THREE YEARS, OR A LIFETIME, I WANT YOU TO KNOW HOW EXCITED WE ARE AT THE PROSPECT OF PUT- TING OUT A MAGAZINE AGAIN, PUTTING IT OUT WITH AND FOR THE SAME PEOPLE WHO HAVE BEEN WITH US IN THE PAST. THANK YOU.

This taped message was introduced and followed up by a trained tele- phone communicator, who adhered to a step-by-step script that specified the introduction, responses to questions, and closing remarks to be used. The script serves as a "road map" for the communicator to follow through the stages of each call, allowing for detours along the way to answer any questions that might arise and providing instructions for returning smoothly to the main thrust of the conversation. For scripting purposes, the telephone call is broken down into modular units—the introduction to the prospect is one, the explanation of the offer is another, each answer to a question still another. To facilitate a natural flow from point to point in the course of a call, each of these modular segments must be available at the communicator's fingertips, clearly labeled for easy access. For a very simple script, this can be accomplished easily with two or three sheets of paper, laid out for maximum readability. The script used for the Norman Cousins program fell into this category (see Figure 1-1).

For a more complex script, which involves many answers to questions or objections or substantial variations in the offer to be made, a flip-chart format is usually appropriate (see Figure 1-2). Each script segment goes onto a separate card, and each card is headlined legibly and is visible at all times.[1]

The calls made to sell Norman Cousins' new magazine were direct and to the point, but still responsive to consumer needs. When the phone was answered, the communicator asked for the individual whose name was on the prospect list. Then the callers introduced themselves and explained that they were "calling with a specially recorded taped message that Mr. Norman Cousins asked me to play for you. The tape runs about two minutes. May I play it for you now and ask for your reactions and questions after you have heard it?"

If the prospect agreed, the tape was played. As it turned out, thanks to the very careful selection of lists, virtually everyone agreed to listen to Cousins' message.

When the tape was over, the communicator came back on the line with: "Did you hear that all right?" (making sure that the tape had been clearly transmitted), then asked, "May I tell Mr. Cousins he can count on your support for a three-year charter subscription?" The other available subscription terms were then offered if the first was not accepted. If an order was taken, the new subscriber was thanked and told that "Mr. Cousins will be writing to you shortly to thank you himself." If the prospect was not interested, the call was politely terminated.

A typical respondent who signed up for a three-year subscription said (and this is a direct quote): "I've read Mr. Cousins' editorials for years, and even though I've never met him, I like the guy. I trust him."

[1] Where a company today has computer facilities, many marketers are utilizing CRTs (cathode-ray tube or video terminals) with the necessary computer software programs for scripting, with all the possibilities and responses "branching" on screen for easy access by the communicator.

CAMPAIGN COMMUNICATIONS INSTITUTE OF AMERICA, INC.

"World Review" Telo-communications Program
Official Telo-communicator's Calling Script

Instruction:

This script gives the only acceptable approach. We ask that you use the introduction(s), responses to questions, and closing as worded without deletions, additions or change!

Introduction to Person Answering Phone:

Hello, may I speak to _____ (name of prospect on card) please? (*You are to speak to the prospect's wife or husband and make offer if the prospect is not available.*)

If you find you have inadvertently called a business office or doctor's office, say: I'm sorry I did not realize we were calling _____ (name of prospect on card) at his office. This is Mr(s) _____ calling with a specially recorded taped message from Mr. Norman Cousins about his new magazine, may I call _____ (prospect) at home? What is his home number please? We do not wish to disturb him now. (*If you are not given home number—record on card and terminate conversation.*)

This is Mr(s) _____ calling with a specially recorded tape message that Mr. Norman Cousins asked me to play about his new magazine.

Introduction to Prospect or Spouse:

Hello Mr(s) _____, this is Mr(s) _____ calling with a specially recorded taped message that Mr. Norman Cousins asked me to play for you. The tape runs about two minutes, may I play it for you now and ask for your reactions and questions after you have heard it Mr(s) _____?

If Yes: Thank you Mr(s) _____, it will be on in just a moment.
If No: I'm sorry Mr(s) _____, thank you for your time. Good-bye.

Figure 1-1.   Simple three-page communicator script for Norman Cousins' World magazine campaign.

If Asked Who Is Norman Cousins?

Norman Cousins is the past editor of *Saturday Review*. This taped message is about his new magazine, which he thought you might be interested in. May I play it for you?

If Asked What is Tape About:

Mr. Cousins has prepared this taped message so that he could tell you about his new magazine. He tells it much better than I. May I play it for you now?

If Asked What Will Magazine Be Like?

Mr. Cousins describes his plans for the magazine on this taped message—from this description it will be different from *Saturday Review*. May I play the tape for you now? He describes his plans much better than I can.

If Asked Where Did You Get my Name?

I'm really not aware of the exact source Mr(s) _____ . However, I'm sure Mr. Cousins felt you might be interested in this new publication—perhaps because of the other types of magazines you subscribe to.

If Prospect Agrees. . . .Play Tape Message

After Tape Say:

Mr(s) _____ , may I tell Mr. Cousins he can count on your support for a three-year charter subscription? Or for two years, one year, or lifetime? (NO-TATE RESPONSE ON CARD.) *If takes subscription, say:* Thank you Mr(s) _____ , Mr. Cousins will be writing to you shortly to thank you himself. (*Check address as it appears on card.*)

If Needs More Information, Say: Fine Mr(s) _____ , may I send you a letter from Mr. Cousins which describes the new magazine in more detail? (*If Wants Letter—check address as it appears on card.*)

If Not Interested After Hearing Tape Message:

Thank you for your time Mr(s) _____ ,

If Wants to Discuss With Husband or Wife:

Fine, Mr(s) _____ may I call again and play tape for _____ (name of husband or wife)? Or would you prefer if we sent you a detailed letter from Mr. Cousins which describes more about the magazine and you may decide then if you wish to subscribe? (NOTATE RESPONSE ON CARD.)

Figure 1-1. Simple three-page communicator script for Norman Cousins' **World** *magazine campaign. (Cont.)*

CAMPAIGN COMMUNICATIONS INSTITUTE OF AMERICA, INC.
LOUISANA NATIONAL BANK
PANEL 1B--SELL TBS/ENTREE/SAVINGS TO SELECTED ATM FILE
COMMUNICATOR SCRIPT

INTRODUCTION TO HOUSEHOLD		1
INTRODUCTION TO PROSPECT		2
INTRODUCE TAPE		3
IF HESITANT ABOUT TAPE	(1 of 2)	4
IF HESITANT ABOUT TAPE	(2 of 2)	5
AFTER TAPE	(1 of 2)	6
AFTER TAPE	(2 of 2)	7
OFFER		8
IF HESITANT ABOUT THE BILL SYSTEM		9
TBS CLOSE	(1 of 3)	10
TBS CLOSE	(2 of 3)	11
TBS CLOSE	(3 of 3)	12
IF NOT INTERESTED		13
ENTREE CLOSE		14
ORDER TERMINATION		15

ANSWERS TO ANTICIPATED QUESTIONS/OBJECTIONS LNB--THE BILL SYSTEM

"WHO CAN BE PAID VIA THE BILL SYSTEM?"	16
"HOW FAST WILL LNB PAY?"	17
"ARE THERE LATE CHARGES?"	18
"IS THE BILL SYSTEM SAFE?"	19
"CAN I ADD MERCHANTS TO MY LIST WHENEVER I WANT?"	20
"CAN I PRACTICE BEFORE I BEGIN?"	21
"WHEN CAN I CALL?/WHAT ARE THE HOURS?"	22
"CAN A BUSINESS ACCOUNT USE THE BILL SYSTEM?"	23
"IS THERE PROOF OF PAYMENT, LIKE A CANCELLED CHECK"	24
"WHAT IF I MAKE A MISTAKE/HAVE A PROBLEM?"	25
"HOW DO I KEEP A RECORD BEFORE I PAY THE BILLS?"	26
"DO I HAVE TO CALL FROM MY HOME PHONE?"	27
"WHAT IF I HAVE A 'ONE-TIME' PAYMENT?"	28
"WHAT DO YOU MEAN BY A PERSONAL I.D. CODE?"	29
"HOW WILL I KNOW MY PAYMENT CODES?"	30
"WHEN IS THE PAYMENT ACTUALLY MADE?"	31
"IT SOUNDS SO CONFUSING"	32
"NO MONEY/CAN'T AFFORD?"	33
"NO INTEREST/NO NEED/I LIKE THE WAY I PAY BILLS NOW	34
"NO HURRY/I'LL THINK ABOUT IT"	35
"WILL I RECEIVE MY BILLS EACH MONTH?"	36
"I'M NO LONGER WITH LNB"	37
"CAN I PAY BILLS ALL AT ONCE/ONE AT A TIME?"	38
"WHAT HAPPENS IF OVERDRAFT?"	39
"WHY DO I NEED A PERSONAL I.D. CODE?"	40

Figure 1-2. Complex flip-chart–type script used in Louisiana National Bank campaign. Note the use of the flip-chart to allow the communicator to answer involved questions.

But what happened if all did not go according to this smooth flow? Included in the script were a series of predetermined responses for the consumer's most commonly posed objections. If the number reached turned out to be a business office (which can happen with a list drawn largely from magazine subscription records), the communicator explained the purpose of the call briefly and requested the prospect's home number.

If asked "Who is Norman Cousins?", the communicator identified him as the past editor of *Saturday Review* and politely terminated the call. If they didn't know him, then there was little point in trying to sell him. Happily, the question would come up almost immediately in the call presentation if it was going to come up at all, so valuable phone time was not wasted playing a taped message to a highly unlikely prospect.

If asked what the tape was about or what the magazine would be like, the communicator politely suggested that the tape offered the best description of the new magazine and repeated the request to play it.

And for anyone who requested more information, the communicator offered a detailed letter from Mr. Cousins that described the magazine. Arrangements had been made with a word processing firm to produce a three-page letter on Norman Cousins' letterhead and bearing his signature that, albeit at greater length, gave essentially the same information as the telephone tape had. The same firm produced the personalized acknowledgments that were sent out to customers who ordered subscriptions by phone.

Tracking and Measurement Each call was carefully accounted for—the communicator recorded on a tally sheet which of the following occurred:
- An order was taken (and for what subscription term).
- The prospect was not interested.
- The prospect was unavailable at the time.
- The prospect wanted to receive literature.
- The prospect asked to be called back at a later time.

If the attempted call was not completed, the communicator indicated whether:
- There was simply no answer.
- The line was busy.
- The party was not available at the phone number provided.
- Phone contact was permanently impossible due to death, deafness, or other difficulty.

The other crucial set of information recorded by the communicators was the reaction of the people to the new project. The give-and-take of telephone contact allows questions to be quickly answered and creates the sales-promoting intimacy that is missing from other direct-marketing efforts. It also allows prospects to express their enthusiasm or their qualms as well as their suggestions for the product being offered.

Results The initial testing phase was completed by the end of December, and the results were nothing short of astounding. In the space of 100 communicator hours (the previously agreed-upon maximum), there were 877 completed calls out of a total of 2,206 attempted dialings. And out of these 877 individuals reached, an extraordinary 299 placed orders for the magazine—a 34 percent response rate! Furthermore, 77 percent of these orders were for three-year subscriptions at $25 each, with two people taking lifetime subscriptions for $200 each. The full figures for the original test marketing program are shown in Table 1-1.

The testing also revealed which of the center's list segments were most productive. From highest to lowest response, the ranking was:

1. *Saturday Review*
2. Common Cause
3. *New York Review of Books*
4. SANE
5. Norman Cousins' personal list
6. Contributors of $25 to CSDI
7. *Smithsonian*

Program Roll-out With this successful test completed, the next phase of the program called for fast action. Specifically, a larger list universe of potential prospects had to be compiled while the calling to the remaining 8,000 names already in-house from the center lists and Cousins' personal file proceeded.

The assumed characteristics for identifying high-potential individuals had proven valid. Now it was necessary to find further list sources of people with similar interests. The strong response from the *Saturday Review* segment of the center's list suggested that a look at their subscriber

TABLE 1-1. *Original Results of Test Marketing Program*

Result	Number	Percentage
Lifetime subscription	2	0.2
3-year subscription	230	26.2
2-year subscription		
1-year subscription	67	7.6
Literature requests	166	19.0
Not interested	239	27.3
Special (will decide later, after publication)	122	13.9
Requested call-back	51	5.8
Total completed calls	877	100.0
Total dialings	2,206	100.0
Completed calls	877	39.8
Not available	395	17.9
Don't answer/line busy	900	40.8
Permanently unreachable	34	1.5

profile would be valuable. This information showed that *Saturday Review* subscribers were particularly likely to be people who held a graduate degree in education or English literature, who attended ballet or concert performances and/or were museum goers, and who worked in the field of education.

With this information in hand, brainstorming on the part of CCI and Cousins and associates produced several dozen promising sources to be investigated, including magazine subscriber lists, membership lists from cultural and political institutions, and lists of contributors to selected charitable causes. These potential sources were contacted, and where the institutions were willing to rent their lists for use in telemarketing, an arrangement was made to make calls to a sample of the names to determine whether the list was fruitful enough to justify a large-scale phone campaign and/or a direct-mail effort.

Phone plus mail–A critical new balance. A major innovative feature of the *World* magazine campaign is the fact that the phone was in the forefront of the sales effort. Telemarketing had in the past been used as a sort of cleanup operation, brought in after a mass mailing to increase the response rate. Here phone contact was the prospect's very first encounter with the new product. The fact that this approach was so dramatically effective proved that magazine-buying habits could be altered as the result of direct contact by the new phone marketing medium.

Even more exciting, phone proved to be an excellent tool for *pretesting* the response efficiency of direct-response lists. CCI management had long contended that the telephone would consistently produce 2½ to 5 times the positive response rate of direct mail. To test this theory, 30 select lists consisting of 2,000 names each were rented for testing from a variety of sources. For each list, 100 to 200 names were chosen at random for telephone solicitation, while the remainder received promotional literature by direct mail. The results of this split test of mailing lists consistently matched CCI's expectations. Take, for instance, the figures shown in Table 1-2.

Thus phone became an important money-saving tool in direct-mail marketing. It became clear that a phone response rate of 5 percent or less would yield a mail response rate too low to justify the expense of mailing. From this point on, as a potential mailing list was considered, it was first phone-tested and only then ranked on the basis of these results as good, poor, or borderline for a direct-mail effort.

This winning combination has since been used many times for many different products. The campaign often starts off with personal telephone

TABLE 1-2. *Split-Test Results*

List source	Phone response rate, percent	Total completed calls	Mail response rate, percent	Total mailing
Atlantic Monthly	12.2	313	1.5	48,967
Bulletin of Atomic Scientists	12.4	3,151	1.5	9,332
Change magazine	13.7	1,884	2.9	5,887
Common Cause	15.3	221	4.6	28,292
Daedalus	13.7	9,067	2.0	7,809
Harper's	11.4	404	2.6	29,842
The Progressive	15.4	136	5.3	1,153
Show magazine	11.2	233	3.1	70,368

calls bringing a one-to-one message from a respected figure to the consumer. These calls allow the marketer to evaluate the drawing power of available direct-response lists and to refine the presentation of the winning sales points of the product by listening to the responses and questions coming from the other end of the phone. With the in-depth information about markets and product positioning gained in these exploratory phone calls, a subsequent mail campaign can follow phone's lead and produce substantial profits.

Flexibility of the medium. The fluidity of a phone program allows for continual testing of innovative ideas at very low expense. As new lists became available from different sources as the months progressed, each was tested and evaluated. If the response was about 15 percent or higher, it was deemed suitable for a large-scale phone campaign. If it was lower than that but still comfortably between 8 and 15 percent, it was recommended for mailing.

It seemed that a very specific psychographic profile was needed to find the degree of interest needed to spur the purchase of a magazine that the prospect had never seen. However, in search of additional subscribers, this hypothesis was put to the test at one point in the program. An attempt was made to work from demographic lists compiled from census data by three different list brokers. Sophisticated computer analysis had provided lists that take the national census information, which deals with relatively broad census tract divisions, and narrow it down to individual zip-code areas. This allows marketers to select from nearly 38,000 zip-code segments, basing their choice on over 100 separate criteria.

In the *World* magazine program, the names were chosen within selected metropolitan areas on the basis of highest possible median education level, high median income, and guaranteed presence of a phone in the household. The test calls indicated, though, that this approach wouldn't work—the correct "Cousins profile" needed to produce results was far too specific to be gleaned from simple demographic data. There was now proof that prospects had to know Cousins to trust his magazine—and that he was its best salesperson!

Several tests were also conducted using different taped messages as the program progressed. The tapes were updated periodically to keep the information about the new magazine as up-to-date as possible. For instance, when U Thant, former Secretary General of the United Nations, and Buckminster Fuller, the world-renowned architect and philosopher, agreed to be members of the new magazine's editorial board, this fact was added to the tape—as was the magazine's name, once that was settled on (note that the original, successful Norman Cousins tape does not mention the name of the magazine at all!). In the earliest stages, the magazine was identified as *Review*. The fledgling publication then became *World Review* and, by the time it reached publication, had been christened simply *World*.

An interesting approach tried out in the *World* program and used later for many other programs with great success was tailoring the taped message to the particular interests of the individuals on the list being called. For instance, Mr. Cousins adapted his basic message to stress *World*'s coverage of developments in the educational field and the literary world for a tape to be played to a list of professors of English.[3] A similar tailored approach was taken for members of the World Federalist organization, a group to which Mr. Cousins belonged that was dedicated to the goal of world citizenship.

By the time *World* magazine appeared on the newsstands and in subscribers' mailboxes in June of 1972, telemarketing had completed 143,203 calls to prospects, with a total of 22,323 subscription orders taken directly over the telephone. This means that over 15.5 percent of all the people contacted had ordered subscriptions to a magazine they had never seen! And of this number, over 47 percent ordered three-year subscriptions (see Table 1-3).

Figuring total income and dividing by the total number of orders, we find the income per order was $18.64. The cost of telemarketing per order per list was at a high of $12.84 to a low of $7.00.

---

[3] See Appendix F.

TABLE 1-3.   *Summary of the Orders Taken between December 1971 and June 26, 1972 (143,203 completed calls)*

Order	Number	Percentage of total
3-year subscription	10,570	47.4
2-year subscription	290	1.3
1-year subscription	11,417	51.1
Lifetime subscription	46	0.2
Total	22,323	100.0

Of course, these figures are affected by the collection rate—how many of those initially ordering by phone sent in their check when the invoice arrived. Telephone can produce orders, but there is no way for the buyer to enclose a check in a phone call. In many recent programs, this problem is taken care of by accepting credit card orders. Once the buyer has given both the okay and his or her credit card account number, the sale is consummated.

However, in the *World* campaign there was still a question about how many orders would fall through because the money never arrived.

The surprising answer was that fully 92 percent of the phone customers had indeed paid for their subscriptions by the time the first issue was in the mail, a phenomenal rate. This collection rate is further testimony to the enthusiastic response achieved by bringing the right product to precisely the right list of prospects. The figure also reflects favorably on the low-pressure sales techniques employed. The people who ordered were not hyped into saying "yes" only to realize upon reconsideration that they were bullied into the purchase. Instead, they were being offered a product in a dignified manner and allowed to make a rational buying decision.

Even with these collection adjustments, then, the figures remain impressive, especially when you keep in mind the fact that we are discussing the magazine business here. If the full-rate subscription price pays for the expense of procuring the subscription, you have essentially done very well, since you will then be selling those subscribers to the advertisers, who provide your profit.

Don't forget the economic bonuses involved in the phone sales program. First and foremost of these are the hundreds of subscribers who responded at full subscription rates to the literature sent to them at their request after the initial phone contact. Also significant as cost considerations are the enormous savings brought about by eliminating costly mailings to unproductive lists through telephone pretesting and the market research data compiled by the communicators; all of which, taken together, represents a healthy dividend over and above the simple cost-per-order figure.

And what about the qualms that Norman Cousins felt initially about becoming involved with telephone sales efforts that disturbed people in their homes? Well, there were a handful of complaints—there always will be when you give people an avenue to voice them with ease—but very few indeed, considering the number of calls made.

Summary Did the appearance of *World* magazine signal the end of Norman Cousins' use of telemarketing? Not by a long shot! The combination of telephone and mail subscription solicitation techniques continued throughout *World*'s brief life as an independent publication and beyond.

You see, while Cousins was successfully getting his own venture off the ground, trouble was brewing back at *Saturday Review*. The new owners were unable to maintain a healthy circulation for their four weekly magazines and experienced further difficulties in providing the quality editorial product that Cousins had made the hallmark of the magazine when he was editor. By August 1973 *Saturday Review* went bankrupt, and who stepped in? —Norman Cousins!

He took over the helm as editor and publisher, bailing out the ailing magazine by merging it with his own healthy publication to create *Saturday Review/World* (a name later shortened back to *Saturday Review*).

With this new acquisition, though, he inherited a problem as well. In their attempts to save the magazine, the new owners had built up a large number of "bought" subscribers, who had paid very little for short-term trial offers. Cousins' goal now was to trim away the inflated circulation figures produced through this technique and get back to the kind of faithful readership that had constituted the loyal, reliable following of *Saturday Review* in the past. To accomplish this task, he once more turned to the phones.

The objective of the telephone program he undertook was to sell cut-rate subscribers on full-price subscriptions to the newly resuscitated *Saturday Review/World*. Taking his cue from the first successful phone campaign, Cousins recorded two separate tape messages.

The first, addressed to previous *Saturday Review* subscribers who had stayed with the magazine under its new management, said, in essence, "I'm back. We're going to return to the kind of publication we used to be."

The second, addressed to those who had bought subscriptions during the new management's reign, said basically, "The magazine you know is going to change. Here's what it's going to be from now on."

In all, more than 20 different variations on these recorded messages were used, to obtain new subscribers and to convince current subscribers to renew with longer-term subscriptions. This effort produced orders from over 25 percent of the individuals contacted.

Implications for the Marketer *Saturday Review* weathered this stormy period in its history and continued on as a vital part of American publishing for another 10 years.[4] It is safe to say that without the power of telemarketing and the creativity and courage to use it effectively, its dedicated readership would have been left without a distinctive voice for their interests and concerns.

For marketers, the lessons gathered through this innovative program extend into many areas. Certainly the use of telephone as a means to test the drawing power of a direct-response list before using it for mailing has powerful ramifications, particularly for marketers who are trying to reach prospects with relatively specialized interests. Not only does the telephone response indicate the potential for selling the product to the people on a given list; it also allows you to assess the quality of the list itself. People change residences frequently, and of course there are deaths and other factors that can make many of the names on a list worthless within a surprisingly short time. Testing by phone will uncover problems of list quality much faster and at far less expense than waiting for mail packages to be returned with "Not at This Address" and "Return to Sender" stamped on them.

At least equally important in this case history is the demonstration of the sales potential of a taped message. Remember that, before Cousins and *World*, tapes had been used by us only in the context of political campaigns or fund-raising appeals. Now the door was open to bringing the persuasive personal sales messages of noteworthy spokespeople into consumers' homes by phone, and that capability has been employed with great success over the years by such major companies as American Express, Prentice-Hall, Colonial Penn Insurance Group, Encyclopedia Britannica, the Canadian Olympic Coin Program, Xerox Publishing, and Montgomery Ward.

[4] *Saturday Review*, still plagued by financing and advertising problems, finally closed its doors during the business recession of 1982. Cousins had not been its active leader for its last five years.

Futurism. The telephone's ability to reach "just those people interested in Norman Cousins" or just those who ski, or ride motorcycles, or hang-glide, or surf, sail, or scuba, "or listen to opera" will be made doubly effective by combining the power of the video screen with the instantaneous response of the phone. Special "life-style" video magazines, already tested in Florida, Ohio, and Texas, may change "publishing" as we have come to know it—especially if there's a "printing machine" attached to your TV set! It may eventually be easier to renew your magazine subscription by punching a few buttons on your TV hand control, but most people will still need reminding—and selling. Good ol' "pots"—plain old telephone service—will be around for a long time yet!

chapter two

Bank Marketing–
A New Frontier

In this chapter, we will look at the fastest-growing realm of telephone use, marketing "business-to-consumer." Here purchases are generally smaller, with many differences in the techniques used to get your message across and close the sale. However, you will also find important similarities between consumer and business programs, not the least of which, as in the Norman Cousins campaign, is the compelling effect produced by the right taped message to the right list.

- "Can we really expect people to trust us when we're only a voice on the phone to them?"
- "My offer isn't all that simple. How are people going to understand what we're selling over the phone?"
- "Telemarketing is fine for a $15 item, say, but you can't sell anything with a high ticket price over the phone—can you?"
- "Is telemarketing consistent with my bank's image?"

These are the sort of questions that predictably come up when business executives in the financial marketplace first attempt to grasp the enormous possibilities that telemarketing opens up for their banks or firms.

Each question involves preconceived notions of the limitations of this medium. These notions are rooted largely in our own familiarity with the phone as a part of everyday life. In this case, the old axiom that "familiarity breeds contempt" is particularly apt. Modern and future-oriented executives will readily believe miracles can be performed with a new piece of high-tech hardware but too often fail to see the potential profit-makers near at hand—the phone on the corner of the desk, for example.

To determine the ways in which telemarketing answers questions of concern to bankers, let's look at some case histories in one of today's hottest marketing areas—consumer banking.

Once upon a time, banking was a relatively sedate, noncompetitive business, but that's all behind us now. Dizzying interest rates have forced banks to find new sources of capital. Their search for cheaper ways to buy money has placed new importance on the consumer banking business— which, in turn, has led to the development of expanded customer services to attract consumer deposits in this new, aggressive marketplace. However, building image identification and customer loyalty for a specific banking institution is not an easy task.

With a large number of banks from which to choose and an increasingly demanding and sophisticated public to deal with, financial institutions are initiating nontraditional promotional strategies in their fierce competition for an increased share of the market. The variety and complexity of giveaway programs and new, unfamiliarly convenient banking services has made it necessary for bank marketers to both sell their services and explain them in depth. This means greater use of print and broadcast advertising, of course, but in addition, several banks have gained an edge over their competition by employing telemarketing as one element in their media mix. The telephone contact goes beyond filling the function of advertising, which can only deliver a message—phone responds immediately, to answer questions and take the order.

In fact, the essence of direct marketing is its ability to reach out and sell products and services without the physical presence of a sales force. One of the major difficulties to be overcome in this type of selling situation is defusing the prospect's skepticism about the reliability of a company he or she can't see. A retail store, for example, is more than a place to look at merchandise, select it, and pay for it—the store building and staff set the tone for the offering, inspire confidence in the product, and provide some assurance to the buyer that there will be a human being available to deal with if something should go wrong.

It would be hard to think of an institution that relies more heavily on customer confidence than a bank, or one that has used the physical presence of its branch offices and staff more effectively as a symbol of the security and trustworthiness they are offering. With or without a marble-columned bank building to inspire consumer confidence, financial products and services are not easy to market. First off, they tend to be complex. Most people are not comfortable dealing with the ins and outs of banking transactions, and do so only reluctantly. At the same time, they must feel absolutely secure in their choice of a banking institution—after all, they are dealing here not with a one-time purchase but with the choice of someone to handle the bulk of their hard-earned money. This branch of marketing is further complicated by government regulations, which set forth the strict guidelines for all transactions by financial institutions.

Yet telephone, the most interactive of the direct-marketing media, has entered the difficult arena of consumer banking and succeeded in selling expanded services, including "Now" accounts, debit cards, ATM[1] cards, automatic savings, credit cards, and bank-by-phone services to existing bank customers.

One professional telemarketing program has generated orders with billions of dollars in a money market fund investment vehicle. People—individual investors or companies thousands of miles from the office of the Dreyfus Liquid Assets Fund (which is making the offer via print advertising)—respond by a combination of mail and phone with orders in the magnitude of $50 to $100,000 and more!

This prospect of broadening market penetration into a national market or geographical area where one is not represented in the flesh holds special appeal to bankers hard-pressed to bring in new revenues. The lessons learned in testing this concept in the financial community are equally important for any business interested in reaching out to new parts of the country, or the world, to find new customers.

Case History: Banking on the Bayou

"Banks do a lousy job of selling. But we have been experimenting with new ways of selling bank services, and now we know how to cross-sell products like they should be sold."

The speaker is Jerry D. Turk, Vice President and Marketing Director of Louisiana National Bank, which conducted a pioneering telemarketing campaign to generate new customers for an innovative new banking service.

---

[1] Automated teller machines.

Louisiana National Bank is heavily involved with consumer banking—the consumer market accounts for nearly 40 percent of its total deposits. LNB is also identified in its market with electronic and "plastic" banking services. It was an early issuer of bank-sponsored credit cards and was also one of the first banks to provide access to automated teller machines for its depositors.

Marketing Objectives   In a highly competitive market environment, Louisiana National Bank had established a distinctive reputation as a leader in providing innovative banking services. In order to reinforce this strong positive image, attract new customers to the bank, and strengthen its customer-service relationship with its current customer base, LNB decided to introduce an automated system for paying bills by telephone—a service that at that time was virtually unknown to the public. Jerry Turk summed up the strategic implications of adopting and actively promoting the new system: "The more unique products and services we offer, the better chance we have to attract customers from our competition."

Appropriately dubbed the "Bill System," the service allows subscribers to call a special number and order payment of any or all of their bills directly from their account, without writing out and mailing a check. There is a modest monthly fee for this service.

This "bank-by-phone" service is positioned right at the cutting edge of today's expanding movement toward electronic banking transactions conducted without ever entering a branch office. Only recently, an experimental system was introduced in a small test market that employs interactive cable television technology to provide bank-at-home service to subscribers. While two-way cable systems are still in the developmental stages, two-way telephone is available to effectively reach every banking customer in the country, and innovative telephone technology makes it possible today to transact business without even speaking to a teller. "The Bill System is a move toward source data capture, with the consumer recording payment information through his telephone," Mr. Turk explained.

Another important factor weighing in the bank's decision to implement a bank-by-phone system is that it provides a low-capital alternative to offering an electronic fund transfer service. As Mr. Turk pointed out, there is no terminal expense involved with bank-by-phone: "The phone company has already taken care of that. Every home and office has a phone, and in our market about 30 percent are touch phones that allow direct input to the computer."

There are substantial benefits, both to the bank in terms of personnel costs and to the customer who gains in 24-hour convenience. However, while the system would offer advantages once it was sampled and accepted, there were major hurdles to be cleared before this could be expected to occur. As bank officials fully realized, convincing people to adopt this unfamiliar new system for dealing with their hard-earned money would not be easy. As Jerry Turk notes, "Changing habits is one of the toughest things the human animal does. People are basically reluctant to change. Think about your golf grip, your tennis grip, or the way you shave or comb your hair. So to expect customers to fall all over themselves to pay bills by phone would be stupid. We had to change first. We had to change our way of selling." The new competitive selling stance at LNB involved a carefully orchestrated multimedia campaign, with telephone as a prime element in the overall mix.

This medium seemed particularly logical considering the fact that it was telephone service they were selling. However, there was some feeling within the bank's executive offices that telephone was not an appropriate sales vehicle for a financial institution. Results of the initial test program, though, caused a substantial shift in attitude.

There were two stages to the marketing process involved in launching the Bill System. First, consumers had to be sold on the new service's advantages—a task that was in essence educational. Then, when the idea had been successfully sold, the sale had to be closed. Louisiana National Bank launched an extensive, high-impact promotional campaign that saturated the market with the Bill System message in a short time frame, to build product familiarity. "Advertising had a tremendous task to accomplish," Mr. Turk recalls. "Television was our prime vehicle—our flag waver—and print carried the details. . . . When we introduce a new service of this magnitude, we bombard the market with advertising. We spend all we can afford for the first 13 weeks."

Once advertising had done its work in raising awareness, a medium was needed for translating that awareness into action. Customers could, of course, sign up for the Bill System at their branch bank, but direct-response mechanisms were better suited to tapping the prospect's enthusiasm with immediacy and impact. This called for direct mail and direct, outgoing telephone contact.

The marketing campaign began with a press conference explaining and demonstrating the system, which sparked significant local and national media coverage. Demonstrations of the Bill System for customers were also arranged in branch offices, to help acquaint them with the new service. Combined with the major broadcast and print advertising exposure, the sense that something important and exciting was happening at LNB was communicated to the entire market area.

To capitalize on this, direct mailings featuring the Bill System were sent to current LNB customers. The bank made an introductory offer of six months of Bill System service free to new subscribers, after which there would be a small monthly fee.

The direct-mail piece included an application form that was to be filled out with the account numbers of merchants the subscriber intended to pay through the Bill System, a personal identification number, and check-offs for type of phone (rotary or Touch-Tone) and service charge method (per bill paid or flat monthly fee). This form could be filled in and mailed to the bank, or the recipient could call the bank at a number provided in the mail piece and dictate the information to a bank representative, who recorded it and sent out a verification form subsequently. (See Figures 2-1 and 2-2.)

The outbound telemarketing program was aimed at increasing response from those LNB customers who did not respond to mail. The call would reach these individuals, focus their attention on the bank's offer, concisely but persuasively explain the benefits and features of the Bill System in a one-to-one personal sales message, and then answer any of a wide range of questions that might be holding the individual back from accepting LNB's offer. Rather than attempting to organize an outgoing call program themselves, LNB arranged with an outside telemarketing agency (CCI) to create the phone campaign and test it, that is, to do all the creative work involved in preparing the program and to make the calls via WATS lines from CCI's New York offices.

Telemarketing Strategies   The first requirement for selling any product or service through direct-response media is the target list of potential customers, and this factor is critical in the strategic design of a telemarketing campaign. The methodology of telephone contact allows marketers to zero in on precisely those individuals with the greatest potential interest and to make the offer in the most convincing, personal way. At the same time, the economics of the telephone medium demand that you reach *only* those "best prospects"—otherwise the costs of nonproductive contacts will quickly wipe out any incremental profits generated over the phone. Selecting and calling the "right list" is the critical element in any telemarketing campaign—some marketers feel that more than 70 percent

I want to pay your bills for you - FREE for six months

Dear Customer:

How much time and money do you spend each month to pay your bills? There is the cost of stamps and envelopes. Then, there is the hassle of licking, addressing, stuffing and mailing. But, for the next six months we're going to save you time, money and hassle.

Because you are already a valued customer of LNB, we would like to give you the opportunity to pay your bills by phone free for six months. After that time, we will simply bill you either 15¢ per bill paid or $1.50 per month. Here's how to get on The Bill System.

1. Read The Bill System brochure and the special form enclosed in this envelope entitled "Two Easy Steps".

2. Decide which merchants such as utilities, doctors, department stores, you would like to pay each month and write the merchant addresses and your merchant account numbers in the space provided on the form.

3. Then just call 389-3773 and read your list to our Bill System teller or mail the form to us in the return envelope.

We will open the account for you and within five days you will receive your Bill System payment kit. Then you can pay your bills the easy, convenient way---through The Bill System.

Sincerely,

J. D. Parker

J. D. Parker

P.S. Enclosed with this letter you will find Bill System practice instructions. Pick up your phone right now and try The Bill System. It's easy and it's fun, too.

J. D. PARKER · LOUISIANA NATIONAL BANK · P.O. BOX 3390 · ENTRÉE/24 DEPARTMENT · BATON ROUGE, LOUISIANA 70821 · 504/389-3554

Figure 2-1. *Louisiana National Bank mailing piece.*

Two easy steps and your Bill System™ account is open.

STEP #1

Fill in the form below.

To help you complete your payment list, we've listed the four most-frequently paid companies. However, you may add any additional merchants you would like to pay.

STEP #2

Phone 389-3773.

A *Bill System* representative will answer. In a few days you can be paying your bills the easy, convenient way. Through *The Bill System.* And, it'll be *free* to you the first six months!

FOR BANK USE ONLY PAY CODE	MERCHANT NUMBER	MERCHANT NAME	ADDRESS	YOUR ACCOUNT NUMBER*
		Gulf States Utilities	Address on file at LNB	
		South Central Bell*	Address on file at LNB	
		Baton Rouge Water Works*	Address on file at LNB	
		LNB-VISA/BankAmericard	Address on file at LNB	

*NOTE: Include route number from your Baton Rouge Water Works bill and area code, phone number and customer code from your South Central Bell bill.

TYPE OF PHONE: *(Please check one below.)*
☐ Rotary Phone ☐ Touch Tone

SERVICE CHARGE METHOD: *(Please check one below. Your first six months are free.)*
☐ 15¢ per bill paid ☐ $1.50 per month

PERSONAL IDENTIFICATION NUMBER _____
You select your own code. It may be any four (4) letters or numbers you wish.

If you wish to mail this form to us. please fill in below and mail to: The Bill System Department. P.O. Box 3399, Baton Rouge, Louisiana 70821.

Name _____

Phone Number _____

Checking Account No. _____

Figure 2-2. Louisiana National Bank mailing piece requesting consumer information.

of the success or failure of any call effort can be traced to the efficiency of the list.

For this reason, the most effective telemarketing tactics call for contacting people who are already familiar with your company or organization. This familiarity may be stimulated as part of the campaign—by sending a persuasive mailing piece and then following up by phone. However, the *best* productive universe for calling is generally your current customer list. This has been demonstrated over and over in practical situations and has recently been further documented in a survey conducted by a researcher at San Jose School of Business,[2] who contacted a representative sample of over 1,300 consumers nationwide and asked their opinion of telephone solicitations. The overwhelming majority indicated that they were pleased to receive telemarketing calls from merchants they had dealt with previously, as long as the product was worthwhile and relevant to their needs.[3]

This receptivity to telephone contact on the part of consumers already familiar with the caller's business, in addition to the demanding economics of telephone as a marketing medium, point clearly to a strategy of *cross-selling*—calling established customers and offering them new and/or different goods and services in addition to their present purchases. In most cases, cross-selling is preferable to *prospecting*—contacting noncustomers and attempting to establish a new relationship through telephone contact. (Keep in mind, though, that there are instances where telephone prospecting can be quite profitable—when the profit margin on the order is large enough to support the marketing costs or when the value of new customers over their buying lifetimes is great enough to justify the relatively high expense of producing the initial order—if the list is right, prospecting can be very profitable.)

For most banks, including Louisiana National in the program we are discussing here, cross-selling is the way to proceed in developing economically effective telemarketing programs. The telephone effort was directed toward increasing acceptance of the Bill System among current holders.

Another strategic consideration was making sure that the telephone commitment to join the Bill System was an active commitment that the subscriber would indeed make use of the service agreed to by phone. In order to prompt such an active commitment, the telephone call included a request for highly personalized information from the respondent. The telephone communicator would request account numbers of local mer-

[2] See Appendix E.
[3] See Appendix B: The Report of the FCC on consumer response to telephone selling.

chants that the new subscriber would like to pay via the Bill System. In addition, since a customer might have more than one account with LNB, subscribers were asked for the number of the checking account from which they wished to pay their bills. As a final aspect of the "immediate involvement" strategy, new subscribers were asked to select a personal identification code—an easy-to-remember combination of numbers and letters that would serve as identification when they wanted to access the system. Those who agreed to join the Bill System were sent a complete enrollment package by mail, which gave details on how to use the system. However, thanks to the detailed screening and information-gathering activities undertaken during the initial telemarketing contact, the individual's involvement in the system was well assured—they were usually part of the Bill System by the conclusion of the phone conversation.

List Segmentation   There was no difficulty in producing an appropriate list for calling. LNB had its customers classified in market-segment groups by existing type of account activity. This broke down into two basic units— the Entree file (customers who used the Entree card to access automated teller machines) and the LTF file (customers with non-Entree Card checking accounts or other LNB savings accounts). The combined universe for the two files was 14,500 individual customers.

For initial test calling to sell the Bill System, names were taken from the Entree file, since these customers were already oriented to electronic banking through their use of the automated teller machine.

Creative Strategy   The telemarketing campaign for the Bill System was more than an exercise in sales—it was an effort to build customer confidence in an unfamiliar financial service. A key to overcoming the skepticism and reticence on the part of the bank's customers was to bring them reassurance and explanation from a figure who was totally believable—the president of Louisiana National Bank.

In order to bring his personal message to each of the Bill System prospects, Mr. McCoy recorded a brief message to be played by telephone communicators to those phone respondents interested in listening. The tape would serve not only as a "door-opener"—virtually everyone who was called and told that the bank president had recorded a special message agreed to listen—but as a powerful demonstration of the confidence and commitment of LNB to this innovative Bill System service.

The telemarketing agency responsible for developing the program prepared a selection of tape scripts in conjunction with LNB management.

The tape of Mr. McCoy that was finally selected was one of three creative approaches tested during the campaign's initial stages. The other tapes recorded and tested featured J. D. Parker, the bank's popular television spokesman, and Mr. McCoy, together with a local lawyer who delivered a testimonial. The two tapes with Mr. McCoy, whose title and role as a respected civic leader provided an impressive degree of authority and credibility, proved most effective. The one with him alone was chosen because it was shorter.

The following is a transcript of that taped message:

HELLO, I'M CHUCK McCOY, PRESIDENT OF LOUISIANA NATIONAL BANK. I'VE CHOSEN THIS SPECIAL WAY TO REACH YOU BECAUSE I WANT TO PERSONALLY INTRODUCE YOU TO THE "BILL SYSTEM"—THE EASIEST, FASTEST WAY YET TO PAY YOUR BILLS.

NOW—INSTEAD OF WRITING CHECKS, BUYING STAMPS, STUFFING AND ADDRESSING ENVELOPES, AND REMEMBERING TO GO MAIL THEM— YOU CAN PAY ALL YOUR BILLS QUICKLY AND EASILY BY PHONE. ANY PHONE, ANYWHERE. YOU JUST TELL US WHAT BILLS YOU WANT TO PAY—AS MANY OR AS FEW AS YOU'D LIKE—AND WE TAKE CARE OF THE REST.

THE COST OF THIS SERVICE WILL SURPRISE YOU—ONLY 15 CENTS PER BILL PAID OR $1.50 PER MONTH TO PAY AS MANY BILLS AS YOU LIKE. WE'RE SO CONVINCED YOU'LL FIND THIS THE EASIEST, MOST CONVENIENT WAY TO PAY YOUR BILLS THAT WE'RE OFFERING IT TO YOU AB-*SOLUTELY FREE* FOR THE NEXT SIX MONTHS.

IN A MOMENT OUR REPRESENTATIVE WILL BE COMING BACK ON THE LINE TO ANSWER ANY QUESTIONS YOU MAY HAVE AND ENROLL YOU IN THE BILL SYSTEM. I'M PROUD THAT THIS SPECIAL SERVICE IS AVAILABLE ONLY WITH US. AND SINCE YOU ARE ALREADY AN LNB CUSTOMER, IT MAKES GOOD SENSE TO TRY THE BILL SYSTEM FOR YOURSELF AND SEE JUST HOW EASY BILL PAYING CAN BE.

WE ARE SO CONVINCED THAT YOU WILL FIND THIS THE EASIEST, MOST CONVENIENT BILL-PAYING SERVICE AVAILABLE THAT WE'VE ARRANGED THIS SPECIAL TRIAL OFFER TO LET YOU USE IT FREE FOR THE NEXT SIX MONTHS. I HOPE YOU WILL DECIDE TO TAKE ADVANTAGE OF THIS FREE INTRODUCTORY OFFER AND SEE FOR YOURSELF JUST HOW GREAT THE BILL SYSTEM IS.

The script developed for the telephone communicators took special pains to enable customers to express any fears they might have about the possibility of machine errors, a major stumbling block in gaining acceptance of an automated bill-paying system. Working closely with knowledgeable bank officials, the creative people at the telemarketing agency prepared accurate, easy-to-understand responses to these questions, allowing the communicators to offer authoritative answers during their one-to-one presentation. In all, answers to 30 different questions were included in the final script, organized in flip-chart form so the communicators could quickly find the information they needed.

The call went as follows:

Communicators were to determine whether direct mail had been received and to screen for interest in listening to a brief tape message recorded by Mr. McCoy that detailed the new bank-by-phone service benefits. The communicators returned on the line after the tape to answer questions and stimulate enrollment in the service. (See Figure 2-3.)

Those individuals called who accepted the offer of the Bill System were promptly sent an authorization form to sign, along with a complete kit of materials explaining precisely how to use the service.

Results The first step in testing the Bill System program was actually *pretesting*. By taking the draft script and three alternative tape messages and making as few as 10 to 15 calls, recording these calls, analyzing the results, and then making revisions and retesting, a smooth, effective script presentation was developed. Remember that one of the crucial aspects of this program was answering consumer questions about the new service. No matter how hard the experts try to predict which questions will arise

CAMPAIGN COMMUNICATIONS INSTITUTE OF AMERICA, INC.

LOUISANA NATIONAL BANK

PANEL 1B--SELL TBS/ENTREE/SAVINGS TO SELECTED ATM FILE

COMMUNICATOR SCRIPT

INTRODUCTION TO HOUSEHOLD	1
INTRODUCTION TO PROSPECT	2
INTRODUCE TAPE	3
IF HESITANT ABOUT TAPE (1 of 2)	4
IF HESITANT ABOUT TAPE (2 of 2)	5
AFTER TAPE (1 of 2)	6
AFTER TAPE (2 of 2)	7
OFFER	8
IF HESITANT ABOUT THE BILL SYSTEM	9
TBS CLOSE (1 of 3)	10
TBS CLOSE (2 of 3)	11
TBS CLOSE (3 of 3)	12
IF NOT INTERESTED	13
ENTREE CLOSE	14
ORDER TERMINATION	15

ANSWERS TO
ANTICIPATED QUESTIONS/OBJECTIONS
LNB--THE BILL SYSTEM

"WHO CAN BE PAID VIA THE BILL SYSTEM?"	16
"HOW FAST WILL LNB PAY?"	17
"ARE THERE LATE CHARGES?"	18
"IS THE BILL SYSTEM SAFE?"	19
"CAN I ADD MERCHANTS TO MY LIST WHENEVER I WANT?"	20
"CAN I PRACTICE BEFORE I BEGIN?"	21
"WHEN CAN I CALL?/WHAT ARE THE HOURS?"	22
"CAN A BUSINESS ACCOUNT USE THE BILL SYSTEM?"	23
"IS THERE PROOF OF PAYMENT, LIKE A CANCELLED CHECK"	24
"WHAT IF I MAKE A MISTAKE/HAVE A PROBLEM?"	25
"HOW DO I KEEP A RECORD BEFORE I PAY THE BILLS?"	26
"DO I HAVE TO CALL FROM MY HOME PHONE?"	27
"WHAT IF I HAVE A 'ONE-TIME' PAYMENT?"	28
"WHAT DO YOU MEAN BY A PERSONAL I.D. CODE?"	29
"HOW WILL I KNOW MY PAYMENT CODES?"	30
"WHEN IS THE PAYMENT ACTUALLY MADE?"	31
"IT SOUNDS SO CONFUSING"	32
"NO MONEY/CAN'T AFFORD?"	33
"NO INTEREST/NO NEED/I LIKE THE WAY I PAY BILLS NOW"	34
"NO HURRY/I'LL THINK ABOUT IT"	35
"WILL I RECEIVE MY BILLS EACH MONTH?"	36
"I'M NO LONGER WITH LNB"	37
"CAN I PAY BILLS ALL AT ONCE/ONE AT A TIME?"	38
"WHAT HAPPENS IF OVERDRAFT?"	39
"WHY DO I NEED A PERSONAL I.D. CODE?"	40

Figure 2-3. Communicators' call script for Louisiana National Bank.

when they contact the public, there are always many issues that never occur to them and others that, in fact, are perfectly clear from the start. Only pretesting and careful analysis of the results can produce a script as comprehensive and reliable as the one prepared for the Bill System.

Once the script and tape were determined, calls were made to several hundred LNB Entree-card customers, offering them the Bill System. The results were extraordinary: over 35 percent of those contacted agreed to join, and the costs per order were far lower than expected. Expanding the volume of calling would bring in economies of scale that promised to further reduce the per-order cost.

The bank had tried other sales techniques to bring in new account customers but found the telemarketing campaign to be especially successful in two highly important areas. First, the cost per new account opened was less than for any of the other media tested. Secondly, the efficient cross-selling program produced a large number of new, income-contributing accounts that might not have been brought in by other means. As Mr. Turk summarized the results, "Selling the Bill System by telephone was a natural. We're especially pleased with the results."

Program Expansion   Based on these very positive results, a further experiment in cross-selling was tested. Instead of offering a single additional service to present customers, communicators would now offer a choice of three, including the Bill System, an automatic savings plan, and an Entree card for those who did not already have one. Names to be called would be drawn from the bank's complete customer file, with notations to indicate which services the individual already used. In this way, the appropriate combination of services could be offered to each prospect during a truly personalized marketing call.

The Bill System was new and exciting, so this continued to be the lead-off for the sales message. However, the customers were offered the additional services even if they turned down the Bill System. About 70 percent of the prospects were in fact offered all three services, and the strong customer response to this new strategy indicated that a multiple-service sale was not only possible but far more profitable than the "single-service" call.

In the first *multiple-service* calling effort, over 6,500 prospects were contacted in a two-month period, and nearly 27 percent placed orders. This strong response drove the cost per order below $20, and thanks to the multiple-service agreements made in a single call, the cost per service sold was below $10.

Summary   The results of the LNB telemarketing experience clearly indicate that consumers are willing to purchase sensitive and complex financial services directly over the telephone and that trained communicators
can function as effective representatives of a banking institution or any
other industry when they are well trained and work with expertly prepared
script materials. On the financial end, the numbers speak for themselves.
Multiple-service offers in a single telephone contact added very little to the
cost of the call, yet they maximized the return on the investment very
effectively by increasing the profit potential inherent in each contact.

As to the fears of some of Louisiana National's officers that telephone
selling was incompatible with the bank's image, they were proven un-
founded not only by the strong customer response but by an independent
survey[4] as well. This sampling of those who had been called to determine
their reaction to the phone presentation revealed that the number of
people who responded negatively to the idea of LNB engaging in telephone solicitation was negligible. The communicators received overwhelmingly high marks for courtesy and informativeness. And, touching
closer to the bottom line, a sampling of those who had accepted the offer
were asked, "Would you have opened a Bill System account even if the
service had not been offered to you over the phone?" Over half of those
responding said unequivocally that they would not have tried it if they had
not been called, and over 20 percent more said "maybe," indicating that
the phone call was the catalyst that secured their participation.

Case History: New Money
from New Markets

In an era when major metropolitan areas are blanketed by a wide variety
of both commercial and savings banks, the prospect of expanding into
new markets is particularly appealing for the banks. However, specific
government regulations prohibit banks from building branches outside the
area of their charter, which is limited to a single state. As consumers
become more accustomed to banking without human interaction (by
using automated teller machines, for example), the banks have also found
"loopholes" in the law that involve them in nationwide banking networks:
the time appears ripe for developing continuing relationships with customers throughout the country who may never see the inside of a "branch
office" of their bank!

---

[4] See Appendix G for the survey questionnaire and response.

Until recently, no bank had successfully offered its services to customers in areas where it did not have offices to personally service accounts. However, a recent experiment conducted by one of the largest financial institutions in the world indicates that, by using telephone to provide the personal contact needed to inspire consumer confidence, even high-ticket, relatively complicated transactions can be completed without face-to-face contact, even in geographical areas where the bank doesn't have a branch or office.

Marketing Objectives   The world of consumer banking has changed drastically in a relatively short period of time. As interest rates on Treasury bills and other secure investments soared, the return on money left in traditional savings accounts in the early 80s was legally restricted from rising, creating an enormous gap between the current "price of money" and the return available to savers. Money began draining from banks as consumers with even a few thousand dollars to invest turned to other investments, especially money market funds, to find realistic interest rates in a period of double-digit inflation.

In response, the role of the bank changed. Options involving time deposits were created to offer attractive interest rates to consumers through their local banks. In the process, banks became more than a place to leave your money—they took on the role of investment counselor. The average consumer usually needs professional advice on where to keep his or her money to "get the most out of it." Issues such as liquidity and the variety of available interest rates makes banking transactions far more complex than they ever were. As consumers look to their banks for more than simple savings and checking accounts, the bank expands its role into an advisory capacity, both educating and serving the consumer.

This dual capacity has had an enormous impact on the marketing function in the banking community, and it has made telephone a far more important aspect of the bank's interaction with the public.

The telephone test program we will examine here was conducted in a period of escalating interest rates, when banks were offering as much as 15 percent interest on an investment of $10,000 in a six-month certificate of deposit (CD). This ability on the bank's part to offer interest rates more than double those legally available through a passbook savings account provided a product attractive enough to have a reasonable chance of luring out-of-state money to the New York bank that conducted the test.

Of course, banks across the country were offering $10,000 six-month CDs at comparable interest rates, but the product to be test-marketed in

this program offered certain features that were not generally available:
- First and foremost, the bank worked out an arrangement that allowed people with less than the $10,000 minimum required for a CD purchase to receive nearly the same high yield on a substantially smaller investment. If the customer invested at least $3,000, the bank made up the difference (up to $7,000) and charged 1 percent interest for this "loan." This let someone with as little as $3,000 in savings earn a double-digit return by investing it in a shared CD, and it required tying up the money for six months only.
- Federal banking regulations governing this type of investment require substantial interest penalties for early withdrawal. However, this New York bank was willing to offer a money-back guarantee with no penalty if the buyer wished to cancel within the first month. This was a privilege not available elsewhere.

By its nature, a certificate of deposit will spark questions in the mind of the consumer considering it as an investment. There are restrictions on withdrawing money, set amounts that can be invested, interest rates that fluctuate often, and other features that make it different from other possibilities. With the modified form of CD described above, the number of questions multiplies. The telemarketing program provides answers to the consumers' questions promptly and authoritatively, thanks to prescribed replies drafted through the combined efforts of bankers and professional telemarketers.

These same answers could, of course, be provided in printed materials, but the effect would not be the same. On a practical level, the booklet that contained them would have to provide all the answers to all the common questions—an individual who may need replies to only one or two specific objections might be put off by the surplus of explanatory material. There is also a unique quality to direct interpersonal contact, a quality that gives more meaning to an answer and more appeal to the transaction.

Finally, the interest rates that are such a crucial consideration in making this type of investment decision change frequently. In order to pass up-to-the-minute information of this nature on to the consumer, a marketing system responsive to change is required; the ease of changing the data incorporated into a telephone script makes this medium the natural resource to draw upon.

The telemarketing program created to sell innovative savings certificates was designed to test two key concepts—aspects of using the medium that had not been tested before by the bank.

First, could telemarketing be used to sell a certificate of deposit? There were a string of questions involved here: Would consumers be willing to make commitments for major investments directly over the telephone? Without the detailed expertise of a professional banker, would telephone communicators be able to deal with the public effectively in this sensitive transaction? Previous experience indicated that it could probably be done, but the effect of the magnitude of the sum being invested was an entirely unpredictable factor.

This program was far more ambitious than testing consumer reaction to major investment marketing by telephone. The overriding aim was to explore the possibility of developing remote customers for a wide range of banking products and services. If a bank can successfully overcome the barrier of geography, then the profit potential opened up by this market expansion is enormous. Unlike other businesses, banks were unable to open branch offices in locations outside their current prescribed territories. The hope of "going national" with their services depends on the willingness of customers to abandon the idea that it is necessary to go and "visit your money" at a brick-and-mortar bank branch.

To convince people to make that initial change in banking habits from a local to a nonlocal banking institution required a strong product offer— something that could not be acquired from a local institution. The special CDs fit the bill nicely on this score.

To make it work, though, there had to be personalized selling activity in the remote areas targeted for testing. That's where telemarketing came in. The telephone representatives could provide all the information and individual service that would ordinarily be offered in a face-to-face meeting with a branch banker; if an unforeseen question arose, the communicator could record it and have a professional banker call back with the answer within hours. What was missing in this arrangement was the physical presence of a bank and a banker. How much difference would that make? Only testing would tell.

List Segmentation Bearing in mind the legal requirements regarding out-of-state bank marketing, three test regions were selected.

Two lists were tested within these regions:

■ Remote bank customers: individuals who had been customers of the bank and had moved out of the New York area but still maintained some connection with the institution—a checking or savings account, for instance, or a bank-sponsored credit card.

■ Prospecting lists: individuals selected on the basis of a favorable demographic profile, that is, 40 years of age or older with an income of $35,000 or more.

Telemarketing Strategy The marketing program designed to sell these certificates involved a totally integrated direct-marketing package—direct mail, an incoming "800" number, and outgoing WATS-line calling—all timed and structured to complement each other in a synergistic campaign.

The program progressed in three stages:

Stage 1. The new program relied on an initial direct-response mailing to introduce the high-yield savings certificate within the geographical areas to be tested.

The mail package explained the basic advantages of the program and offered further information by calling a toll-free "800" number. There were also premium items offered in some of the test mailings—ranging from a hibiscus plant to a book to a fairly expensive folding umbrella—as an incentive to respond.

Stage 2. When the prospect called the "800" number provided in the mailing piece, the operator took the basic name, address, and telephone number information—and then went beyond, in an unusual application of the "800" number concept. The telephone representative volunteered to answer any questions the caller might have about the certificate program and then offered to reserve a certificate in the caller's name right then and there. This was a unique approach to incoming-call handling—using an active, selling script to try and close on the incoming call, as opposed to the standard, reactive information-gathering function usually performed by "800" number operators.

If the caller was not interested in making a commitment at that time, the phone representative proposed calling back in a few weeks with the then-current interest rates. The communicator also asked, "What would be a good time for a bank representative to call?" If there was a premium being offered, the phone rep also took any selection of style or color in this call.

Stage 3. The names of those who had called in to the "800" number were removed from the list so that the remaining names of people who had received a mailing could be used for outbound telemarketing. This list processing had to be completed quickly—it was important to make the calls soon after the mailing piece was received to capitalize on its impact. The sooner the better!

An additional use of outbound telemarketing explored "follow-up calls" to boost final sales response. Those who agreed on their incoming telephone call to purchase a certificate but had not yet sent in payment three weeks afterward constituted a separate calling list. In any telemarketing effort, more people say "yes" than finally send in orders—or pay for them. These individuals were contacted to determine why they had not mailed in a check, to answer any additional questions that might have arisen, and to resell the certificate if possible.

Creative Strategies   The first step in the outbound call was to repeat the basic benefits and features of the program, using then-current interest rates to tell the prospect precisely what return to expect on the investment he or she was considering. This information, which changed every week as interest rates fluctuated, was prepared in table form for the communicators' ready reference. The telephone contact allowed an up-to-date sales presentation that would not have been possible through a mail-only campaign. It also helped move the prospect toward a close—the high interest rate being quoted "could only be guaranteed for a limited time"; if there was "interest" in the offer, it would be wise to "act now."

As always, the communicator had scripted replies ready to respond to the most commonly raised objections, including questions about the safety of purchasing investment vehicles (a) by mail, or (b) from an out-of-state bank; (c) the relative merits of this savings certificate versus some locally available product, or (d) investment in mutual funds; (e) further explanations of the regulations regarding penalties for early withdrawal; (f) minimum deposits; (g) taxability of interest; and so forth. If a question came up that was not included in the script, the communicator offered to have a bank representative call back the prospect within a day with the appropriate answer.

Control and accuracy—crucial considerations. Maintaining accuracy in the answers given to prospects over the phone is always an important consideration in both the design and the execution of a telemarketing campaign. For a program dealing with government-regulated financial transactions, the need for absolute accuracy in every statement made by every communicator takes on critical importance. Any mistakes can have not only negative impact on the individual contacted but legal implications as well.

The keys to establishing and maintaining accuracy as flawless as possible are the following:

■ *Develop scripted responses* in close cooperation with the experts. In this case, for example, the telemarketing professionals cooperated with the professional bankers. Only by combining the expertise in communicating with people over the telephone with the in-depth product knowledge of the financial experts could reliable, accurate, and comprehensive answers be crafted.

■ *Train communicators* to follow the scripted responses to the letter. They should not make attempts at interpretation or expansion beyond the written text before them when dealing with such sensitive material.

■ *Constantly monitor* to ensure that the communicators are indeed following the script. This entails live monitoring by trained supervisory personnel and taping (with a "beeper") a segment of the calls for later analysis.

■ *Establish a backup system* whereby questions that are not covered in the script or issues that simply become too complicated or detailed can be referred to a more authoritative source—in this case, a bank representative. If the communicator notes the question accurately and a return call can be made with the answer within a short time frame, then none of the effectiveness of the initial phone call will be lost.

A unique closing strategy. The form of the close in this transaction was both important and interesting. If the prospect agreed to purchase a certificate, he or she was immediately assured that the bank had accepted their firm financial commitment. While the bank could not issue a certificate until it had received the remittance, the communicator *could* issue a certificate *number* right over the phone, in effect reserving a certificate in the individual's name. The customer was told where to fill in this number on his or her check and on the registration forms that had previously arrived in the mail and was urged to send the forms and a check as soon as possible to "lock in" the interest rate being offered at the time. The rate that actually pertained was the one in effect on the day the remittance was postmarked. That way, the customer did not suffer a penalty for banking by mail by risking a drop in interest rates while the check was in transit. This was significant, since at that time interest rates could change by a point in a week.

With a comprehensive script in hand and thorough training in the program before going on the phones, the communicator could perform nearly every function that a far more highly paid bank officer would have fulfilled in a face-to-face meeting with the prospective investor. This was confirmed by an assistant vice president of the bank, whose name was included in the prospect list for quality-control purposes. He posed some tough questions to the communicator who called him and then wrote a letter to the communicator and his employers, which read in part:

"At first I played the part of an ordinary prospect, asking for clarification on the 1 percent loan and other issues. But alas, you were so in control that I couldn't resist the temptation to wrestle with you by tossing out a couple of questions that I knew were not on your script. You held your ground quite nicely. Your responses were sharp, to the point, and authoritative—no nervous stutter or hesitation. . . . Congratulations on a job well done."

Results The level of response produced from the two distinct market groups or segments contacted—those who maintained some financial relationship with the bank and those who were noncustomers—was predictably different. However, each was extremely promising, given the nature of the task being undertaken in each of these markets. Remote banking customers were being introduced to an entirely new source of banking services, so each sale in this market segment represented the opportunity to establish a new, long-term customer relationship.

On the incoming "800" number direct-response calls, over 18 percent of the bank's current remote customers agreed to invest in a certificate and received their certificate number at the time of their call in. Noncustomers made a purchase commitment on 6 percent of their incoming calls.

A similar ratio was evident in the outbound calls made to nonrespondents. Approximately 1.6 percent of the current remote customers contacted agreed to purchase a certificate, compared with 0.5 percent of the noncustomers. Bearing in mind the nature of the investment—anywhere from $3,000 to $10,000—this closing rate was remarkable.

There is one note of caution to be sounded in reviewing these figures. They do not reflect the nonfulfillment rate—those who agreed to participate but failed to send in their payment. This statistic is certainly important in evaluating the net program results, as is the bank's level of profitability on the investment being marketed. Unfortunately, neither figure is available at this time, due to the proprietary nature of the information. Suffice it to say that bank officials were pleased enough with the bottomline results to plan a large-scale roll-out of the campaign.

Alternative strategy tested. Another strategy for marketing the modified CDs that was tested but rejected involved an ingenious but complex offer of money-management assistance for current customers. The program began with test mailings to the same two list segments outlined above—remote customers and demographically selected noncustomers outside the bank's primary area. The direct-mail package explained that the bank was offering a new investment system that could potentially double an individual's return on savings. The recipient was alerted to the fact that a bank representative "would call soon" with details, and the letters were signed by an account executive at the bank.

A list of those who had received mailings, complete with the name of the individual account executive who had signed the personalized letter, was passed along to a professional telemarketing agency. Communicators using scripted presentations called the prospects, asked whether the mailing had arrived, and offered to explain in more detail the offer being made. The key to taking advantage of this offer was the preparation of a "Cash Management Analysis," a personal program prepared by the bank account executive, indicating not only where the prospect's assets were currently but how they could be redistributed using the bank's new investment vehicles to produce at least twice as much interest while maintaining acceptable cash reserves. This analysis would be prepared free of charge.

The program required the prospect to furnish detailed information on personal income and savings to the communicator on the phone. Despite the sensitive nature of personal financial information, prospects who were interested in the concept as a whole did not balk at supplying the required background on their personal finances. Clearly, the communicators were accepted as a trusted representative of the bank.

When the telephone information was gathered, it was passed back to the account executives at the bank, who produced personalized analyses using standardized forms, all of which was processed into neat, individualized financial plans and mailed out to the prospects.

The next step was another phone call. About a week and a half after the mailing, the communicator called to make sure the "Cash Management Analysis" had arrived and offered to go through it line-by-line and answer any questions. If the prospect indicated interest in following the recommendations contained in the analysis, the communicator arranged to have the account executive call the prospect to make arrangements for the financial transactions involved.

This marketing approach produced a favorable response from a large number of individuals—but the costs were too high. In order to complete a sale, three phone calls (two from telephone communicators and one from the account executive) and three mailings (including the fulfillment package sent after the order was taken) were required. Data factoring in the value of the customer over the buying lifetime absorption or the expenses involved were unavailable to allow the overtime. Valuable conceptual lessons came out of this heavily service-oriented approach, but the simpler three-stage approach was finally selected for the final roll-out of the program.

Summary   The test effort outlined was a substantial success, and plans were under way to launch an expanded, heavily financed campaign, using print, radio, television, and direct-mail advertising to produce the leads for phone follow-up. However, by this time interest rates had taken a dramatic downturn. The differential the bank could offer between a shared six-month certificate of deposit and a passbook savings account dropped, until it was only 1 or 2 percentage points—not enough to effectively compete for the consumer's business against local branch banks. The roll-out was shelved because the product it would have offered was, in effect, no longer available.

However, there was still considerable interest in finding the right product to take advantage of the lessons learned in the program. Testing was continued to explore innovative ways of marketing other longer-term investment vehicles, offering attractively high interest rates to the consumer with phone as a major element in the marketing media mix. In addition, telephone's unique personal contact capabilities were brought to bear in several difficult selling situations in the consumer and corporate markets, including "rolling over" certificates of deposit, setting specific appointments for small business owners to discuss cash-management systems with a bank officer, and later introducing the All-Savers certificates to the consumer market.

Implications for the Marketer   The proven ability to market high-ticket investment vehicles by phone to remote markets expands the horizons for telephone marketing far beyond the stereotyped applications of selling subscriptions or taking incoming orders.

First, this experience reinforces the assertion that telephone communicators can handle complex products when given proper training and backup materials—and neither training nor materials need to be overly elaborate. Expanding the number of officers at bank branches is an extremely expensive proposition. However, by splitting off the selling function and establishing a telemarketing system to handle it efficiently and reliably, the selling process proceeds far more successfully. The same principle applies in many other businesses where face-to-face selling is only one function of a busy individual's duties. By implementing a system of personalized telephone contact, prospects receive a more immediate and better quality of service for the most part, and other important business functions can be handled by the individual freed from the "face-to-face" selling responsibility.

The lesson gleaned from this study regarding territory expansion is also pertinent for a wide range of marketers. Combined with direct mail, telemarketing can increase market penetration dramatically at very reasonable expense. One of the quickly understandable reasons for proceeding into new markets by telephone is the minimal additional overhead involved in testing unknown waters. Instead of spending money up front to hire additional field representatives, pay for travel and lodging, or perhaps even establish a branch office in a new location, marketers can enter a new region through direct mail and/or advertising and use *telephone* to offer the personal contact needed to close the sale.

Historical as well as traditional approaches to offering and selling investments and securities—be they money market funds or IRAs—are undergoing radical change.

Nowadays depositors are more personally involved with their cash cards and ATMs than with a "personal banker." Bankers Trust Company in New York sold its entire branch operation when it sensed the implications of the new electronic banking revolution. Citicorp beefed up its "Marketing Department"—and ordered thousands of electronic tellers! All of this is but a prelude to the control of all consumer banking directly from the home via the "little black box." Monthly statements available for the asking on your TV screen: debits, credits, charges, or placing orders all will involve the telephone—cable or instrument—on your personal home TV screen, connected with a home computer and home printer. Telephone testing will add a new dimension—the customer can "see you" and "order or reject" immediately! Bank sales "personalities," extra-special and responsive customer-service systems, and "believable" offers will dominate the screen and telephone relationship—for the new levels of response made possible by "interactive marketing."

Selling credit card protection by phone. Another banking service that has been marketed successfully by phone is a credit card insurance policy. This coverage protects the holder from liability from unauthorized use of credit cards that have been lost or stolen. Federal law says that a card holder may be liable for up to $50 charged on each missing card before the issuer is notified. However, with this insurance coverage, the card holder receives the following benefits:

- Protection from liability on any credit card the consumer holds (not just bank-sponsored cards) as soon as the covered individual calls a single toll-free 24-hour telephone number

- Emergency cash and airline ticket arrangements if needed
- Immediate notification of all card issuers of the loss or theft, and ordering of replacement cards

This type of service was first offered to the public in the early 1970s. By 1978 two major companies had developed a commanding leadership position in the marketing of credit card insurance—Safecard and CCSB. Between the two, they had approximately 3 million customers. It was at this point that another important factor entered the picture—a major New York City bank.

The time was ripe for a major expansion of this market. Previously, banks had been restricted to offering their customers only one of the two bank-sponsored credit cards—Mastercharge (now Mastercard) and VISA. In 1978 this restriction was rescinded. The bank in our case study, which previously had offered only Mastercharge, went after the newly opened VISA market segment through an aggressive direct-mail campaign to a nationwide audience—a move that caused substantial consternation among local banks, who felt that their territory was being infringed upon by this huge New York banking institution.

The file of the bank's credit card holders quickly grew to approximately 6 million names—3 million of which were active customers.

A bank vice president working in the personal banking division prepared a business plan that showed the bank that it would increase earnings by developing its own credit card protection service. In order to test this hypothesis, he organized a program of direct mailings.

The total mailing audience was 100,000 bank customers. This group was divided into 30 cells to test variables in offer and price. The mailing itself arrived in a standard business envelope, just as any other piece of mail from the bank would look.

Overall response rate was a respectable 2 percent, producing the first 2,000 customers for the protection plan. The best combination of response rate and profit margin came at the level of a $27 fee for three years of coverage.

Further testing was done in the form of inserts in regular credit card statement mailings. These produced a response rate of approximately 0.5 percent—a profitable rate given the fact that there was no additional postage charge entailed in the promotion.

However, despite the positive and profitable response the bank was generating through their mail program, there was still a problem in using this route to build a new business division—the rate of customer growth was too slow. In order to justify the investment in servicing these protection plan customers, a much larger subscriber base was required. In order to produce a large number of new customers in a short period of time, the bank turned to a professional telemarketing agency.

A natural marketing service. The first challenge to face when confronted with a 6-million-name card holder file was identifying those portions that would hold the greatest promise for telephone contact. In consultations between the bank and the telemarketing agency, an interesting feature of the credit card division's operating procedure came to light, which offered a niche seemingly custom tailored for outbound telemarketing.

After an individual applied for a bank credit card, there was a six-week time lag between receipt of the application by the bank and receipt of the card by the customer. Three weeks were involved in checking the individual's credit, making the decision on whether or not to issue the card, and entering the new account in the computer system. However, there was another three-week period *after* the customer was accepted—the interval used to produce the cards, process them, and mail them out.

The positioning of telephone in this process was dictated by the need for immediate follow-up of the initial acceptance. Once those new individuals had been approved, their names and phone numbers were available for telephoning. The telephone communicators could identify themselves as representatives of the bank, give the customer the good news that his or her application had been accepted and cards were being prepared, and then make the natural transition into a discussion of the need to protect the new credit cards.

Working in close collaboration, the bank and the telemarketing agency developed a script that was an effective sales tool and yet maintained the required prestige image and absolute integrity and accuracy necessary in any bank-marketing program. The communicators first congratulated the prospects, informing them that their applications had been approved and that the new cards should arrive in about a week. They even told the new card holders how high a credit line had been approved.

Then the call moved into the sales presentation, first offering a capsule explanation of the coverage being offered and then, if the party was interested, explaining each of the benefits in detail. Enrolling in the plan was extremely simple—the fee would just be billed to the customer's new charge account. And the coverage became effective with the agreement over the phone, so the customer was instantly committed to the insured service.

The results of the calls to this market segment were extraordinary—the positive response rate in the initial test was nearly 36 percent. This level settled down somewhat as the testing progressed, but remained at nearly 30 percent on a projectable basis.

While the success of this effort was clear, it was also distinctly limited in the number of potential calls, due to the relatively small numbers of new cards issued. The marketing search for further likely prospects for the service led to another seemingly natural group—those individuals who had reported their credit cards lost or stolen. This group amounted to approximately 10,000 bank customers each month.

The telephone communicators' script was modified to be responsive to the different situation involved in contacting these new prospects. The communicators once again provided an informational announcement— they told the card holder that replacement cards had been issued and should be received within a week or two. Having filled this "customer-service" role, the communicator then went on to discuss the ways in which Protection Plus could make the experience of losing credit cards less traumatic, should it ever happen again.

While the response of this group was lower than that of the new card holders, it was still very high indeed—well over 20 percent accepted the offer—and was extremely profitable for the bank, as far as it went. Once again, though, the list was distinctly and irrevocably limited. There was an enormous potential universe out there, in the form of the 6 million bank customer names on the total card holder file. However, a high telephone order response rate was the only way to justify the marketing expense involved in telephone contact to such a broadly based list. A test program was called for to determine how great a percentage of this mass audience could be profitably contacted and how the "segmented," receptive individuals "willing to buy" could be identified.

A million calls in a year. The bank credit card holder file offered 40 different demographic criteria on which list segmentation could be based. Test cells were developed to probe the reactions of individuals based on a single demographic factor or a combination of demographic factors. All list handling and tabulation was handled by the bank's sophisticated computer system.

The result of the testing was highly encouraging—approximately 1 million of the total 6 million names on the master file fit the demographic profile for economically feasible telephone contact.

Recruiting, hiring, and training the necessary telephone representatives to call a million people was a massive undertaking. As a result, the bank expanded its program to tap a number of telemarketing agency resources. As the year progressed, as many as eight different companies were involved in the calling. The bank even attempted to set up its own in-house facility, an effort that the bank's vice president says taught him that the fees charged by telemarketing agencies for their services were surprisingly reasonable, given the nature of overheads and the labor-intensive effort involved in making professional-quality, fully accountable calls. Nevertheless, he suggests that the experience was valuable as a source of greater understanding of the telemarketing process as a whole, whether conducted in-house or via a telemarketing agency.

Each agency worked in its own style and adapted the already tested basic information package describing the protection plan to its own mode of operation. In the course of the year, agencies were dropped or added, depending on the results of their calls and the quality of their presentation as monitored by the bank. By the end of the year, only two agencies were left, having performed at a level that was consistently professional enough to meet the bank's needs and, at the same time, sales-effective enough to keep the overall response rate of the million-call effort at over 20 percent.

In the course of a single year, this massive telemarketing effort expanded the protection plan's customer file by a factor of 10! It had, in effect, built a highly profitable business for the bank, taking a promising concept and adding a steady influx of paying customers in a very short time frame.

It is also interesting to note the results of price testing done in the course of the telemarketing effort. Through the mail, the strongest response came when offering three years of service for $27—any fee over that level caused a sharp drop-off in response. However, by phone, no substantial customer resistance was encountered until the price went beyond the $36 level. Needless to say, as intelligent marketers, the bank maintained the cost for Protection Plus coverage at $36 for three years—adding a six-month bonus period at no further charge to justify the higher price level. This experience speaks strongly of the difference in consumer response between mail and phone. The addition of personal, individual telephone contact was persuasive enough to support a 33 percent price increase over the mail-feasible level.

Telephone as a service medium. There was a time when *the bank* or *the banker* was regarded by the American consumer as a family consultant, like the family doctor or lawyer. This relationship has changed dramatically in the last few years. According to Devin Scott, CCI's Vice President for Financial Services, the bank has become a retail chain, and consumers shop for CDs as they shop for winter coats or new appliances.

But underneath this new consumerism lies an ingrained need for the family financial consultant.

How will the banks provide this kind of personal service and regain the kind of loyalty that draws a lifetime commitment from a customer household? Again and again, the need is stated: *service* (attention must be paid)!

Telemarketing provides a natural medium for the kind of customer-service-oriented, interactive dialogue that supports the needs of customers and promotes the products and services provided by contemporary banks. As with any advertising or marketing medium, effectiveness is a function of careful planning on the part of the bank marketer. What is the bottom line for profit on any given product or service? When does the life of a customer, and the "cross-sell" potential, have to make way for simple, expedient short-term transactions to gain vital investment capital?

Whatever the need, telemarketing, in combination with other direct-marketing disciplines, provides an immediate and controllable force to shape the future of any bank's success in an increasingly demanding marketplace.

chapter three /

"800" Success Stories: 3 Companies—25 Million Incoming Calls

The incoming or direct-response call via the "800" WATS network at AT&T continues to enjoy the largest share of the telemarketing boom. New, specialized directories of companies—large and small—seem to come out every month. Ma Bell supposedly passed its ten-thousandth "800" customer somewhere in 1980, yet imaginative new uses for the concept continue to expand. Our first book, *Telephone Marketing*, details the early "800" route to sales for companies like McGraw-Hill's Sweet's Catalog Files and the Lane Furniture Dealer support program. Financial services offered by Dreyfus Liquid Assets are today valued in the billions, due in great measure to its combined multimedia programs of print advertising and "800" calls. In structuring the campaign for the '76 Olympic Coin program, we learned the inherent problems of the system in attempting to answer 10,000 calls per hour on nationwide TV during the NFL game on a Sunday afternoon! And we learned about the impact on incoming calls for All-State Insurance during the first snowstorm in Atlanta in a century—when the "800" facility was closed down!

The program we're proudest of is still bringing in much-needed dollars for UNICEF from concerned citizens who respond via the "800." This chapter describes the entry of the package goods conglomerates and a major electronic manufacturer to the spectrum of "800" users. It provides details and a very specialized knowledge to its discussion and analysis of these very original and successful campaigns. The bulk of the material was prepared by Aldyn McKean, probably the leading "800" expert and editor of the *AIS "800" Report*—certainly the leading newsletter dealing with telemarketing. McKean also functions as a New-York–based consultant with a background in all aspects of the use of the telephone medium but specializing in incoming-response programming.

Since the introduction of the "800" number in 1967, the number and diversity of applications of toll-free calls have grown at an astounding speed. The range of marketing and service activities that are now performed over toll-free lines is truly remarkable. It is hard to believe today that when first introduced, "800" numbers were perceived principally as a device for businesses to hold down long-distance bills and avoid collect calls in their internal communications.

Within a few years of the birth of "800" numbers, the travel industry began to use them as a means of encouraging customers to make reservations by phone. Soon television commercials appeared in which viewers were urged to order inexpensive novelty items by dialing an "800" number. As "800" began to appear in a vast array of advertisements, a new term, *direct response*, was added to the lexicon of marketing.

As the traditional direct-marketing tools of planning, testing, and analysis came to be applied to toll-free telemarketing, the effectiveness of the "800" number was lifted to a new plateau. Indeed it is the early and systematic use of planning, testing, and analysis that distinguishes the three operations discussed in this chapter from most other "800" number campaigns of the late 1970s.

Case History: Customer Service by Telephone

In San Diego a homemaker wants to know if Crisco shortening can be used a year after the can is opened. An amateur pastry chef in New Orleans wants to know how much Duncan Hines cake mix to use to fill a 12-inch pan. A senior citizen in New Hampshire wants to know how to remove a stain caused by spilling Downy fabric softener directly on a white shirt.

Help in each of these dilemmas was a quick, toll-free telephone call away. In each of these instances, the consumer called an "800" number and spoke to a Procter & Gamble consumer-services representative, who offered appropriate advice: "You should not use Crisco from a can that has been open for longer than nine months." "You'll need to use a package and a half of mix for a 12-inch pan. You should also add three-eighths of a cup of regular flour to the batter." "The stains can be removed by dampening the stained area, rubbing it with a bar of soap, and rinsing." In each case, a problem with a P&G product was averted or corrected. Potentially dissatisfied customers were pleased with the help they received from the consumer-services representatives and thus remained loyal buyers of P&G products. That is precisely the objective of Procter & Gamble, which seeks to build and maintain large market shares through brand loyalty.

How the Program Originated   In the early 1970s, P&G's market research turned up some facts with startling implications. At that time, the company, which did not widely publicize a customer telephone number, heard from its customers almost exclusively by mail. The market research teams found that of the consumers who had problems or complaints concerning Procter & Gamble products, only 40 percent bothered to communicate with the company. Of the 60 percent that did not complain, a majority were likely to cease purchasing the brand with which they had experienced problems.

Most of the 40 percent who did communicate their problems were appreciative of P&G's response and continued to buy the brand in question. However, many of these people expressed unhappiness over the length of time it took for P&G to respond.

It was clear that it would be beneficial for the company to hear from more of its customers. It was decided that an effort would be made to encourage a greater percentage of the customers who experienced problems with P&G products to communicate with the company. It was also felt that something should be done to shorten the reaction time.

The solution, it appeared, was to publicize a toll-free telephone number. But how should the number be publicized and how extensively?

The Test Begins   It was decided that a test of an "800" number customer-service operation should be conducted. Accordingly, in 1974, "800" numbers began to appear on Duncan Hines brownie mixes.

In the initial months of testing, several important discoveries were made. First of all, the telephone consumer-services representatives were spending considerable time dealing with questions that had not emerged as significant when communication was received only by mail. Chief among these was a variety of questions concerning the need for special baking instructions in very high altitudes. These questions were so frequent that today all Duncan Hines mixes come with instructions for high-altitude baking.

Another surprise was how eager consumers were to use the telephone to obtain information. The number of consumer contacts concerning the brownie mixes nearly doubled in the first months in which the "800" numbers appeared. In addition, many calls were received about products—particularly Duncan Hines cake mixes—that did not at the time carry "800" numbers.

Perhaps the most interesting finding emerged from market research follow-up studies of customers who had used the "800" numbers. It was found that over 90 percent of these people were satisfied with the responses their queries had received.

The Test Expands Eighteen months after the "800" numbers first appeared on brownie mixes, each of P&G's six operating divisions chose one product on which to further test the "800" number concept. In 1976 and 1977 the toll-free numbers were added to the packages of the chosen products. In no case was a division's major brand used for the test, as it was felt that this might generate an unmanageable volume of calls.

By 1976, P&G's market research teams had generated an immense amount of data related to the telephone calls being received. A record of the number of calls received on each product was kept by the hour, day, week, and month. A record of the types of calls—whether questions, complaints, or compliments—was also kept. Market research again indicated that over 90 percent of the customers who contacted P&G were satisfied with the response they received and would continue to use P&G brands.

An extensive analysis of the data that had been generated was then undertaken. The number of calls received on each of the six products was correlated with the product's sales volume as well as with the volumes of mail that had been received about the product in prior years. This process allowed P&G's analysts to estimate the volume of calls that could be expected on other products, based on those products' projected sales volumes and previous histories of generating mail.

In addition, it was found that the cost of handling a telephone contact averaged significantly less than the cost of dealing with a similar mail contact.

All this information was then studied in an effort to determine if it would be cost-effective to print "800" numbers on all of P&G's products. Several factors had to be weighed. The total cost of the consumer-services operation would increase if "800" numbers were printed on all products, because the number of consumer contacts would increase. However, the cost of handling each contact would decrease. In addition, the increased number of customer contacts would yield increased customer satisfaction and hence greater brand loyalty. After carefully weighing all these factors, P&G's management decided to print "800" numbers on all P&G products.

The Roll-out Begins By the end of 1978, a plan had been developed whereby "800" numbers would gradually be added to all P&G products. By June of 1979, 60 percent of the products carried "800" numbers. By the end of 1980, 90 percent had numbers, and by June 1981, every P&G product displayed an "800" number.

Each of the six divisions—for example, paper products, bar soap, laundry products, and so on—was assigned a different "800" number. Consumer-services representatives were hired and given extensive training in the products of the division they handled. Food-division service reps made Duncan Hines cakes in P&G's test kitchens. Other reps gave Lilt home permanents to volunteers in P&G's lab.

Representatives were then given extensive training in telephone etiquette, listening skills, and interpersonal relations—with particular emphasis on handling irate customers. In addition, the representatives were given scripted answers to the most commonly asked questions as well as detailed fact sheets about each of the products.

The Results The results of P&G's "800" number operation have been impressive. In 1981 there were half a million contacts made between consumers and P&G. Approximately 75 percent of these were by phone. This compares with the average of 160,000 contacts per year that P&G experienced prior to installing in-WATS lines. Where previously the company heard from only 40 percent of dissatisfied customers, today analysts estimate that that figure has reached 80 percent. Research shows that 30 percent of the people who contact P&G today have never before bothered to communicate with a consumer goods manufacturer in the past. Thus the company is hearing from people who are perhaps reluctant to write letters. About half of the communications received are requests for information, a sixth are expressions of praise or gratitude, and a third are complaints about anything from product performance to the plots of soap operas sponsored by P&G.

What's more, the cost per contact is 40 *percent lower* than it was when correspondence was by mail. Even though the total number of consumer contacts has increased threefold, the total out-of-pocket costs for handling them have increased by only 20 percent. Research continues to indicate that over 90 percent of the people who contact P&G are satisfied with the response they receive. While these benefits alone would more than justify the cost of establishing and running the operation, there have been significant side benefits that were not anticipated.

Products improved. P&G constantly hears from its customers of ways in which it can improve its products or make them more useful. The printing of high-altitude baking instructions is one example. Another example occurred with Crest and Gleem toothpaste. Consumers frequently complained that when they attempted to get the last bits of toothpaste out of the tube, the tube would crack open. As a result, the tubes were strengthened.

These are complaints that were never heard about in the mail—not because they did not exist but because they were not serious enough to warrant writing a letter.

Quality Control Improved–recalls avoided. In the fall of 1979, a spate of calls were received from consumers who complained that the plastic tops on Downy fabric softener were splintering when they were twisted on and off—resulting in a dangerous situation in which consumers might cut their fingers. P&G quickly identified the supplier of the defective caps. It was discovered that this supplier had recently changed the chemical composition of the caps, which resulted in their becoming more brittle.

Because the telephone gave consumers an immediate communications link with P&G, the company was warned of the problem before it became serious. Indeed, most of the fragile caps were in the factory and were simply replaced. In this way P&G avoided what could have been a costly recall as well as potentially even more costly lawsuits.

Major problems more easily managed. When major problems with a product do develop, they can be more easily managed with less customer aggravation because of the in-WATS telephone system. A case in point is the suspension of sales of Rely tampons. When studies suggested in the summer of 1980 that the tampons might be a contributing factor in the occurrence of toxic shock syndrome, P&G voluntarily suspended sale of the brand and offered refunds to women who had already purchased Rely.

When news of the possible dangers of using Rely was broken to the public, P&G was ready. A tape was prepared to handle the most frequently asked questions, such as "How do I get a refund?" If the caller had questions that were not covered on the tape, she was directed to call another number where representatives were standing by from 8:00 A.M. to 8:30 P.M. Central Time. In this instance, research suggested that approximately 85 percent of the people who contacted P&G about Rely were satisfied with the response they received. Once again, what could have been an extremely distressing situation was made less so by "800" numbers.

New product ideas received. Not all consumer complaints result in changes in the product about which the complaint was made. Sometimes wholly new products result. Many consumers complained about having to go to their washing machines at the rinse cycle in order to add Downy fabric softener. The result was the development of Bounce, a rayon sheet impregnated with softener that can be added to the clothes in a dryer.

Another example is provided by Attends. Consumers requested that a large-sized Pampers-style disposable diaper be created to aid in the care of incontinent adults. The result was Attends.

Again, these were problems that did not show up in the mail but came to light only after the telephone program was instituted.

Advertising suggestions received. A final benefit of the "800" number customer-services operation is that among the 80,000 consumer testimonials P&G receives each year are ideas that can be used in ad campaigns. All favorable comments on P&G products are forwarded to the appropriate advertising agencies. Past consumer praise has developed into major ad campaigns for Ivory soap, Joy dishwashing liquid, and other products.

Virtually all aspects of Procter & Gamble's marketing efforts have improved as a direct result of the toll-free telephone customer service that the company provides. The gains that P&G has achieved have been made possible in large part by the careful planning and testing that went into creating the telephone operation, as well as the research and analysis that accompanies it.

Case History: Dealer Locator Program for the Spacemaker

In the summer of 1979 the marketing staff of General Electric's range, dishwasher, and disposal division had a problem. The division's product development team had come up with a new microwave oven called the Spacemaker. The name derived from the fact that, rather than taking up counter space, the unit was designed to be installed over an existing range. It was, in fact, a range hood and microwave in one unit.

While this feature solved a consumer problem, it created headaches for GE's dealer organization. In order for a unit to be installed, the existing range hood had to be removed; in many cases a 120-volt line on its own circuit had to be brought to the site of the installation, and the new unit had to be put in place. Many dealers were dubious that a non-counter-top model would sell, while others were incapable of providing installations because of the required electrical work. The result was that, when the Spacemaker was introduced, only a small percentage of GE's dealers carried it.

The problem for GE's marketing team was to devise a means whereby consumers who were interested in the unit could find a dealer who did carry it.

GE Turns to "800" Numbers To inform consumers about where they could purchase a Spacemaker, GE had two options. Print ads could be purchased that listed all the dealers, or ads could encourage consumers to call a telephone number to find out the location of their nearest dealer.

Publishing dealer locations in print ads would have required GE to use up a substantial portion of the Spacemaker's ad budget to buy the space necessary to list the dealers. Since the Spacemaker was a new and unknown product, it was felt that the ads should present the sales message in as strong and undiluted a fashion as possible. Thus the listing of dealers was rejected.

The idea of using an "800" number in the ads was considered. The critical unknown was whether or not consumers would actually take the trouble to go to their telephones and dial an "800" number in order to find out where they could buy the Spacemaker. Only time would tell. It was decided that a three-month test should be conducted with the target date for the beginning of the test to be October 1979.

In-house or Out-of-house? Once the decision had been made to use "800" numbers, it then had to be decided who would take the calls. Should GE attempt to set up its own telemarketing operation and handle its own calls? Or should the operation be turned over to an outside service bureau?

Using an outside service bureau offered several advantages:

Quick start-up. With an outside service, the phones, lines, and telephone reps would already be in place. Thus the time necessary to get the program off the ground would be much shorter.

Cost saving. By combining the call volumes of several clients, an outside service can generate enough calling activity to make most efficient use of labor and phone lines.

Experience. Finally, a service that has handled similar campaigns would be in a better position to predict call volumes, anticipate any likely problems, and effectively manage the program.

These advantages of out-of-house operations were balanced against the primary disadvantage: the loss of control. With an out-of-house operation, GE would have no direct control over the number of WATS lines used, the quality of the telephone representatives, and the reporting of results.

It was decided that, particularly given GE's lack of experience in "800" number telemarketing, the advantages of an outside service center would outweigh the loss of control.

Enter Dialogue Marketing   The marketing team at GE made contact with such a center,[1] which specializes exclusively in handling dealer locator calls on its "800" lines.

The agency offered several capabilities that would be beneficial to GE's program.

Specialized operation. The company does not take order calls or any type of call other than dealer location inquiries. Thus all personnel, from management to phone reps and clerical people, are specialists in that type of operation.

Computerized system. Dealer files are maintained in company computers and each phone representative can access the file through a video terminal unit. Cumbersome and time-consuming hard copy or microfilm files are thus avoided.

Geo-match locator program. This is an efficient program whereby callers can be matched with their nearest dealers based on zip codes. The representative who takes the call simply keys the caller's zip code into the computer system, and the name of the dealer located closest to the caller appears on the video terminal screen.

Rotation of dealer names. In those instances in which there is more than one dealer in the same area, the computer system will automatically give the names on a rotating basis. Thus all dealers are treated fairly.

Short calls. The system is able to keep its calls to an average length of one minute. This is accomplished through careful training and monitoring of phone reps as well as a computer program that saves key strokes. When the caller's zip code is entered into the system, the corresponding city and state automatically appear on the video terminal and are also entered. The phone rep merely corroborates that they are correct but does not need to

[1] Dialogue Marketing, Peoria, Illinois.

key them in. This keeps call times to a minimum and thus decreases telephone costs.

On-the-fly on-line updates. The dealer list can be updated on the fly. Thus any changes are entered into the system and available to the telephone reps within minutes after the company has been notified.

Follow-up reports. A variety of follow-up activities improve the effectiveness of the dealer locator program offered. Reports can show by the day of the week and hour of the day how many calls were received. Reports can indicate which medium generated the calls, how long the calls lasted, and which phone rep handled each call. A monthly breakdown of the number of referrals to each dealer is provided. It's also possible to send dealers a "hot prospect" card with the name and phone number of anyone who was referred. Thus the dealer can call the prospect and say that the desired product is in stock.

Setting Up the Operation   Having hired an outside telephone service center to handle the calls, GE began putting together the dealer list. This was a crucial part of the campaign, and GE wisely assembled the full list two months before the ads would appear. This allowed time for the service center to enter the list into its computer system and then check and recheck it for accuracy.

Space was purchased in a variety of magazines. These included home-improvement magazines (*Better Homes and Gardens, Good Housekeeping*, and *House Beautiful*); women's magazines (*Ladies Home Journal* and *McCall's*); culinary magazines (*Bon Appetite* and *Cuisine*); and periodicals such as *Reader's Digest, National Geographic,* and *Money* magazine.

The Campaign Begins   By October 1979 the Spacemakers were in the dealers' warehouses and the dealer lists were on file at Dialogue. The ads appeared that month and continued through December. In that time 36,000 calls were received! Clearly consumers were willing to use the telephone to help find the product.

Extensive Follow-up Analysis   GE made extensive use of the data supplied by the phone. All callers were asked where they had seen the ad, and this information was used to evaluate the cost-effectiveness of the advertising in the various magazines. It was found that the magazine that produced the greatest number of calls per dollar of advertising was *Better Homes and*

Gardens, followed closely by *House Beautiful.* The culinary magazines proved to be cost-effective, as did the women's publications.

In the first half of 1980 it was found that *Sunset* magazine and regional publications such as *Southern Living* were also effective vehicles for Spacemaker advertising.

In addition to the media tracking, GE's analysts spent considerable time studying the relationship between calls and eventual sales of GE products. The number of calls received each month from the various metropolitan areas across the country was compared with the number of sales of Spacemaker units for the same month in the same areas. It was discovered that a significant correlation existed between the number of calls and the number of sales. Thus it was shown that the dealer locator operation played a substantial part in Spacemaker sales.

Impressive Results   The results achieved by GE's efforts were singularly impressive. Prior to the introduction of Spacemaker, GE had lagged behind its competitors in its share of the microwave-oven market. One year after Spacemaker went on the market, GE was the brand leader in microwaves.

Not a Perfect Operation   Though GE achieved enviable results, its campaign was not without flaws.

Lack of emphasis on phone number. The ads designed by GE's advertising agency for the campaign were not direct-response ads. They sold the Spacemaker unit, but they did not sell consumers on making telephone calls. Indeed, the phone number was buried at the bottom of the ads in small type. Given the correlation that was shown to exist between phone calls and sales, the failure to emphasize the phone number may have cost GE significantly.

Sourcing problems. Instead of using different "800" numbers in different magazines, the designers of the campaign had the telephone reps ask where the ad was seen. This is not the most accurate method of sourcing a call. In fact 10 percent of the callers said they had seen the ad in magazines or other media in which no ad had appeared. An additional 3 percent had been told about the ad by another party and did not know where it had appeared. Thus 13 percent of the calls were not attributed to their actual sources. Had different phone numbers been used in different media, virtually all calls could have been accurately sourced by asking the caller what number was dialed.

Lack of dealer follow-up. Perhaps the most surprising of GE's oversights was the failure to take advantage of the opportunity to notify dealers. GE did not opt to send hot prospect cards to dealers. Thus dealers had no way to follow up with prospects, and sales were certainly lost.

GE Expands the Use of "800" Numbers The success achieved with Spacemaker has prompted GE to use "800" number telemarketing in other areas. Since Spacemaker's debut, GE has used "800" number dealer locator campaigns to launch its Quick Fix System for home appliance repair and to introduce a wide-screen television. In the television operation, hot prospect cards *were* used, with excellent results.

GE has become so convinced of the power of "800" numbers that it now maintains a fully staffed "800" number customer-service center called the GE Answer Center.

Case History: Cap'n Crunch Hoists Sales with "800" Promo

From July to November of 1981, the Quaker Oats Company ran a promotional sweepstakes to boost the sales of its Cap'n Crunch dry cereal. The results of the sweepstakes once again provide eloquent testimony to the power of "800" numbers. During the promotion, sales of Cap'n Crunch increased by more than 30 percent. The brand's share of the ready-to-eat cereal market rose from 2.9 percent to 3.9 percent. Though sales have since slackened slightly, Cap'n Crunch is still doing very well.

Quaker Sought Kids' Involvement Quaker began looking in 1980 for an unusual promotional strategy that could give Cap'n Crunch a boost. The company wanted something that would involve children under 12, could be easily understood by them, and would encourage trial purchases of the 18-year-old brand.

Lee Hill, Inc., the Chicago-based promotion and merchandising agency, was hired to develop and execute the promotion. The Hill organization came up with a sweepstakes called "Find LaFoote," in which youngsters obtained maps suggestive of pirate treasure maps either from a box of Cap'n Crunch or by mail from Quaker. The cartoon character pirate Jean LaFoote was shown on the maps, but in different locations on different maps. The recorded voices of Cap'n Crunch and his crew informed youngsters who called an "800" number of LaFoote's true location.

Anyone with a map showing LaFoote at the right location won a Huffy bicycle (worth approximately $100 at retail).

The promotion was tested successfully prior to the national campaign. Based on the initial test, it was estimated that 10 million calls would be received during the four months of the national sweepstakes. In order to accommodate that volume of calls and leave room for some stretch, 300 lines were installed. Each line terminated in a Dictaphone 620 automatic answering machine. The answering machines were chosen over a computerized answering system because the computer system was not cost-justifiable for a one-shot promotion.

Call Projection Proves Drastically Low   During the first three weeks of the promotion it became apparent that the projection of call volume had been extremely low. That projection was revised to 18 million and an additional 100 lines were ordered. Illinois Bell was able to install the extra lines in only four days.

Even with 400 lines, it was possible to answer only about 40 percent of the calls on the busier days. Call traffic was at the maximum level that could be handled approximately 14 hours a day for about a month. During this time approximately 1 million call attempts were made per day, and 400,000 per day were completed. It is assumed (based on the final results of the promotion plus the fact that most of the callers were children) that many of the callers who reached busy signals were repeat dialers who kept calling frequently until they got through. When it was all over, *24 million calls* had been taken. That's 10 times the number of responses in some of the most successful mail-response sweepstakes. The Quaker sweepstakes achieved participation from half of the households in the United States with children under 12. Sales of Cap'n Crunch increased by 30 percent, with only a modest drop-off after the end of the sweepstakes.

Why It Worked   By almost any standard, the "Find LaFoote" sweepstakes would have to be termed an enormous success. How was it accomplished?

Effective promotional hook. Perhaps the most important single factor in the campaign (for which credit must go to Lee Hill, Inc.) was the presence of a brilliantly effective and simple promotional hook: a map that could make a child an instant winner of a bicycle. All too often "800" number promotions are designed with very little incentive provided for placing the call. Other promotions have attempted to generate calls by encouraging people to "Call for more information" or to "Call today for a great new idea."

Compare the appeal of those approaches to "Call to find out if you're the winner of a new bicycle."

Testing and planning. Another key ingredient in the program's success was the months of careful planning and testing that preceded it. Though the initial projections of response to the national promotion proved extremely low, even these projections would not have been possible without a test. Any attempt to estimate response to the national sweepstakes without first conducting a test would have to have been based on the results of national sweepstakes with mailed-in responses. Such sweepstakes are often considered successful if they generate 500,000 responses; 2 million responses is a rarity. Even doubling those figures would not come close to being as accurate as the projection based on the test.

Phone company commitment. The organizers of the sweepstakes were fortunate in being located in Chicago, which is served by Illinois Bell, one of the few local operating companies with a strong commitment to providing good service to telemarketers. In very few other cities would it have been possible to turn up 100 lines on four days' notice. Quaker and Lee Hill, Inc., made the most of their situation by consulting with representatives of Illinois Bell early and often. The top management of Illinois Bell was kept constantly apprised of the progress of the sweepstakes, and it was this involvement of top managers that made it possible to add extra lines rapidly.

Lack of "800" Marketing Expertise The one flaw in the planning of the sweepstakes was the rather surprising failure to involve anyone with hands-on experience in "800" number telemarketing and knowledge of past promotions. An experienced telemarketer with knowledge of the results of such promotions as Johnnie Walker and Barclay cigarettes would have known that national "800" number campaigns can generate more response than would be predicted by extrapolation from tests in isolated markets. Such a person might very well have advised that the estimate of 10 million was too low and that 300 lines would not be nearly enough.

Despite the failure to actually predict call volume, the Cap'n Crunch sweepstakes stands as a remarkable success based on the increased market share captured.

Only the Beginning The three stories presented here are only the beginning of what will doubtless be a long and varied series of unusual and original applications of the "800" number. As these examples illustrate, it is possible to achieve a great variety of marketing goals with "800" numbers. All that is required is a little creativity and a lot of careful planning and testing.

These consumer "800" programs emphasize the need for planning and expertise—and many companies are finding both in short supply. The industry is still in transition and in its learning stages; pinpointing and finding knowledgeable telemarketers is keeping specialized recruiting agencies busy searching among the approximately 60 incoming direct response "800" agencies. Planning for an "unknown" number of incoming calls can still be treacherous and costly—witness the continuing number of "800" service bureau bankruptcies, with interruption of service, consumer dissatisfaction, and economic dislocation for both client and customer in the past few years.

The future looks brightest for the phone carriers, mostly AT&T, which is heavily promoting its "800" and "900" message-center service ("900" numbers constitute a totally automated response system). Though still an AT&T central office monopoly, "800" calls won't find the other carriers too far behind. Satellite technology is pushing their telephone signals into today's world with many foreseeable benefits for both consumers and business.

chapter four /

Marketing
Communications Services

Case History: S Is for the Services
She Gives You. . . .

One of the most intriguing organizations to become involved in telemarketing in recent years is the telephone company itself. The Bell System sales department has discussed the advantages of "Phone-Power" for client companies for at least a decade. Only in the past few years, though, has the phone company employed and promoted sophisticated telemarketing techniques to sell its own special services to local customers.

The "marketing" of basic telephone service is mostly a matter of order taking. Virtually everyone in the United States finds the need for at least one telephone in the home. As the result of deregulation, competitive phone companies and new common carriers—manufacturers and merchandisers offering discount equipment or rates to subscribers—already pose a visible threat to the past absolute domination of basic telephone calling service and phone products that the Bell System traditionally enjoyed. A major marketing effort by Bell in this regard had been commercials designed to increase usage of existing services by emphasizing the need to "reach out and touch someone." There will be an increasing emphasis on direct marketing and telemarketing in merchandising the

AT&T Design Line™ telephone and new telecommunications services directly to the subscriber, either at home or in the office.

The recent growth of expanded Bell System convenience services created "luxury" options that were prime candidates for direct-marketing promotional efforts.

In earlier years the choices available to phone company subscribers were pretty much limited to the number of extensions desired, the class of service needed (also highly standardized), and possibly a colored or Princess™ model phone. Today, the telephone company offers the following specialized products and services, each of which is currently sold via direct marketing:

Gift certificates. These are relatively new to the phone company and are being positioned for year-round gift giving. These certificates are good for payment toward any Bell System product, service, or local or long-distance calling that is being marketed through broadcast, print, and direct marketing.

Design Line telephones.™ The variety of telephone instruments now offered through the telephone company itself has grown dramatically. Bell provides anything from a real oak country-kitchen phone to a Mickey Mouse or Snoopy-shaped phone. This is an area in which significant competition developed after court rulings took away Bell Telephone's monopoly on supplying phones to be used with their network, opening the door for customers to own their own phones instead of renting them from the phone company. Extensive promotional efforts to increase consumer acceptance of Bell's own Designer phones have included the full range of advertising media, direct mail, and telemarketing.

Custom Calling Services. Developed in the late 1970s, the Bell companies' Custom Calling services include:

- **Call forwarding.** If Call Forwarding customers will be away from home but available at another phone number, they can dial a code number and the number where they can be reached and their incoming calls will automatically be transferred to the new location.

- **Call waiting.** If a Call Waiting subscriber is on the line and receives another incoming call, he or she will hear a tone indicating that there is a second call coming in. The first call can be put on hold while the second call is answered. Call Waiting thus virtually eliminates busy signals for incoming callers and helps subscribers avoid missing important calls.

- **Three-Way calling.** This service allows the user to set up a three-way telephone conference.

- **Speed calling.** Frequently dialed numbers are abbreviated, so that they can be called using only a 1- or 2-digit code.

Since Custom Calling services are available only to customers in electronically equipped offices, mass media advertising cannot be utilized effectively. However, these services have proven to be very successful products for telemarketing. Marketing efficiently under these circumstances requires the ability to target markets with precision, personalization, and persuasiveness. That is the extra dimension that New York Telephone brought to its promotional efforts on behalf of Custom Calling, in a combination of direct mail and telemarketing conducted through both an in-house operation and an outside agency.

Marketing Objectives The person in charge of New York Telephone's Direct Marketing Center is Staff Supervisor Woody Manzer. He explains the dramatic expansion of Bell System direct marketing in terms of reaching the "nonmobile market."

"Most of the people who call us for phone services are mobile customers," Mr. Manzer points out. These are the individuals who change residence with some frequency. When they call to start or change their service, the phone company representatives have the opportunity to explain the various special services currently available and to attempt to make the sale while taking the basic service order. In this sense, the telephone company has been selling its special services through a form of telemarketing all along.

However, the mobile market is limited. According to Mr. Manzer, "mobile customers account for about 20 percent of our population. But the other 80 percent are nonmobile. We don't have the opportunity to tell them about special services, so we had to find another way to reach them.

"In April 1979 we started experimenting with direct mail," Manzer continues. "Custom Calling services were relatively new and didn't lend themselves to mass advertising because they were limited in their availability. So instead, we tried a mail piece, and drew a 1 to 1.5 percent response. We were only geared for mail orders, but we felt that there was great promise in telemarketing as well. Four to five months after we began sending out direct mail, we began experimenting with outbound calls.

"Clearly, our objective was to test telemarketing's ability to establish a customer-service contact with select segments of our house list and to knowledgeably and cost-effectively sell a range of consumer services."

Telemarketing Strategy The initial stages of New York Telephone's telemarketing efforts did not go smoothly. The key problems that had to be overcome included developing an effective script to enable the communicator to respond to a wide range of complex technical questions.

Despite the lackluster economics of the program, the phone company's commitment to the telemarketing concept led it to continue experimenting.

In the next phase, proven interactive marketing concepts were applied and the program took off.

A central factor in the eventual success of the Custom Calling marketing effort was a synergistic combination of direct mail and telephone. The calls were timed to follow within two weeks of a mail drop—the information presented in the mailing, which described a by-and-large unfamiliar group of services, was still fresh in the customer's mind when the phone call was received.

Creative Strategy   In addition, the telephone script was written to build upon the strengths of the earlier mail piece. The mailing met the need to explain in depth the way the Custom Calling services work (see Figure 4-1). And since this was a mailing to the customers of New York Telephone, the letters were read! In the telephone call, the communicator could answer questions if necessary but did not have to go into a long description of the services being offered unless requested to. In this way, the outbound call could concentrate on the benefits of the services and the cost savings of buying all the services at once.

List Segmentation   As we already mentioned, Custom Calling services are available only in the limited number of exchanges that have the special wiring required—in the New York Telephone territory, this is approximately 30 percent of the total customer base.

To increase the cost-effectiveness of the telemarketing effort, a decision was made to narrow down the target universe. A combination of in-house data and outside lists were used to segment the customer base according to demographic, life-style, and telephone usage characteristics. And the range of factors available for analysis is astounding. According to Mr. Manzer, "There is the possibility of over 150 different variables that can be used."

To date, one of the most reliable indicators of response to the offer is telephone usage. "Predominant traits we find in the buyer profile are high toll usage and high telephone service usage—such as more than one telephone station in their home. We're looking for the up-scale universe— people who are computer-oriented, technically oriented—people who like gadgets."

NEW YORK TELEPHONE

Home Communications Center
65 West Red Oak Lane
White Plains, N.Y. 10604

MR JOHN DOE
1234 MAIN STREET
ANYCITY, NY 00000

DEAR MR JOHN DOE

    - You're busy at the office and you've tried to call home to say you'll
be late ..... but the line is busy.

    - You're out for the evening. You left the children with the sitter
and you're calling home to make sure everything is all right ..... but you
can't get through. When you finally do, you get a garbled message about
an important call.

    - You're planning a trip. The travel agent calls about a last minute
change. Now you have to make arrangements with other people to accommodate
your new plans. You spend a lot of time contacting people and calling
them back.

    Do these scenarios sound familiar? Well, New York Telephone can help
you solve these annoying and counter-productive communications problems with

CUSTOM CALLING SERVICES

    You can personalize your phone service and maximize its efficiency
by choosing the problem solving features that address your communications
needs.

    With CALL WAITING never miss another important call. Whether you're
trying to call home or someone is trying to call you, calls will always
get through. If you're on the phone and someone is trying to reach you,
you'll hear a gentle "beep" to tell you a call is waiting. You can take
the waiting call by pressing the receiver button and putting the first call
on "hold". You can even switch back and forth between calls.

    Use CALL FORWARDING to transfer your incoming calls to another number.
If you're at the club for the evening or out of town for a week, you
won't have to miss important calls any more. Just dial a simple code and
the number where you're going to be. Calls will go there automatically.

    Save time dialing with SPEED CALLING. Fast and convenient, you dial
just two digits instead of seven for those frequently called numbers.

    Ever have to talk to more than one person at a time? Coordinating
schedules or arranging for family get togethers can be made easier with
THREE-WAY CALLING. Put your first call on "hold" by depressing the
receiver button, dial your second call and when that person answers depress
your receiver again. Immediately, you have a three-way conversation.

    To order any or all of these Custom Calling Services, just dial toll-
free 1 800 942-1818 and ask for operator 35.

    You'll be on your way to a personalized and efficient home communica-
tions system.

                      Sincerely,

                    Leslie Wasserman

                    Leslie Wasserman
                    Manager

P.S. Custom Calling Services are programmed from our central office so
     there's no equipment to buy and no installer visit. A one time
     service charge applies and you can save up to 24% when you order
     more than one service.

Figure 4-1. Initial mail piece explaining Custom Calling.

Testing   The first successful test of telemarketing entailed completed calls following up the mailing piece shown in Figure 4-1. The program offered customers the two-service package indicated or the option of selecting any single service. The charge for the full package was $6.62 per month; for Call Waiting alone, $5.11; for Call Forwarding, $3.14. A $16.50 installation charge was required for either or both.

The script used in this effort is shown in Figure 4-2. It was developed through a slow process of testing, revision, retesting, and re-revision, until

---

CAMPAIGN COMMUNICATIONS INSTITUTE OF AMERICA, INC

New York Telephone
Custom Calling Service
Communicator Script
JANUARY 1981

Introduction to Prospect

Good (morning/afternoon/evening) Mr(s) _____ . This is (NAME) for New York Telephone's Custom Calling Services. Right now we're offering a 20 percent discount on two low-cost telephone services.

Continue without pause to "Introduce Offer"

Introduce Offer

With our Call Waiting service, Mr(s) _____ , you never have to worry about missing other calls while you're on the phone. If someone tries to reach you while you're on the line, you'll be able to hold the first call, answer the new one, and even switch back and forth between the calls. With our other service, Call Forwarding, you can leave home without missing a single phone call because you can have all your calls transferred directly to any other telephone number you choose. In addition to the convenience, this is also a good security measure because callers won't be able to tell that you're not at home. And right now, with our 20 percent discount, you can give yourself both these services for a combined monthly charge of $6.33 plus a one-time connection charge. Would these new phone services make things more convenient for you, Mr(s) _____ ?

> *If definitely not interested:* **go to "Not Interested"**
> *If hesitant:* **go to "Resell"**
> *If Yes, say:* Well, Mr(s) _____ , the services can be connected to your
> telephone line directly from our office. And I can arrange to have it working
> within two weeks. So, may I take care of that for you, Mr(s) _____ ?
> *If Yes:* **Go to "Process Order"**
> *If No:* **go to "Resell"**

Figure 4-2.   CCI communicator's call script for New York Telephone Company campaign.

Resell

You know Mr(s) _____ , not only does Call Waiting let you talk as long as you want *without* missing other calls but it also makes sure *you'll* get through when *you* call home. And, as I mentioned, many people use Call Forwarding for the convenience and freedom it offers but also as a security measure when they're not at home. Of course, if you prefer to have only one of these services, the cost would be $4.89 a month for Call Waiting or $3.00 for Call Forwarding. Would one of these features be better for you, Mr(s) _____?

> *If Yes:* go to "Process Order"
> *If No:* go to "Not Interested"

Process Order

Record service(s) ordered and say: Fine, Mr(s) _____ . I'll make the necessary arrangements today and you can expect to have your service(s) working in two weeks. *If customer has requested more than one order, get other name(s) and telephone number(s).* The installation(s) will be done in our central office for a one-time charge of $16 (for each line). In the meantime, Mr(s) _____ , we'll send you a letter confirming your order for Call Waiting/Call Forwarding telling you the exact date your service(s) will be connected. All right, Mr(s) _____? (LISTEN AND RESPOND.) Tell me, Mr(s) _____ , would you prefer to pay the installation charge in one payment or in three installments? (RECORD.) It's been a pleasure speaking with you and I'm glad we could be of service. Thank you for your time and have a good (day/evening).

> *If negative reaction to service charge, say:*
Well, Mr(s) _____ , we do have an optional billing plan where you can spread the connection fee over three months. Would that be more convenient for you? (RECORD.)

Not Interested

Is there any special reason you're not interested in taking advantage of either of these services, Mr(s) _____? *Record reason and if possible go to appropriate question/objection card. Otherwise, say:* Thank you very much for taking this time to talk with me, Mr(s) _____ , and have a pleasant (day/evening).

Figure 4-2   CCI communicator's call script for New York Telephone Company campaign. (Cont.)

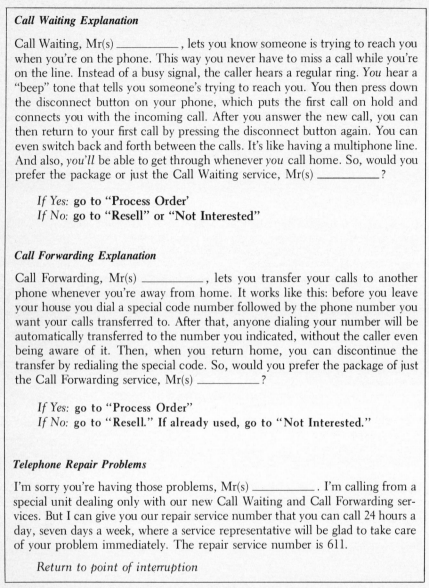

Call Waiting Explanation

Call Waiting, Mr(s) _____ , lets you know someone is trying to reach you when you're on the phone. This way you never have to miss a call while you're on the line. Instead of a busy signal, the caller hears a regular ring. *You* hear a "beep" tone that tells you someone's trying to reach you. You then press down the disconnect button on your phone, which puts the first call on hold and connects you with the incoming call. After you answer the new call, you can then return to your first call by pressing the disconnect button again. You can even switch back and forth between the calls. It's like having a multiphone line. And also, *you'll* be able to get through whenever *you* call home. So, would you prefer the package or just the Call Waiting service, Mr(s) _____ ?

> *If Yes:* **go to "Process Order'**
> *If No:* **go to "Resell" or "Not Interested"**

Call Forwarding Explanation

Call Forwarding, Mr(s) _____ , lets you transfer your calls to another phone whenever you're away from home. It works like this: before you leave your house you dial a special code number followed by the phone number you want your calls transferred to. After that, anyone dialing your number will be automatically transferred to the number you indicated, without the caller even being aware of it. Then, when you return home, you can discontinue the transfer by redialing the special code. So, would you prefer the package of just the Call Forwarding service, Mr(s) _____ ?

> *If Yes:* **go to "Process Order"**
> *If No:* **go to "Resell." If already used, go to "Not Interested."**

Telephone Repair Problems

I'm sorry you're having those problems, Mr(s) _____ . I'm calling from a special unit dealing only with our new Call Waiting and Call Forwarding services. But I can give you our repair service number that you can call 24 hours a day, seven days a week, where a service representative will be glad to take care of your problem immediately. The repair service number is 611.

> *Return to point of interruption*

Figure 4-2. CCI communicator's call script for New York Telephone Company campaign. (*Cont.*)

Connection Charge/If Objects to Charge

Well, Mr(s) _____ , the one-time connection charge of $16 applies if you take one or both of our new services. But we do have an optional billing plan that lets you spread the connection fee over three months. Would that be more convenient for you? (RECORD.)

> *If customer requests payment breakdown info:*
> *Connection Charge:* $16
> > 1st month: $\frac{1}{2}$ = $8
> > 2nd month: $\frac{1}{4}$ = $4
> > 3rd month: $\frac{1}{4}$ = $4

Return to Point of Interruption

Too Expensive

Well, Mr(s) _____ , we are offering a 20 percent discount on our new Custom Calling services. And you can also spread the $16 installation fee over a three-month billing period if that's better for you, Mr(s) _____ . So, if one of our services would be convenient for you, I can have it connected and working in about two weeks. Would that be all right, Mr(s) _____ ?

> *If Yes:* **go to "Process Order"**
> *If No:* **go to "Not Interested"**

Who Are You?

Mr(s) _____ , I work for Campaign Communications Institute, a leading communications agency. And because we're communications experts, New York Telephone has asked us to call their customers to introduce them to the new Call Waiting and Call Forwarding services. If you have any questions at all about this, I'll be happy to have a telephone representative contact you.

Return to Point of Interruption

Figure 4-2. CCI communicator's call script for New York Telephone Company campaign. (*Cont.*)

it worked smoothly from the communicator's standpoint, contained answers for all the likely customer questions, and produced acceptable response levels (see Figure 4-3).

The required economic response level was clearly agreed upon in advance. Based on previous efforts in telemarketing, it had been determined that 0.65 services ordered per calling hour would be the response rate needed to provide a reasonable profit. In fact, the program produced 0.73

New York Telephone

Panel Name_____

Panel #_____

NAME/ADDRESS CHANGE:

_____
_____
_____
_____

☐ Order   Comm_____   Date_____

   ☐ Call Waiting $3.95
   ☐ Call Forwarding $2.42
   ☐ Package of both services $5.11

Service Connection Charges   ☐ Single Payment
       $16.25   ☐ Installment Billing

Comments_____
_____
_____

☐ NI   ☐ SBM   ☐ SPECIAL   ☐ LIT REQUEST

Comments_____
_____
_____
_____

                              Comm_____   Date_____

DATE	TIME	COMM	RESPONSE CODE			PASS SYSTEM	REQUESTED CALL BACK (RCB)
			NA	DA	BY	WDD	____ / ____ AT _____
			NA	DA	BY	WDN	
			NA	DA	BY	WED	WHY?_____
			NA	DA	BY	WEN	
			NA	DA	BY		Comm_____ Date_____

CCI

Figure 4-3.   CCI communicator's call record card.

services per hour, substantially exceeding the requirements for profitability.

In summary, the results of this program were as follows:

- 4 percent of customers contacted placed orders on initial calls.
- 50 percent of these ordered the full package.
- 0.73 features were ordered per calling hour.

Program Expansion Since the initial success, the direct-marketing efforts undertaken by New York Telephone have grown steadily. In addition to the calls made through outside agencies, Mr. Manzer established New York Telephone's Home Communications Center in Westchester County. These company representatives have more product training than those who work for the telemarketing agency, and are therefore given more freedom to deviate from the established script—although they do follow a scripted presentation.

For 1981, Mr. Manzer estimates that his direct-marketing division sold over 20,000 features, individually and in combination. And of that total, 80 percent were produced through *outbound* telephone calls (incoming "800" number calls are considered part of the 20 percent mail response).

Summary The telephone company faced a difficult marketing situation as it expanded its range of services. It would have been relatively simple to purchase space and media exposure to introduce the new services, but given the limited availability of these features, this broad-based advertising was obviously inappropriate. Good marketing sense dictated the need for a direct-marketing approach, which resulted in a classic target-marketing case history and a very profitable venture.

In 1981, Mr. Manzer's direct-marketing division substantially exceeded annual goals and proved the effectiveness of direct mail and telemarketing as a viable distribution channel to reach the nonmobile customer.

Implications for the Marketer There is certainly a valuable lesson to be learned from New York Telephone's ongoing commitment to testing multiple marketing strategies. Quite simply, it requires time and perseverance to perfect a telemarketing program—or any direct-marketing venture—before it becomes profitable. But a measured amount of patience and continued effort was richly rewarded in New York Telephone's case.

There is also a bright future to be discussed. The telephone company is expanding its direct-marketing programs. Building on its growing expertise, Designer phones and gift certificates have been marketed successfully via integrated direct-mail and telephone efforts. To sell additional gift certificates, for example, computer profiling was brought into play to identify past buyers and target them for further marketing attention.

The success of the Custom Calling program is also leading to a search for expanded market segments. Mr. Manzer indicated interest in utilizing other select lists of people in occupations that would be particularly well served by Custom Calling. For example, police officers, nurses, or other service-related occupations on call every day would be a high-potential market segment for Call Waiting and Call Forwarding. The same is true for doctors, actors, and many other professionals who depend on the phone for their livelihood.

The telephone company experience is just one example of the numerous communications services that, due to their limited availability, are highly suitable for direct-marketing attention. For many years, cable television has been sold by outbound telephone; today the phone is used to sell alternative-carrier long-distance telephone service. What is true within the fast-moving consumer communications sector is true throughout marketing today: when there is a select audience for goods or services, a professionally conducted, tightly focused direct-marketing effort utilizing both mail and telephone will produce the greatest return on marketing investment.

chapter five

Nonstore Marketing

Case History: Montgomery Ward Auto Club

A basic strength of marketing via telephone contact is the ability to make the most of your customer list through offers of additional goods and services. Calling individuals with whom you have an affinity or an established business relationship increases the acceptance of your telephone sales message dramatically and produces a far higher order rate than "cold" calling.

At the same time, the telemarketing contact serves a public relations function, reinforcing an ongoing relationship between supplier and customer.

In the area of consumer marketing, credit card customers are particularly desirable as telemarketing prospects. It requires only that they agree to your offer—the additional charge is simply added to their account, and the payment is processed automatically, added to the monthly statement.

As we will see in this chapter, there's an additional advantage to credit card customers—but only if the customer's file is properly respected. Marketers will discover a wealth of information in the credit application if it is available. As long as that information is strictly guarded against any possible invasion of privacy, it can be used to the customer's advantage by allowing special offers to be placed that may prove beneficial to that customer.

The most up-to-date and sophisticated direct-marketing company serving the consumer sector today is Signature, a direct-response subsidiary of Montgomery Ward. Signature currently includes a wide spectrum of direct-marketing ventures, including the Montgomery Ward Auto Club, Ward's Credit Card Security Services, the Charg-All Security Plan, Ward's Wide World of Travel, Signature's F.I.T. Vitamins, and others. In 1981, Signature's revenues approached the $200 million mark.

The thread that binds these disparate elements together is the aggressive and innovative application of a fundamental direct-marketing principle—offer the right product to the right list of prospects. And the man who has led Signature in developing marketing strategies that successfully bring together attractive offers and an appropriate audience in a cost-effective manner is Richard E. Cremer, president and founder of Signature and voted Direct Marketer of the Year in 1981.

As Mr. Cremer explains it, Ward's large-scale involvement in direct marketing is a return to the principles upon which the company was founded. "Montgomery Ward started in 1872 as a true mail-order operation—the world's first," Mr. Cremer explains. "In the years since I joined the company, which was in 1953, it completed its evolution from a mail-order organization to a retail organization. Even though it still had a catalog and 9 mail-order houses and 2,000 catalog stores, they really didn't fit the definition of direct-response marketing, because most all the catalog sales are generated by customers going to a catalog store, placing an order, and picking it up at the catalog store three days later. That really is a retail sale. I've always considered the catalog division of Ward's a retail store between the two covers of a book—not at all a direct-response business.

"And so, the company evolved from a 109-year-old mail-order company to really a 100 percent retail organization, until Signature initiated their reinvolvement in true direct-response marketing. That was in February 1972.

"At that time, we really didn't have something called 'Signature'—we had an idea. The idea was to offer credit insurance and to do it through direct-response marketing, through statement inserts and/or direct-mail offers to the Montgomery Ward credit file.

"Actually, the idea for credit insurance was not new to me at that time—it had occurred to me when I first joined Ward's, working in the collection department right after the Korean War. Unemployment was high—there were a lot of layoffs and a lot of people out of work—and it occurred to me as a collector that I was certainly driving a good many customers away from Montgomery Ward in carrying out my responsibility. I thought that it would be great if we could find some insurance that would make the credit payments for those people who had lost their jobs. I wasn't able to do anything about it at the time, but some 15 or 16 years later when I arrived in the corporate headquarters as the assistant corporate credit manager responsible for credit policy, I had an opportunity to do something about it, and I did."

When the credit protection plan met with great success, all of it through direct-response marketing, Mr. Cremer's brainstorm became the first step in the creation of a thriving and diversified direct-response business. In 1975 it was decided to start an auto club as well.

Mr. Cremer's philosophy in creating the Montgomery Ward Auto Club was the philosophy that has guided every one of the company's marketing ventures: "Montgomery Ward enjoys a wonderful reputation in America. So I want to posture everything we do in direct-response marketing so it will add luster to the name Montgomery Ward. As we create additional services, our customers tend to become more loyal in all of their purchasing. And so we devised the club to be the best auto club there could possibly be. How do you do that? It was very simple. We joined every other club. We developed a big chart summarizing all the available benefits and then designed our club to be equal to or better than all the other clubs. When completed, the study had a package of services claimed to be the finest benefits offered in the auto club field. It was a bit more expensive than the other clubs, but it did add 'luster' to the Ward's name.

"I believe that it's appropriate when you put a fine name like Montgomery Ward on the product that it be something you can be proud of. We've done the same with our other clubs as they developed, including our credit card registration service. We aren't the only people in the industry who offer that service to consumers, but we do it a little better, just as we try to do almost everything we do a little better."

Telemarketing Objectives The Montgomery Ward Auto Club grew rapidly—in the first three years, over a million members registered. This, however, entailed fairly deep penetration of the charge card files. After repeat mailings, the response numbers declined from their previous peaks, and so, Mr. Cremer explains, "We thought that if we could find some new ways of selling the auto club, we might reach some of our customers who might not have joined because they didn't read our direct mail. I've seen some interesting research that indicates that the responses you get on a direct-mail offer come from only about half the people, and the other half don't even read it."

Several tactics were tried to increase awareness of the club. Sweepstakes promotions were launched to boost readership of the direct-mail pieces (see Figure 5-1).

Tied into this effort were magazine advertisements. This was a complex undertaking—the magazine offered a three-part package offer: (1) enter the sweepstakes; (2) apply for a Montgomery Ward Charg-All card; (3) join the Montgomery Ward Auto Club (only Charg-All customers are eligible for auto club membership).

The surprise came in the number of existing Charg-All card holders

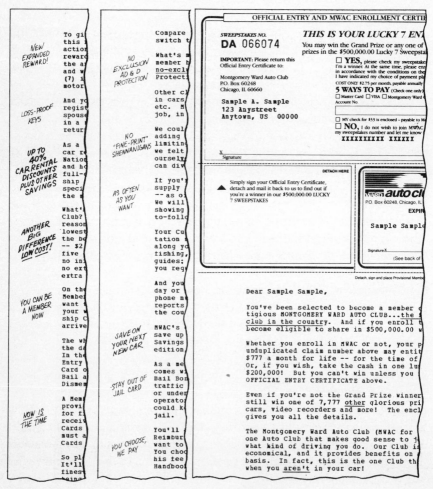

Figure 5-1. Sample Montgomery Ward Auto Club mailing letter.

who chose to join the auto club through the magazine offer—in one *TV Guide* advertising test, this number reached 25,000. These were the same people who had been offered a chance to join the club through statement inserts and direct-mail countless times and had never joined. Mr. Cremer remembers, "I knew that we would enroll some auto club members who had an account at Ward's through the *TV Guide* ad, but I never dreamed that 25,000 of our Charg-All customers would choose to learn about the club through a magazine instead of all the direct mail we'd been sending. And so I became a real believer in multimedia. There are some people who read direct mail and there are some people who will read statement inserts, but there are some people who won't read either. But they might just join the club through a magazine insert—or a phone call."

List Segmentation It is interesting to note that the initial product offering that gave birth to Signature sprang from the credit experience area of Ward's. The sophisticated list segmentation techniques that have been a cornerstone of Signature's success came from the very same source.

Mr. Cremer explains that, while working in the financial division, during the early 1960s, he "became aware that there were some finance companies—American Investment Company was the first—that had devised a scoring system that would help credit managers decide which credit applicants to approve and which to reject. The scoring theory was that you would take a group of accounts that had been on your accounts receivable program for a number of years and separate them into those that were good and those that were bad—and by "bad" I mean they weren't making their payments. Then you collect the credit applications for each group of accounts and keypunch all the data from the credit application onto punch cards for both groups, keeping them separate. Then, through multivariate linear regression analysis, you would find out which of the characteristics in each account seem to discriminate best in separating the good ones from the bad ones."

The system was instituted in the credit area, and in tests over time it proved to be highly accurate in predicting the future performance of credit applicants.

As Mr. Cremer explains, this successful effort led to "the discovery that, when we applied the same principles to telemarketing, we could identify a segment of our credit customers that could be telephoned and we could receive enough positive responses from them to cover the cost of making the phone calls, create an environment in which the telemarketing company made a profit, and still generate members for us at an affordable price."

Montgomery Ward became a pioneer in the use of multivariate linear regression analysis to develop a reliable profile of prospects most likely to respond to a given offer. Their universe for direct marketing was already highly select—it consisted only of Montgomery Ward Charg-All credit card holders. The fact that these individuals were all approved credit customers meant that there was a substantial pool of data to draw on in analyzing their buying preferences:

■ Credit card application information, including income level, family size, occupation, sex, home address, and so on

■ Past purchase and payment history (except for newly opened accounts)

Based on this information, Ward's research can extract 70 different factors deemed significant in building a customer profile.

This method of analysis was first proven successful in marketing Signature products and services through the mail. However, marketing by telephone required an entirely new customer-profile analysis. First, a more highly responsive list was needed to justify the expense of making personal telephone contact, as opposed to a mass mailing. Second, and more important, it was found that the characteristics of a phone-responsive prospect would be different from that of a mail buyer. This was an important concept to test—that not only are there in-store buyers and direct-response buyers but that there is a further distinction between buyers who respond to each of the direct-response media.

To accomplish this sophisticated list segmentation, an initial test was undertaken to provide data for the multivariate analysis.[1] The objective of this effort was to generate 500 Montgomery Ward Auto Club *telephone* buyers. The profiles of these individuals could then be fed into the computer to determine the factors they had in common. The resulting buyer profile could then be matched against the larger file of Charg-All customers to cull those who would be responsive in a larger telephone roll-out campaign.

For this initial test, a random selection of names from the top 60 percent of Montgomery Ward's credit card file (based on the previously successful mail-buyer profile) was provided for telephone calling. Calls were to continue until 500 orders were taken. An important element in the structure of the test was a two-part segmentation based on mailing activity—one panel contained people who had previously received mail and the other, people who had not received a mail invitation to join the auto club.

Creative Strategy   In the same test calling effort, a variety of creative strategies were tested as well. These were all based on the belief that a taped message incorporated into the telephone presentation would be

---

[1] The test was undertaken by Signature's telemarketing agency, CCI.

crucial to the success of the call. The auto club is a fairly complex product. There are many benefits to be explained, and a taped message allowed standardization of the explanation. A tape also provided the opportunity to present the message in the words of a respected spokesperson for the club. Another potentially powerful element in the tape was a testimonial from a satisfied club member.

To determine which strategy or combination of strategies would be most effective, six different taped messages were created:

A. Long copy, no customer testimonials (running 4 minutes 18 seconds)

B. Shortened version of above, no testimonials (3 minutes)

C. Different copy approach, no testimonials (2 minutes 30 seconds)

D. Third copy approach, with testimonials (8 minutes 20 seconds)

E. Fourth copy approach, with testimonials (6 minutes 25 seconds)

F. Message from Zsa Zsa Gabor (see Figure 5-2), spokesperson in advertising campaign for Montgomery Ward Auto Club, no testimonials (1 minute 30 seconds)

HELLO. THIS IS ZSA ZSA GABOR.

WHEN I BECAME A MEMBER OF THE MONTGOMERY WARD AUTO CLUB, IT REALLY WAS A SPECIAL OCCASION. NOT OFTEN DOES ZSA ZSA DO ANYTHING THAT HALF A MILLION PEOPLE HAVE DONE BEFORE HER (CHUCKLE).

THIS PERSONAL PHONE MESSAGE IS SPECIAL, TOO. IT MEANS I CAN INVITE YOU TO JOIN ME.

I LIKE HAVING SOMEONE ELSE PAY THE BILLS, AND I BET SO DO YOU. WHEN WE'RE MEMBERS OF WARD'S AUTO CLUB—THEY HELP PAY FOR MANY OF THE EXTRA EXPENSES OF DRIVING A CAR, ESPECIALLY WHEN THEY BREAK DOWN OR GET INTO ACCIDENTS.

AND, IF YOU'RE JUST THE LITTLEST BIT LIKE ME, DRIVING A CAR IS NOT JUST FOR GETTING FROM ONE PLACE TO ANOTHER. IT'S TO BE ENJOYED LIKE EVERYTHING ELSE IN LIFE. MONTGOMERY WARD HAS DESIGNED AND ROUTED CAR TRIPS JUST FOR ME, AND THEY'LL DO IT FOR ANY OTHER CLUB MEMBER—ALL YOU HAVE TO DO IS ASK.

THERE'S A VERY NICE TELEPHONE COMMUNICATOR COMING BACK ON THE LINE WHO'LL TELL YOU ALL ABOUT THE MONTGOMERY WARD AUTO CLUB.

I HOPE YOU BECOME A MEMBER. MAYBE WE'LL MEET SOME DAY ON A WONDERFUL CRUISE TO MEXICO, HAWAII OR SOME OTHER BEAUTIFUL PLACE. IT'S POSSIBLE. MONTGOMERY WARD EVEN HAS SPECIAL VACATION PLANS JUST FOR AUTO CLUB MEMBERS ONLY.

UNTIL WE DO, GOOD-BYE AND THANK YOU, DARLING, FOR LISTENING TO ME.

Figure 5-2. Zsa Zsa Gabor tape script, Montgomery Ward Auto Club.

The first five versions of the taped message featured Richard Cremer, president of the auto club. The script recorded for the first no-testimonials message was as follows:

MONTGOMERY WARD AUTO CLUB
TAPE TEST SCRIPT A

HELLO. THIS IS DICK CREMER, PRESIDENT OF THE MONTGOMERY WARD AUTO CLUB. I'M GLAD YOU AGREED TO LISTEN TO MY MESSAGE BECAUSE OUR CLUB IS A VERY SPECIAL SERVICE FOR OUR GOOD CHARG-ALL CUSTOMERS LIKE YOURSELF—AND ONLY FOR CHARG-ALL CUSTOMERS.

AT THE HEART OF OUR AUTO CLUB IS THE EMERGENCY CARD SERVICE AND TOWING PROTECTION IT PROVIDES. MOST OTHER CLUBS WILL TELL YOU THAT TO BE COVERED YOU HAVE TO CALL THEIR AUTHORIZED SERVICE STATIONS AND IF YOU'RE TOWED, IT MUST BE TO THEIR—THE CLUB'S—STATION. WE'RE DIFFERENT—MONTGOMERY WARD'S AUTO CLUB ALLOWS YOU COMPLETE FREEDOM OF CHOICE AND REIMBURSES YOU FOR UP TO $30 FOR EACH CALL.

HAPPILY, DRIVING YOUR CAR DOESN'T JUST MEAN AVOIDING BREAKDOWNS—DRIVING CAN AND SHOULD BE PLEASURABLE, AND THE MONTGOMERY WARD AUTO CLUB CAN HELP YOU GET THE MOST ENJOYMENT FROM YOUR CAR. IF YOU'RE PLANNING A VACATION OR BUSINESS TRIP, WE'LL SUPPLY YOU WITH MAPS, ROUTINGS, AND GUIDEBOOKS TO MEET YOUR SPECIFICATIONS—AND AT NO EXTRA COST WHATSOEVER.

HERE'S ANOTHER MAJOR ADVANTAGE OF BEING A MONTGOMERY WARD AUTO CLUB MEMBER. AT NO ADDITIONAL COST, YOU'RE COVERED BY A $5,000 ALL-RISKS, NO-EXCLUSION ACCIDENT INSURANCE POLICY. AND YOU'RE COVERED FOR ANY TYPE OF ACCIDENT—ON THE JOB, IN YOUR CAR, EVEN IN YOUR HOME.

THERE'S LOTS MORE—UP TO $100 IN CASH PAID TO YOU IF YOU HAVE AN ACCIDENT THAT DISABLES YOUR CAR WHEN YOU ARE 50 MILES OR MORE FROM HOME. ALSO, DISCOUNTS ON CAR RENTALS, MOTELS, AND HOTELS, SPECIAL COST-SAVING VACATION PACKAGES TO PLACES LIKE HAWAII AND MEXICO, UP TO 50 PERCENT OFF ON MERCHANDISE OFFERS—ALL EXCLUSIVELY FOR MONTGOMERY WARD AUTO CLUB MEMBERS.

IF YOU WISH TO BE REPRESENTED BY AN ATTORNEY FOR A TRAFFIC VIOLATION, YOUR LEGAL DEFENSE IS COVERED BY AS MUCH AS $500 LEGAL DEFENSE REIMBURSEMENT.

BUT THE BEST PART IS THAT YOUR AUTO CLUB IS BACKED BY WARD'S, AND OUR CLUB COVERS ALL OF THE CARS OWNED BY YOU OR YOUR SPOUSE AT NO EXTRA CHARGE.

THE PRICE FOR ALL THIS PEACE OF MIND IS ONLY $2.95 A MONTH, WHICH IS SIMPLY BILLED TO YOU ON YOUR REGULAR CHARG-ALL ACCOUNT EACH MONTH.

I HOPE YOU DECIDE TO JOIN US—JUST TELL THE TELEPHONE COMMUNICATOR YOUR DECISION AND PLEASE—BE SURE TO ASK ANY QUESTIONS YOU MAY HAVE.

THANK YOU AGAIN—NOW HERE'S THE COMMUNICATOR. . . .

MONTGOMERY WARD AUTO CLUB
MODIFIED TAPE CODE B (SHORTENED VERSION)
HELLO. MY NAME IS RICHARD CREMER, PRESIDENT OF THE MONTGOMERY WARD AUTO CLUB.

PLEASE LET ME TELL YOU ABOUT OUR CLUB. IT WAS FORMED JUST TWO YEARS AGO—IT WAS DESIGNED TO SERVE OUR CHARG-ALL CUSTOMERS' BEST INTERESTS. THERE ARE MANY GOOD AUTO CLUBS, BUT WE'VE DESIGNED OUR CLUB, EXCLUSIVELY FOR OUR CHARG-ALL CUSTOMERS—LIKE YOU—TO BE THE BEST.

THERE ARE GOOD REASONS WHY HALF A MILLION PEOPLE LIKE YOU HAVE BECOME MEMBERS. LIKE HAVING TOWING BILLS PAID, OR $200 ARREST BOND . . . LEGAL DEFENSE ATTORNEY'S FEES UP TO $500 . . . OR, SHOULD AN ACCIDENT OCCUR 50 MILES FROM HOME, THERE'S UP TO $100 OF EXPENSE REIMBURSEMENT . . . THERE'S EVEN A $5,000 ALL-RISK, NO-EXCLUSION ACCIDENT PROTECTION POLICY AT NO ADDITIONAL COST . . . AND YOU'RE COVERED FOR ANY TYPE OF ACCIDENT—ON THE JOB, EVEN IN YOUR HOME.

BUT, THE BEST PART OF THE CLUB IS THE FUN YOU CAN HAVE USING SOME OF ITS OTHER BENEFITS.

LIKE TRIP ROUTING. OR LIKE OUR 10 PERCENT DISCOUNT AT 3,000 OF AMERICA'S BEST HOTELS AND MOTELS, WITH MORE BEING ADDED DAILY. OR LIKE GROUP TOURS AT SPECIAL BARGAIN PRICES—OF COURSE, FOR MEMBERS ONLY. OR LIKE RECEIVING OUR GREAT MAGAZINE WITH TRAVEL INFORMATION AND LOTS OF MERCHANDISE OFFERS AT UP TO 50 PERCENT OFF—AND A SPECIAL TOLL-FREE PHONE NUMBER WHICH YOU'LL GET TO TELEPHONE CLUB HEADQUARTERS ANYTIME—7 DAYS A WEEK, 24 HOURS A DAY.

WE HOPE YOU WILL SELECT US AND JOIN THE CLUB—IT'S ONLY $2.95 CHARGED TO YOUR CHARG-ALL MONTHLY. YOU CAN CANCEL YOUR MEMBERSHIP WITH US AT ANY TIME YOU DECIDE OUR CLUB IS NOT THE BEST. JUST TELL THE COMMUNICATOR YES AND YOU'RE ON YOUR WAY. IN SOME STATES OUR CLUB COVERAGE HAS BEEN MODIFIED TO CONFORM WITH STATE LAWS. THIS WILL BE EXPLAINED TO YOU BY THE COMMUNICATOR AND WILL BE SPECIFIED IN THE MEMBERSHIP MATERIALS WHICH WE'LL SEND YOU. THANK YOU VERY MUCH FOR LISTENING.

In addition, calls were made without a taped message to those who, after receiving the initial phone contact, asked to receive literature and then received a call back.

Results As the calling progressed, the number of taped messages used was narrowed down, as clear favorites emerged. The first series of calls were made to those who had received a mailing about the auto club a few weeks earlier. This produced substantial evidence to indicate that the long-copy, no-testimonial script and the 2-minute 30-second message without testimonial were significantly more productive. Based on this lesson, testimonial presentations were dropped for a time and the two front-running scripts, along with the existing Zsa Zsa Gabor message and a new Zsa Zsa Gabor message with testimonial (see Table 5-1), were employed in contacting the prospects who had not received a mailing.

Interestingly, the two taped messages that produced initial success were significantly different in total length, yet the timing of the total contact between communicators and prospects (the number of completed calls per hour) remained approximately the same. The explanation? It was suggested that since the longer message tape answered more potential

TABLE 5-1. *Summary—Initial CCI Test Results*

Call volume	Mail plus phone	Phone only	Totals
Completed calls	16,800	1,224	18,024
Completed decisions	12,582	954	13,536
Orders	1,458	42	1,500

Results—mail-plus-phone panel tape codes (see page 87 for descriptions)

	A	B	C	D	E	F	Literature	Total
Completed calls (CCs)	4,416	1,881	8,580	663	762	231	267	16,800
Orders	444	126	780	42	54	0	12	1,458
Percent response	10.1	6.7	9.1	6.3	7.1	—	4.5	8.7
Telephone hours	674.25	255.00	1,117.50	116.25	138.00	41.25	10.5	2,353.75
CCs per hour	6.5	7.4	7.7	5.7	5.5	5.6	25.4	6.9

Results—telephone-only panel tape codes

	A	G*	C	F	Total
Completed calls	254	354	192	354	1,224
Orders	21	9	6	6	42
Percent response	5.9	2.5	3.1	1.9	3.4
Telephone hours	52.50	56.25	22.50	48.00	179.25
CCs/Hour	6.7	6.3	8.5	6.8	6.8

* Gabor tape with testimonial, 3 minutes 30 seconds.

questions, the communicator discussion time after the tape was played was reduced, thus reducing the length of the overall call. Nevertheless, management felt that by increasing productivity in the calling operation, the shorter tape would be more effective. And this proved to be true—in the final 2,494 calls of one test, this message alone was used, concentrating calls on prime evening hours and weekends to maximize the number of completed customer contacts. The order rate remained at 9 percent plus, and the number of completed calls per hour climbed from 6.6 to 7.9.

The initial test, then, determined conclusively that people were more responsive to a telephone offer to join the Montgomery Ward Auto Club after having received a direct-mailing piece. It also pointed toward isolating the most effective thrust for the telephone presentation. In addition, it quantified a continuing problem in building a successful telemarketing program to a tightly targeted market—a large number of those likely prospects have already taken advantage of a competitive offer of a similar product or service.

Of the total 6,008 completed calls in one initial test program, approximately 1,430, or 31.7 percent, were members of other auto clubs. Ward's Auto Club offers several unique features, so a certain number of prospects will be interested in joining it in addition to their present affiliation. In fact, of the 500 initial orders generated, 104, or 20.8 percent, were already members of another auto club. However, the percentage of already enrolled auto club subscribers who then agreed to take on Ward's Auto Club membership was far smaller than the number of nonaffiliated individuals who accepted Ward's offer.

After finding out that the individual contacted was already a member of another club, therefore, a balanced "call time expended" ratio was required. Calling members of this group might still be a profitable course—if the number of acceptances justified the amount of labor and phone time spent delivering the offer. The crucial factor to be considered is the number of orders produced per hour. Calling less-likely prospects can produce an excess of nonproductive calls that can quickly wipe out the profits from membership commitments. This is especially true when the telephone presentation is fairly complex and, therefore, lengthy. Only by testing list segments and selected offers and carefully monitoring the bottom-line results can a reasonable decision be made on when to pursue a sale to a member of another club and when to script the communicator to politely move on quickly to the next prospect. And even when "the answer" has been arrived at by scientific testing, it can change over the course of time, as market factors and product features alter.

Program Expansion   After considering the results of the orders produced in the initial tests and using these select lists to learn how to boost order-production standards while creating new membership commitments in the auto club, the next step involved generating a list of "phone-responsive" prospects.

This test began with two lists of 10,000 names each. List A consisted of established Ward's credit card holders who matched the demographic profile of those who joined the auto club in the previous phone test program. List B consisted of new credit card holders who were not profiled against previous demographic criteria. These new charge customers had no previous buying or payment history to be taken into account when "point scoring" them for demographic suitability.

List A prospects had received a solicitation to join the Montgomery Ward Auto Club within the past year, while List B card holders received the same solicitation 30 to 50 days after becoming a Charg-All customer.

The standards to be met in the telemarketing program were stringent. In order to be cost-effective, a 22 percent order rate had to be achieved, with 10 completed calls per hour—in other words, each communicator had to produce 2.2 orders each and every hour.

For this test effort, the need to balance call presentations to members of other auto clubs against the incremental sales generated by these individuals seemed to call for terminating calls to those prospects quickly. The productivity standards cited above made it necessary to maximize orders per hour absolutely. Therefore, a question regarding current auto club membership was included at the beginning of the communicator script, and those who answered positively were thanked for their time and politely passed by. If this procedure achieved the necessary calls per hour, further calls to this screened-out group could be attempted.

The telephone presentation once again employed a taped message and allowed for call-backs after sending literature to those who requested this procedure on the initial phone contact (see Figure 5-3).

As the calls progressed, it became evident that the productivity rate was falling well below the objective of 10 completed calls per hour. In an attempt to improve these results, script modifications were introduced in the presentation to List A prospects in order to shorten the time per call. In one modified version, a decision was asked for immediately after the taped message was completed. In another modified script, the communicator went through a very brief reiteration of the membership benefits and then promptly asked for a decision.

While both modifications served to increase productivity, the order rate declined anyway, leaving the bottom line virtually unimproved. Finally,

CCI CAMPAIGN COMMUNICATIONS INSTITUTE OF AMERICA, INC. WARD auto club TELEPHONE MEMBERSHIP ENROLLMENT

NAME OR ADDRESS CHANGE

M____

STREET ADDRESS

CITY

STATE

NEW PHONE

AUTOMOBILE DATA

| MAKE | | | |
| YEAR | | | |

ADRS. CHG. ☐

Verif. ☐
CNL ☐
NA/DA ☐

PHONE:

By _____

☐ LIT   DATE ___/___   CODE

☐ NI   COMMENTS _____   ☐ ORDER
☐ SBM
☐ SP   _____ _____   DATE ___/___
☐ X
             _____   COMM CODE

REQUESTED CALL BACK (RCB)

☐ ___/___ AT _____   ☐ ___/___ AT _____
WHY? _____   WHY? _____
OP ____ DATE ___/___   OP ____ DATE ___/___

DATE	TIME	COMM				NOTES:
			NA	DA	BY	

CCI CAMPAIGN COMMUNICATIONS INSTITUTE OF AMERICA, INC. WARD auto club TELEPHONE MEMBERSHIP ENROLLMENT

Figure 5-3.   CCI call record card for Montgomery Ward Auto Club.

93

after only 1,152 completed calls, the program was halted to allow reassessment of the results and to institute program alterations that would bring productivity up to profitable levels.

In summary, the results of the second test are shown in Table 5-2.

Several valuable lessons were learned from these separate test panels. First, the select, point-scored list proved significantly superior to the non-select list. When the new list was prepared (Panel 1), using regression analysis, it produced a 15.1 percent order rate versus the 9.1 percent order rate produced by the best tape message presentation in the first test—a 66 percent improvement.

The important effect of a recent mail solicitation on telemarketing results was also demonstrated dramatically in the second test. Compared once again to the 9.1 percent order rate cited above, the new test produced an 11.3 percent order rate for new credit card holders, who had received a direct-mail package about the auto club within 50 days of the telephone contact. This amounted to a 24 percent increase.

Tape versus Nontape The value and necessity of incorporating a creative taped message in the presentation demanded evaluation—pinpointing the

TABLE 5-2.   *Second Test Results**

	Panel 1		Panel 2		Panel 3		Panel 4	
	Number	Percent	Number	Percent	Number	Percent	Number	Percent
Completed calls	641	100.0	389	100.0	67	100.0	62	100.0
Orders	97	15.1	44	11.3	3	4.5	9	14.5
Literature requests	30	4.7	7	1.8	—	—	4	6.5
Subscribed by mail	5	0.8	18	4.6	1	1.5	—	—
Special	17	2.7	21	5.4	2	3.0	1	1.6
Not qualified†	196	30.6	127	32.7	23	34.3	14	22.6
Not interested	197	30.7	120	30.9	27	40.3	18	29.0
Requested call-back	99	15.4	52	13.4	11	16.4	16	25.8
Total dialings	1,948	100.0	910	100.0	228	100.0	174	100.0
Completed calls	641	32.9	389	42.8	67	29.3	62	35.6
Not available	359	18.4	143	15.7	46	20.2	23	13.2
Don't answer	681	35.0	320	35.2	82	36.0	53	30.5
Xs and check numbers	267	16.7	58	6.4	33	14.5	36	20.7
Completed decisions	316‡	100.0	203	100.0	33	100.0	28	100.0
Orders	97	30.7	44	21.7	3	9.1	9	32.1
Completed calls per hour	7.2	—	7.9	—	7.9	—	7.5	—
Hours	88.5	—	49.25	—	8.5	—	8.25	—

* Panel 1 = Point-scored list; panel 2 = new credit card customer list; panel 3 = point-scored list, immediate decision asked for after tape; panel 4 = point-scored list, communicator segment between tape and decision.

† Doesn't own automobile or belongs to another automobile club.

‡ Completed decisions-completed calls less literature requests, not-qualifieds, and requested call-backs.

TABLE 5-3.   *Results—Nontape Test*

	Number	Percentage
Completed calls (CCs) with decision maker	373	100
Less:		
Requested call-backs	53	14.2
Unqualified respondents	118	31.6
Completed decisions	202	54.2
Orders	57	15.3
Not interested	126	33.8
Subscribed by mail	9	4.5
Special attention	5	2.5
Literature request	5	2.5

Hours, 41
Total dialings, 995
Completed calls per hour, 9.1

very essence of the problem confronting the telemarketer: how to take a *conceptually* successful marketing program and make it productive in order to reach vital profitability goals. The taped messages represented a creative concept that required a fixed time allotment per call—and a fairly substantial one at that. If the communicators could provide all the information themselves and save the two minutes involved in the tape message, following a script that provided answers to questions when necessary but did not require the explanation of every benefit to every prospect; the number of calls per hour could potentially be increased dramatically.

To test this hypothesis, a new effort was undertaken with the following stated goals: increase calls per hour to 11 and achieve an order rate of 22 percent.

Based on the response rate generated in calls to members of other auto clubs, it was decided to screen these individuals out at the beginning of the call. An additional "back-end"[2] number of card holders (how many retained their membership over a determined time span?) factor served to reinforce this decision—cancellations of membership commitments made by phone have often proved higher within this prospect segment.

With these new parameters, 373 completed calls were made, resulting in 202 completed decisions. The results of these calls are shown in Table 5-3.

This new strategy did produce the best combination to date, with 9.1 calls per hour achieving an order rate of 15.3 percent. The productivity

[2] Number of final members achieved after direct mail and payment cycles.

(completed calls per hour) jumped 28 percent over the best rate ever achieved with a taped message (7.2 calls per hour, at the 15 percent order rate). A significant factor in analyzing these results is the fact that almost one-third (31.6 percent) of the completed calls were made to unqualified respondents. Removing these nonproductive calls from the results produces a very different order rate—the figure for qualified prospects accepting the membership offer comes to 22.4 percent! This led to the conclusion that further screening the list to eliminate those who belong to other auto clubs or do not own cars would make for a workable, profitable telemarketing program.

Continuing Refinements The discovery that a taped message was not needed to convince potential members to join the club opened the way to a successful ongoing telemarketing program—but not immediately. Continual refinements in every phase of the program were necessary to improve productivity and, hence, bring profitability to acceptable standards. Some of the areas in which modifications proved significant are:

List segmentation. The profiling of an ideal prospect is not a static, once-in-a-lifetime project. Instead, a new multivariate linear regression analysis is undertaken each year, beginning once again with an undifferentiated list of Charg-All customers and deriving from the results of these calls a revised portrait of the desirable Ward's Auto Club telephone prospect. Changes in the marketplace and the profit itself can bring about significant shifts in this profile. For example, until the 1980 profiling was done, the median target age for auto club customers fell in the 45- to 50-year-old range. A new annual analysis revealed that the most responsive group had shifted downward in age, to the 35 to 40 category.

Another changeable consideration in determining the target universe is the question of membership in other auto clubs. Results of the test cited above indicated that calls to this market segment could not be made profitably. However, a test completed a year and a half later indicated that of those who were not interested in accepting the membership offer, only 15 percent cited another auto club as the reason. This segment of the list has been screened out in the first moments of a call during some stages of the roll-out program and has been given a full presentation of the benefits offered by the Ward's Auto Club in others. In addition to changes in the universe of prospects being called, the rise and fall in response of this other-club group also reflects changes in the Ward's Auto Club benefit package over the years. Notable in this regard is a New Car Buying Service, exclusive to Ward's, which assists consumers in buying the car they want at the best possible price. The uniqueness of this feature at the present time makes multiple auto club membership more appealing to consumers.

Scripts and training. There have been literally dozens of script variations in the Ward's Auto Club program over the years, including further tests of a taped message presentation (to date, still not as cost-effective!). Sometimes a seasonal theme proves a significant drawing card—"With the winter weather coming, your Montgomery Ward Auto Club membership could prove especially important." At other times, stressing a new benefit that has been added for club members or shifting the order in which they are presented has proven effective. From an operational standpoint, it is interesting to note that virtually any reasonable change made in the script (or the addition of a motivating incentive for the communicator!) will boost response for at least a few days—the changes help spur communicators, who may become less enthusiastic with the same material day after day.

Improvements in training also make valuable improvements in the bottom-line results. Experience alone will provide a "learning curve" that enhances communicator performance, as the communicator becomes more expert in the product and hence a more knowledgeable and effective representative. In addition, training to understand the true objection behind the stated objection, to screen out those who are truly not interested in the offer from those who are merely hesitant, and other skill-building forms of instruction can boost productivity and response significantly.

Another strategy offering great potential for maximizing the profitability of telemarketing is the concept of *add-ons*.

Add-ons Once contact has been established with a valid prospect, it would seem to be good business to offer more than one product or service. As the statistics provided earlier in this chapter indicate, only a relatively small percentage of the attempted calls actually result in a sales presentation being made. Making an additional offer once that prospect contact *is* made does add to the length (and hence, the cost) of the call, but it is still far less expensive than making a separate call to make the additional offer. And by increasing the value of the goods and services offered in the call, the profit potential from that call clearly rises as well.

This concept was first tested in connection with the Montgomery Ward Auto Club program in August 1976, with an attempt to offer *TV Guide* subscriptions to auto club prospects. In this test, *TV Guide* was ordered by 16.8 percent of those contacted. However, the additional revenue provided by the subscription sales did not compensate for the lower productivity in generating auto club memberships.

A further test program offered *TV Guide* only to those who said "yes" to the offer of auto club membership. This strategy brought the completed calls-per-hour figure up to 6.9—better, but still not adequate—and the order percentage for subscriptions went up to 18.7 percent.

This experience demonstrates the balancing act required for a successful add-on strategy. On the one hand, offering a greater selection of offers to the consumer increases the chance that an order will be taken. At the same time, telephone time is an expensive commodity, composed of both time on the line and labor costs. Any product presentation must offer a strong profitability level in order to justify the additional time required to make the offer. This aspect of telemarketing is strikingly different from mail-order or catalog marketing, where the consumer welcomes a wide selection and can quickly eliminate unwanted items or categories of items. The telephone offer must be presented verbally, in fairly extensive detail, before the prospect is given the option to say "yes" or "no." The economics of telemarketing make it impossible to offer consumers the opportunity to "browse" through a verbal catalog of merchandise.

Nevertheless, the right add-on offer can have a significant positive impact on profits. To this end, many test programs selling various products such as magazines, vitamins, beauty aids, and credit card insurance have been offered to the prospects being called for auto club membership commitment. The search for the "most effective" pairing of offers is constant, as new products and services surface in the marketplace.

Summary Drawing selectively through multivariate linear regression analysis from a total charge card holder file of approximately 16 million names, the Montgomery Ward Auto Club telemarketing effort has been an ongoing, highly successful campaign for over six years. In 1981 alone, the telemarketing operation produced over 150,000 new membership commitments for the club.

As the value of each member increased beyond the annual registration fee that is charged, a club magazine called the *Montgomery Ward Auto Club* (now called *Crossroads*) was added. While offering advertising pages to outside marketers, the magazine is also the vehicle for direct marketing of Montgomery Ward merchandise to auto club members. Thus, it provides two additional revenue streams.

Another profitable service marketing exclusively to auto club members is a new-car pricing service. For a $10 fee, a member who is in the market for a new car can subscribe to a service that finds a dealer willing to sell the car at $150 over cost!

Maximizing return on the telemarketing investment is a continuing challenge to Montgomery Ward and its telemarketing agency. Whether in exploring ways to increase the value of each member solicited or ways to gain new members in more cost-effective operations, the aggressive and innovative marketing mentality at work here provides a fine example for budding telemarketers.

Implications for the Marketer   There are, of course, a great many lessons to be learned from the growth of Signature from a single-product insurance venture to the diversified, highly successful direct-marketing arm of one of the nation's top seven retailers. However, one of the most significant involves a study that Richard Cremer has agreed to disclose for the first time in this book—a study that dramatically demonstrates the effect of incorporating direct-marketing strategies within the context of an overall retail business.

Richard Cremer explains: "In 1977, we were continually trying to overcome the biases of retailers within our company, who believed that we were transferring sales from their store cash registers to Signature. So we decided to do something about it.

"We identified 600,000 accounts in our Chicago credit center, which covered about 13 states, that amounted to about 20 percent of the 3 million accounts on that file, and we selected them on an nth name basis, so that each and every one of those 3 million accounts had an equal opportunity to become part of the sample. Therefore, we could predict with a high degree of accuracy that whatever we did to those 600,000 accounts would be replicated if we did it to the total universe.

"We then took the 600,000 names and divided them into two groups of 300,000 each, on an nth name basis. We put a flag on Group A, which prevented them from receiving any more direct mail until the flag was removed—and it's still there today.

"Not only did we withhold all of the direct mail generated by Signature, but we also withheld all of the direct mail generated at Montgomery Ward Insurance Group, because they were really a part of the problem, according to the retail stores' thinking.

"I have to tell you that, in order to keep that test valid, our company has given up about a million dollars in profits over the four years since that program was established, profits that would have been generated by Signature if we had continued to mail to those Group A names. But I know it was vital to know whether we were transferring sales from retail sales or not, and this was the only way I knew that we could determine with certainty what happened to the credit purchases of our credit customers when they did get our mail, compared with other customers who were identical in all respects but did not get mail.

"We've kept track carefully now of the credit sales in both groups of accounts on a quarterly and monthly and annual basis, and the group that has been receiving direct mail has *repeatedly* and *continuously* grown in incremental sales over the group that has not. It started in the very first year of the test, with a differential of slightly above 1 percent. It grew to 1.6 in the second year and reached 2 percent in 1981. The difference in the first quarter of 1982 is even greater.

"Now what does that mean? It means that Montgomery Ward is getting at least 2 percent more sales from people that get our mail than from people that don't. Of course, we still had to find out what the *source* of the sales were, to demonstrate whether the increase included incremental retail sales or only direct-marketing responses.

"We began to identify that factor by looking at the auto club members in each group. There were 18,000 auto club members in each at the start of the test, and by the time the test was over, there were 6,000 more auto club members in the group that we were promoting than in the group we weren't.

"Since the dues were $30, those memberships account for $180,000 worth of sales differential. The 2 percent I mentioned before—the sales differential on the 300,000 accounts getting direct mail—amounted to close to $700,000, so the auto club accounted for only $180,000, or 26 percent. Then we did the same analysis for each of our products. We were able to identify only two-thirds of the $700,000 that could be traced to the insurance company or to Signature. That meant that one-third of the $700,000—close to a quarter of a million dollars in incremental credit sales—was produced by the retail and catalog division.

"We believe that we now have proof positive that not only do we generate more sales directly but we generate incremental sales on the retail level, as a result of our direct-marketing efforts.

"I believe this lesson can be carried over not only to direct mail but to telephone as well. The question of the impact of a telemarketing call on the consumer comes up frequently. If you phone people, you're going to phone on a highly selective basis, but you're still going to phone at least four or five times as many people as you get buyers on most products—and if it's a big-ticket offer, you might even phone 10 people to find one buyer. The question is, how do you leave the other nine?

"I happen to believe you leave them happy. If I didn't believe that, I wouldn't be doing telemarketing. We have just described probably the largest study ever conducted in the history of the United States about the effect of direct-response mail on the purchasing habits of customers in retail and catalog. If you use that as an analogy, then I believe those nine people that don't buy on the phone will buy more in retail and catalog stores, because they remember that Ward's thought enough to call and offer them something that they thought was a good buy for them. Even though they didn't buy it, they'll remember Ward's.

"And as a matter of fact, they may even have second thoughts. I've had letters from customers saying that they didn't accept an offer that was made by phone but how could they do it now, because they had changed their minds—they'd like to have it. They might even just go into the store in that situation."

The essential message we can take from Mr. Cremer's experience in direct marketing, and telemarketing in particular, is that these marketing contacts are a valuable service to the consumer and are perceived in this way by the majority of those contacted. A research study undertaken by Signature indicated that more than 91 *percent* of their customers who were called appreciated the quality of the telemarketing service calls.[3]

"Most catalogers who have catalog stores," Mr. Cremer explains, "provide those stores with a list of the customers who live in their trade area. The customer data that's maintained in a three-by-five card in all the Ward's catalog stores contains those customers' names, the number of children in the family, where the adults work, and little tidbits of information that permit them to serve that customer on a highly personalized basis. When they have a sale on work shoes with steel toes and they know they've got 30 or 40 people in their territory that have been buying steel-toed shoes, they've got a good chance of making a number of sales if they call those 30 people.

"So selective telephoning is not something that was invented in the last couple of years. It's been going on for 50 years. It's just that it's more marketing-systemized, oriented, highly computerized—and cost-efficient—than it used to be. Retail catalog agencies and catalog stores generate plus sales with 'outgoing phone calls' to their customers, and they

[3] See Appendix H for the full study on consumer response to CCI call programs.

establish a very friendly relationship with them. They oftentimes will call special groups of customers every month with that month's special, and the customers like them to do that, because it's a personal call and they may have missed it in the sale flyer.

"There's nothing more important today to consumers than being able to save money, and if they pass up the chance to save money on a sale on something that is a necessity in their home, they're very distraught about it. They could actually become disturbed with the retailer who didn't get the word to them quickly," Richard Cremer concluded.

chapter six

Incremental Sales to Business

Case History: Seminars for Sale

Seminars in management education are very big business. According to one authority, nearly a million top executives in North America were expected to attend seminars, workshops, or conferences last year. Growing emphasis in the business community on productivity, coupled with rapid developments in high-technology industries, have made organized meetings with expert speakers a key element in maintaining management effectiveness.

The strong demand for seminar programs does not mean that marketing these sessions is an easy task. Success breeds competition, and this is certainly the case in the business-seminar field, where more than 2,000 organizations run some type of teaching session each year—the annual total of seminars offered recently passed the 35,000 mark. The marketplace has become highly competitive and highly cluttered. A busy executive may receive dozens of invitations to seminars every week.

The traditional marketing channel for producing seminar registrations is direct mail. Using highly segmented rented lists of business executives along with their own critically important "in-house" files, marketers can determine the select target universe for a particular seminar topic and direct their mailing to those prospects alone.

The overwhelming volume of sessions being offered has put a serious crimp in this marketing strategy. Even with the finest list selection processes, the end result is still an executive who, while a valid prospect, has far too many potentially interesting seminar offers arriving to consider each of them. What is needed is a strategy to focus that individual's attention on a specific topic or series of seminars, to make that offering stand out from the crowd. Telemarketing fills this role particularly well.

Conventional thinking might suggest that executive-level decision-makers would not want to be interrupted with a "sales" call in the middle of their business day. In a sense, that's true. Once again we return to the concept of the best telemarketing contact positioned as a *service* call. With this kind of script emphasis, business-to-business contact works very well whenever you have an offer (1) properly targeted, (2) providing benefits of interest to the decision maker, and (3) presented in a knowledgeable, responsive, and "businesslike" manner.

To explore the workings of this concept in depth, let us examine the specifics of telemarketing done by CCI,[1] programs developed and refined over the course of a decade and still very much under way today at the American Management Associations (AMA). By using many varied applications of telephone contact and dovetailing these efforts neatly within ongoing direct-mail efforts, a creative multimedia campaign continues to prove its effectiveness.

The American Management Associations is the world's largest organization in the field of management education. The AMA offers courses, seminars, and conferences and produces hardcover books, research studies, multimedia programs for in-house training, tape cassette programs, home-study courses, and a number of other teaching products and services. With major centers in eight key American cities, a worldwide operations network, and a history of serving corporations both large and small since the 1920s, the association has a very strong reputation as the leading institution in the field.

However, when the economy is in a downward trend, companies in the management-seminar field are very vulnerable. It is ironic that educational programs to strengthen profitability through improved management and operations are threatened by the very economic forces they are designed to combat. Nevertheless, when the budget crunch is on, these programs are often considered expendable. High-caliber training pro-

---

[1] Campaign Communications Institute of America (CCI) has been the AMA's telemarketing agency since 1970.

grams are a fairly expensive proposition, whether a $400 registration fee for a two-day seminar on financial marketing or a $10,000 or more fee for a multimedia in-house training program. This represents a substantial capital investment for many hard-pressed company budgets.

Marketing Objectives Traditionally, direct mail has been the primary avenue for generating seminar registrations. In fact, the AMA sends out over 15 million direct-mail pieces every year! However, as the association entered the 70s, it found that the extensive direct-mail effort on behalf of its seminars and conferences was producing a volume of registrations that would often just barely justify giving a particular program at all. Many would fail to reach even the "break-even level," leading to heavy losses and program cancellations.

There was an urgent need to find profitable alternative marketing channels to reach potential registrants and motivate them to "sign up" for the seminar of their choice.

In its search for a solution to this marketing crisis, the association turned to telemarketing. The first tests involved a series of call programs aimed at developing a strategy for soliciting seminar registrations directly over the phone. The first major question to be explored: "Can the AMA reach its market by telephone?" The people who attend seminars are almost without exception upper- and middle-level management. Even for lower-echelon employees, the decision to spend the money for seminar registration must come from the top level of a company or division. Some doubted whether the appropriate level of decision maker would be willing to accept a telemarketing call.

In addition, the profitability of telemarketing was in question when compared with direct mail, which can reach individual prospects at a much lower cost per contact than calling them one by one on the telephone. An added barrier: The AMA was a nonprofit association and sent mail at the lowest postal rates. In order to make economic sense as part of the overall marketing effort, the telephone program had to provide additional revenue either (1) by producing registrations from the same market segment less expensively than mail, or (2) by producing new registrations incremental to those generated through the mail effort.

Telemarketing Strategy and List Segmentation Of the dozens of conferences and seminars conducted by the association each year, the one chosen for the first telemarketing test effort in 1970 was the annual conference on education and training, held in New York City. A mailing piece announcing the conference and inviting registrations had already been sent. Now telephone follow-up calls would be made to a very select list— educators and corporate-personnel training directors who had attended either or both of the previous conferences but had not yet responded to the direct-mail brochure. Most, but not all, of these names were drawn from the vicinity of the conference location.

Creative Strategy   The script prepared for this test was very direct. The calls were following up immediately on a mailed brochure and therefore did not have to go into a detailed sales presentation about the conference itself. The communicator asked for the specific individual on the prospect list, explained the purpose of the call, made sure that the literature about the conference had indeed arrived in the mail, and attempted to complete the registration over the phone. If the mailing piece had not arrived, the communicator offered to send out a new one but could not call back to take a registration, since the test was restricted to a one-week period.

Results   With 157 prospects to contact and only a week to train communicators and make the calls, 96 of the names on the list were reached. It took 241 call-backs and 393 total dialings to achieve this reach rate (see Figure 6-1). You will rarely see this kind of ratio of dialings to contacts in a consumer program—it isn't cost-efficient to pursue an individual consumer with this degree of dedication.

In the production-conscious world of telemarketing, every dialing counts. *Calling private homes*, you will often dial and receive no answer, while this is almost never the case in calling a business. A communicator spends time dialing and listening to the ringing phone when there is no answer on a residence phone. Then additional expense is tacked onto the cost of that potential contact if one must collect the records of those who did not answer and resort them to be recalled for another "pass," preferably at a different time of day to increase the likelihood that the person will be at home.

Generally it pays to continue calling numbers that don't answer the first time in a consumer program. However, there are several factors to consider in determining how many attempts to make for each name, including the total number of names you have available in your calling universe, the amount of money you've already spent in acquiring those names, the profit margin on each individual sale, the response rate you are experiencing in the calling program as a whole, and the total expense of each attempted contact, including phone costs and clerical costs. A similar

CCI **AMERICAN MANAGEMENT** /TOP 40
Associations

LIST_____

CODE_____

BAND_____

Name/Address Change:

Name_____

Title_____

Address_____

_____

_____

Name_____

Title_____

_____

_____

FIRST CONTACT/FUTURE CONTACT

RESPONSE CODE

OP	DATE	REG.	LIT.	SP. LIT.	NI	NA	DA	RCB	/	FUTURE CONTACT: DATE	RE:MTG. #
		REG.	LIT.	SP. LIT.	NI	NA	DA	RCB	/	/	
		REG.	LIT.	SP. LIT.	NI	NA	DA	RCB	/	/	
		REG.	LIT.	SP. LIT.	NI	NA	DA	RCB	/	/	
		REG.	LIT.	SP. LIT.	NI	NA	DA	RCB	/	/	
		REG.	LIT.	SP. LIT.	NI	NA	DA	RCB	/	/	
		REG.	LIT.	SP. LIT.	NI	NA	DA	RCB	/	/	
		REG.	LIT.	SP. LIT.	NI	NA	DA	RCB	/	/	
		REG.	LIT.	SP. LIT.	NI	NA	DA	RCB	/	/	
		REG.	LIT.	SP. LIT.	NI	NA	DA	RCB	/		

COMMENTS:_____

_____

_____

_____

_____

_____

Figure 6-1. Sample CCI call cards for AMA campaign. Notice "future contact" column on right-hand side.

calculation must be made when it comes to agreeing to the prospect's request to "call back later." In that case, there is an additional factor to be considered. "Call back later" is often code for "I'm not interested," and a call-back could be a total waste of time and money.

With a *business-to-business* phone marketing program, the call-result pattern changes substantially. You will rarely call a number and get *no* answer. However, you will often fail to get through to the person you need to contact, and since only that specific individual or decision maker will do, it may take repeated call-backs to deliver your message and get a measurable response. Another factor to consider in the difference between business-to-business and consumer calling is the timing of your call. Consumer calls are far more effective in the evenings, when people are home for the night, while business-to-business calls must be made during regular office hours, are much more costly, and are restricted still further to accommodate late arrivals, early departures, and lunch hours. This can affect your expense picture substantially, since labor costs, telephone rates, and physical plant costs can all vary, depending on "day" or "evening" factors.

To ultimately answer the question of whether to make repeated attempts, or call-backs, and how many times per name, you must accurately determine your total cost per call, measure your response rate, and see how well they balance. Like most forms of marketing, "gut" response decisions, even when they are based on years of experience, will be wrong about as often as they're right. Stick with controlled, statistically reliable testing whenever possible.

Returning to our initial test, results of the 96 completed contacts in the first test program are shown in Table 6-1.

The initial 18.7 percent response rate was very impressive indeed, and it is really only part of the story. It is worth noting that of the sample called,

TABLE 6-1. *AMA Test Results*

Total reached	96	100.0%
Will attend	18	18.7
Requested program literature	5	5.2
Not interested	58	60.4
Registered by mail prior to call	9	9.4
Will register directly with association by mail	6	6.2

nine individuals were not valid prospects, since they had already registered before they received the call. Of the 87 valid prospects, 20.7 percent responded with a registration directly over the phone. Considering only these direct registrations, the test program brought in fees totalling $2\frac{1}{2}$ times the cost of the marketing effort. When we further consider the six prospects who planned to register directly by mail after having their memories jogged by the phone contact and those who responded to the program literature mailed to them after their phone request, it is easy to understand the excitement that this test produced, both for the association and their telemarketing agency.

Some of the side benefits uncovered by the test are also interesting in pointing up the unique benefits of phone. For example, the communicators were able to trace and contact 11 past participants who had changed jobs or moved within the company and to discuss the conference with them. Four of these 11 individuals registered for the conference. We can safely assume that without the persistence of phone contact, most of these people would never have been reached by the association and given the opportunity to participate—as the mail never reached them either.

The communicators were also able to follow through on a contact and reach the person who had taken over the position formerly held by a past participant in the conference. From the 14 people contacted in this way, 3 registrations were taken.

In addition, communicators succeeded in recording the reasons 40 past participants would *not* be attending this year's conference, providing useful feedback with which to plan future sessions and analyze the results of the association's marketing strategy.

Program Expansion   These promising initial results led to the decision to go ahead with two more test programs. The first would offer a choice of seminars, courses, and briefings—13 in all—to be given in the Chicago area in August and September. The list consisted of 400 association members and customers within a 60-mile radius of the meeting site.

The other test was focused in the New York area, where a briefing session on pollution was scheduled. Calls would be made to 269 "cold" prospects who had been sent a mailing piece promoting only this briefing session.

Neither of these tests was successful. For the Chicago seminars, 324 individuals were contacted, and only 7 registered over the phone—a 2.2 percent response rate, when the break-even point was projected at 6 percent. One bright note: of the 7 who did register, 1 had taken over the job of the executive included on the prospect list and hence would probably not have been reached by the association's direct-mail effort, while 4 of the 7 registrations came after the prospect had requested a new copy of the brochure when called the first time and registered when called a second time, again indicating that these were registrants who would not have been secured through the mail. However, the expense-to-income ratio was totally unacceptable—only two-thirds of the marketing costs were recouped in registration fees.

The results for the New York pollution briefing campaign were substantially better. Of the 269 available names, 172 were contacted, and 7 registrations resulted—6 for the pollution briefing session and 1 for a nonrelated seminar. Registration fees were 50 percent higher than telemarketing expenses.

However, neither of these tests lived up to the promise of the education and training conference results. Two other tests were later attempted in the New York area, one for a session on alcoholism and drugs, another on data processing. These also produced unimpressive response rates of 4.1 percent and 2.8 percent respectively, reflecting the general lack of response on the part of the business community to management education at the time. "Discretionary expenditures" are usually the first casualty in a recessionary economy—but one doesn't need the added expense of telemarketing to prove that point!

Analysis and Strategic Decisions   At this stage it was necessary to assess what had been so right about the first program and why the subsequent tests, while producing some registrations, were not successful.

Some of the difficulties were evident in the reasons for lack of interest elicited by the communicators. The first problem was bad timing. Of those who gave reasons for noninterest, over half of the Chicago sample and nearly three-quarters of the New York pollution briefing sample cited conflicts with vacations, budget-planning meetings, and so on (the New York pollution session was held on the brink of the long Labor Day weekend).

Budgetary problems were also cited, and this price resistance seemed to be a valid variable in a tight economic period, since the education conference tested initially was far less costly than the seminars and briefings offered subsequently.

But the major, overriding factor that distinguished the first test from later efforts was the "quality" of the list used. In the first test, in which the attendance lists of previous conferences were called, the prospects were extremely well screened for proven interest and ability to attend. By contrast, the other tests were made to lists of association members and customers who might or might not ever have attended a seminar before, who had not demonstrated their specific interest in the particular topics being offered, and who could not depend on their own past participation as a reason for organizational approval of the expense involved in current attendance.

It had proven economically unfeasible to take a "cold" prospect list that might be suitable for mailing and use it for telephone solicitation. The response standards for a successful marketing campaign by mail are substantially less demanding than those for the phone, which makes the question of list quality the crucial challenge to telemarketers. And again, the difference in cost per contact is particularly pronounced when the mailing is done at the favorable postal rates reserved for nonprofit institutions. For example, at the time these tests were undertaken, to achieve a 25 percent expense-to-income ratio for a mailing piece costing (nonprofit rate) $0.07 each, and selling a $330 meeting required a pull of .85 registrants per 1,000 pieces mailed. To get the same expense-to-income ratio with phone required a pull of 6 registrants per 100 calls—about 70 times more than the needed mail response! It has also been found, in many subsequent test programs, that if an offer does not "pull" well through direct mail, it will generally not do well through phone contact either.

Additional Tests   The initial test programs undertaken on behalf of the association pointed the way to strategic decisions that would maximize the effect of telemarketing by targeting calls to those list segments and products that offered the greatest potential. By combining the ability to pinpoint individuals who might well ignore mail or space advertising with a tool for delivering a persuasive, personal sales message, telephone can multiply the number of positive decisions within a responsive market segment many times over the results possible with other marketing media. By launching programs that combined *top lists* with *top meetings*, therefore, the association expected to boost registrations significantly.

Another consideration that showed promise for the association was the use of phone as an *incremental* medium. There are many people who will respond to personal phone contact and not to an offer made by mail or other mass medium. Again, when the phone rings you answer it! It is often worthwhile to follow up on a mailing that produces a reasonable response with phone calls to those on your list who did not respond. This is particularly true when the list is rather selective in the first place, as with the past attendees of the education and training conference we've described. In doing this, you are contacting the "difficult to sell," and every order you receive is one normally given up as lost without the telephone backup system.

The association, for instance, also offers a steady stream of management training courses and products, which are sold largely to their list of established customers. By registering someone for a seminar who otherwise would not have attended, the phone program can create a new customer for future association services or maintain the enthusiasm of a previous registrant. Many of those who responded by phone *once* could be expected to register by mail in the future, substantially reducing the average cost per sale over the buying life of the customer. Thus, many phone sales efforts are worth more in the long run than the "bottom-line" of the individual campaign would indicate.

There are also several special circumstances that are especially suited to a telemarketing program. For the association, these included the following:

■ **Boosting borderline sessions.** The association has a continuing problem with meetings that receive borderline response through their mailing efforts but have not attracted enough registrants to justify holding the program. Phone contact brings in enough additional positive responses to make the difference between cancellation and continuing with plans for the session.

The costing for this kind of program did not have to compete head-to-head with mail costs in order to be worthwhile, since there was already a group of cost-efficient mail registrations that would be lost if the attendance figures could not be brought up to "break even." The expenditure for this type of incremental program could also be tightly controlled by monitoring the constant progress reports on phone response. In this way, management could stop the calling program as soon as it had generated enough registrants to allow the session to take place or, if the response by phone was particularly good, allow the calls to continue as long as they were profitable.

■ **Quick action.** There were also situations that demanded the type of fast attention that only a phone program can provide. If a topical meeting was organized, one that could be expected to produce enthusiastic response because it dealt with a particularly timely issue, phone calls to a selective list of likely prospects could tap this peak response with more impact and greater speed than a mail campaign. And if there was an exciting new speaker added to a program, phone could carry this message to a prospect who had already received a mailing piece without this vital information.

Another feature of the timeliness of phone: if a list that showed promise for a scheduled program became available too late to be reached by mail, a script and calling program could be developed to tap these hot prospects on short notice.

- **Small market segment.** Certain sessions sponsored by the association appealed to a highly specialized market segment. In order to be most effectively promoted, these meetings had to be presented individually, rather than lumped into a brochure announcing several programs, but the size of the target audience would not justify the expense of preparing a special mailing piece. A telephone campaign tailored to the interests of such a specialized group could be prepared and implemented quickly and inexpensively, producing a response within days of the decision to proceed with a calling program.

Having arrived at a strategic framework for the AMA's telemarketing effort, it was necessary to structure the tactics and engineer the procedures that would translate plans into profits. In the following pages, we'll examine how a battery of business-to-business telephone techniques were brought to bear in campaigns conducted for and by the association.

Profiting from the 80-20 Rule   Having proven that telemarketing was a valid means of registering executives for seminars, the next steps probed ways to increase the efficiency of this branch of the marketing operation. The strategy followed was based on the 80-20 rule—simply put, educational marketers, like most businesses, make 80 percent of their profits from 20 percent of their products and 20 percent of the market. Using this best-product-to-best-list strategy, the association put together a highly successful, long-running telemarketing effort to maximize positive response from each dollar invested in telemarketing.

Of the hundreds of seminars they offer each year, they identified the 40 most popular, based on past attendance figures, and divided these into separate areas of specific business interest. (Initially there were six categories—finance, marketing-sales, purchasing, personnel, management systems, and maintenance management—and this number grew with the addition of insurance, manufacturing, and others as the program progressed.)

To match the products offered as closely as possible with the prospects being called, the computer produced a list of individuals who had attended previous seminars in this group of 40 top-drawing programs. This list, which was already well screened on the basis of past attendance, was further segmented into the separate business-interest divisions described above, allowing the phone operation to match the prospects called with the choice of meetings appropriate to their specific interests.

Having assembled their ammunition and specified their targets, there was still the problem of reaching this select audience, which in this case was made up predominantly of corporate executives. This is a twofold problem—getting past the switchboard and/or secretary to the executive and then catching the busy decision maker's attention long enough to accept the call and listen to your call presentation.

A proven technique to overcome both these difficulties simultaneously is to include a taped message from a corporate figure whose company name and title will be impressive and appropriate to the audience being called.

With this approach, the communicator's personal introduction to the voice that answers the phone changes from this:

"Hello, I'm John Doe calling for the American Management Associations. May I speak with Mr. Smith?"

To this:

"Hello, I'm John Doe calling for the American Management Associations. I'm calling with an important taped message for Mr. Smith from Jack Jones, Vice President for Corporate Affairs at International Conglomerate. May I speak with Mr. Smith?"

On the secretarial level, this approach provides leverage and credibility. Few secretaries will take it on their own authority to dismiss a call with a message from an important corporate executive.

From the boss's point of view, your call with a taped message is likely to be accepted since it appeals to the irresistible force of "peer pressure" and human *curiosity*. The thinking process is likely to go something like this: "What could Jack Jones possibly want with me? What is International Conglomerate into this time? I'll take the call."

For the association's telephone campaign for seminar registrations, a script was developed that could be adapted with minor revisions to accommodate a different executive from each of the individual business-interest areas being called. Here, as an example, is the script recorded by an executive for his "peer" prospects in the purchasing function:

TAPED MESSAGE SCRIPT PRESENTATION
HELLO. THIS IS JACK JONES, VICE PRESIDENT, PURCHASING AND EN-GINEERING SERVICES FOR INTERNATIONAL CONGLOMERATE. I'M TAK-ING THIS OPPORTUNITY TO TALK WITH YOU PERSONALLY ABOUT THE

AMERICAN MANAGEMENT ASSOCIATION'S COMMITMENT TO BUSINESS EDUCATION AND ON-THE-JOB TRAINING.

TODAY, MY COMPANY, LIKE YOURS, IS FACED WITH THE SAME SEVERE ECONOMIC CONSTRICTIONS, SHORTAGES, DISLOCATIONS, AND NEW COST RELATIONSHIPS. OUR MANAGEMENT IS ASKING OUR OWN PUR-CHASING EXECUTIVES TO TAKE ON MORE, TO PRODUCE MORE, TO WORK MORE EFFICIENTLY AND EFFECTIVELY. YOU'RE PROBABLY SET-TING THIS TASK FOR YOUR OWN STAFF RIGHT NOW. BUT ASKING FOR MORE, OR ACHIEVING MORE, DOESN'T NECESSARILY HAPPEN. CON-TINUING TRAINING, EDUCATION, AND COMPANY SUPPORT ARE NECES-SARY IF ANY INDIVIDUAL IS TO SUCCEED. A NEED TO DEVELOP INTER-NAL RESOURCES AND GET THE BEST OF THE BEST OF YOUR PEOPLE REQUIRES YOUR COMMITMENT TO HELP THEM IN EVERY WAY POSSI-BLE. THOSE OF US INVOLVED IN THE PAST WITH THE AMA WOULD LIKE TO HELP YOU MEET THIS COMMITMENT.

EDUCATION, DEVELOPMENT, AND TRAINING HAVE ALWAYS BEEN THE MAJOR CONCERN AT THE AMA, AND THIS IS WHY I'VE CHOSEN THE NEW TYPE OF PHONE MESSAGE TO REACH YOU, AS DIRECTLY AS POSSIBLE, ABOUT THE ASSOCIATION'S COURSES THAT ARE DESIGNED TO HELP MEET THE NEEDS OF EXECUTIVES OF VARIED EXPERIENCE LEVELS. SOME OF THESE COURSES DEAL WITH SPECIFIC SKILLS FOR THE SENIOR PURCHASING MANAGER AND THE DIRECTOR OR MANAGER OF MATERIALS HANDLING. OTHERS COVER A RANGE OF SUBJECTS OF INTEREST TO WAREHOUSING MANAGERS. THE SAME SEMINAR MAY SERVE AS A REFRESHER TO A DIRECTOR OR MANAGER WHO'S RUSTY IN CERTAIN AREAS—OR ACQUAINT HIM WITH THE FUNDAMENTALS OF A NEW AREA OF RESPONSIBLITY.

THE EMPHASIS OF ALL COURSES IS ON PRACTICAL, ON-THE-JOB APPLI-CATIONS, WITH THE NEWEST TECHNIQUES APPLIED TO THE NEWEST PURCHASING AND PHYSICAL DISTRIBUTION CHALLENGES—ALL DE-SIGNED TO HELP YOU AND YOUR STAFF MEET THE NEW ECONOMIC MANPOWER AND PURCHASING AND PHYSICAL DISTRIBUTION PROB-LEMS HEAD-ON.

VERY SOON, A NUMBER OF COURSES THAT I BELIEVE WILL BE OF SPE-CIAL INTEREST TO YOU AND YOUR STAFF WILL BE HELD IN YOUR AREA. OUR TELEPHONE COMMUNICATOR WILL BE HAPPY TO GIVE YOU SPECIFIC INFORMATION ON THEM. I HOPE YOU'LL TAKE A MINUTE TO REVIEW THE CONTENTS OF EACH COURSE WITH THE COMMUNICATOR AND RESERVE SPACE FOR YOUR COMPANY. THANK YOU FOR TAKING THE TIME TO LISTEN.

The message in this taped presentation is certainly loud and clear—and long. Is it worthwhile devoting that much phone time to a prerecorded tape? Does it really make a measurable difference?

The answer probably lies in the level of both the audience and the spokesperson being taped. In any program, a tape from a high-ranking executive adds a personal touch and professional validation to the call contact. In the case of the association's program, the tape had special significance because the spokesperson was an executive of a major corporation, not of the association itself. Unlike product endorsements by movie stars or sports figures, the executive recommendation here is being made by someone with no personal stake in the outcome of the call. The testimonial and relative purity of intent assumed by the listener adds a great deal to the credibility of the message. The tape is especially effective when introducing a product or service to a new customer, who will find the willingness of a respected executive to endorse the product or service a powerful reassurance against understandable initial skepticism.

The Communicator Role AMA program operations were not simple, either for the clerical staff or the communicators. The clerical staff had to "hand track" six or more separate sets of names simultaneously, first looking up telephone numbers and then processing orders and channeling requests for call-backs back into the phone room at the designated times.

The communicators required a different presentation for each market segment to be called, and each presentation involved several separate elements. If a company name only was provided on the prospect list, the communicator needed to know the proper job title to ask for. The introductory elements of the presentation had to be tailored to the particular market segment and to the executive whose taped message was included in the call. For the business end of the call, each communicator needed a list of the appropriate courses to offer in the prospect's area of interest, with a summary of each of the courses to be read to interested prospects. These summaries included a description of the seminar audience, the format, the key subjects to be covered, and the special meeting features or benefits offered.

In addition, the communicators needed up-to-date schedules showing when each course would be given within the next several months in the prospect's geographical area.

The communicator could then take a course registration over the phone or offer to send literature, if requested, on any of the courses. The communicator would finish the call by asking for referrals—"Do you feel any other member of your department might be interested?"—and these referrals might be called subsequently.

While this may seem to be an impossible amount of paper and information to juggle while on the phone, the communicators relied on expertly prepared, carefully structured scripts and quickly learned to respond and provide answers to a prospect's questions with admirable smoothness.

As it was conceived (and as it turned out), this registration-generation program required more than one phone call per prospect to produce positive results. The first call established the individual's interest, offered literature, took whatever immediate registrations were available, and determined whether further calls would be welcome. It was on the second, third, and even fourth attempts that significant numbers of registrations were taken. For example, in the initial testing period of the program, 14 registrations were produced through phone activity—2 from initial calls, 9 from subsequent call-backs, and 3 sent in by mail in response to literature requested over the phone.

This repeated calling plan was oriented as a customer-service program. In the final script that was developed, the phone call was presented to the prospect as "our preferred-member service, designed to provide current information on selected association meetings—those we feel can be most relevant to your organization." This service-oriented approach helps to overcome much of the sales resistance encountered when interrupting busy executives with sales propositions. You are not only offering them courses, you are offering them convenience by bringing to their attention only those courses that fit their individual needs and by taking a registration right over the phone without the bother of time-consuming paperwork.

In the first four years of the program, registration commitments were made in 3.6 percent of the completed calls (bear in mind that many executives are only reached after repeated attempts).

This success rate produced profitable registrations from executives who had not registered by mail and therefore were highly unlikely to attend had they not been contacted by phone. An important factor in the call results was the number of executives who wished to receive future phone calls with seminar offers—this figure ran close to 60 percent, indicating that a healthy majority were strong prospects for future telephone registration.

A call program emphasizing individualized sales presentations and periodic call follow-ups cannot be done inexpensively. On average, the expense-to-income ratio for the program ran at about 50 percent for several years—but this was in accordance with the projected level of expense and was considered acceptable for two good reasons. First, these "cream-of-the-crop" meetings run at a very low cancellation rate, generally between 1 and 2 percent, so the phone-registered individuals can be expected to actually attend in a significantly greater proportion than could be expected for the seminar program as a whole. In addition, these meetings almost always run above break-even in terms of numbers of registrants, so that whatever additional registrations can be obtained by phone represent *incremental income*—almost pure profit, after the marketing expense is deducted. And as the calls progressed, it became clear that virtually no one called had recently subscribed to a meeting by mail, indicating that *those who responded by phone* did indeed represent *added registrations* unobtainable by mail alone.

Other Sources of "Hot Prospects"   The select and compiled list business has grown to enormous proportions and developed an undeniable sophistication in recent years. A marketer can rent lists of individuals who fit into virtually any classification imaginable—or rent all of them at once! However, it has often been shown that the best possible list source is available within your own company, going unnoticed, and failing to fulfill its profit potential. Two such valuable reference sources have been put to good use by the association for many years now.

One of the strongest sources of hot prospects for upcoming seminar programs was discovered to be the list of individuals who have previously registered for a meeting but did not attend, either because they canceled voluntarily or because the total registration for the session was insufficient and the association itself was forced to cancel. These managers have already demonstrated their strong interest in management education. Often their cancellations were caused by practical difficulties that cropped up between the registration and the date of the session—the registrant was needed in the office that week, or a major business development took place unexpectedly, or a personal contingency arose and led to cancellation.

There are always *some* disappointed would-be buyers, in most businesses; whether they ordered out-of-stock merchandise or had to break a sales appointment without immediately rescheduling it or facing some other problem that surfaces unexpectedly. Failing to follow up on such demonstrated interest would seem to be the height of folly, yet that is precisely what happens in business with surprising regularity. It takes an organized, systematic program to recontact these potential buyers and convert them into present customers, and the telephone can be the perfect medium for this effort.

The association implemented an effective telemarketing program to follow up on seminar cancellations to reregister these potential registrants with specific offers of either a new session of the same seminar they had previously been unable to attend or another session in the same field of interest.

This program worked on two levels:

1. Registration department. When a person calls the AMA registration department to cancel, a trained communicator attempts to reschedule that individual immediately into a future seminar.

If the association is forced to cancel a scheduled session, a Mailgram is sent to those who have already registered announcing the change, and a personal phone call is made quickly to verify the cancellation and to attempt to complete a reregistration for an upcoming session.

2. Telemarketing department. Information on all mailed-in cancellation requests and all call-in cancellations that were *not* rescheduled is assembled for a follow-up telephone campaign. As soon as the data is received and processed by the registration department, it is passed on to the phone agency workshop, so the lag time between cancellation and recontact is kept short.

Telephone communicators call the cancelees and offer them a new session of the same seminar, if one is available, or a selection of upcoming seminars on related topics if it is not. If the prospect requests descriptive literature, it is mailed out promptly and followed up with another call about a week later. Calls continue to each prospect until there's a "yes" or "no" decision.

The program has been a major success for the association over the years. In its first five years, it produced over a million dollars in revenue, with costs amounting to less than 20 percent of the total. In a 10-year period, over 100,000 completed calls were made, producing more than 10,000 seminar registrations.

The fly in the ointment in assessing this program is the recancellation rate—those who registered again and had to pull out again without attending. This is a difficult number to track, since it involves segregating the brand-new registrants' cancellation figures from those of the reregistrants. It seems logical to believe that a registrant who cancels once is more likely to cancel again than the average registrant. But taking this into account, let's pose some typical figures and analyze them.

In a representative period, let's say the figures run as follows:

Completed calls	25,000
Registrations	3,000
Average registration fee	$500
Cost of marketing services	$150,000

Experience shows that it takes an average of 1.8 calls to get a decision from the prospect. On that basis, the program outlined above contacted

13,889 prospects and registered 21.6 percent of them for seminars, at a cost of $50 per registrant, only 10 percent of seminar registration fee.

Now let's factor in an extremely high recancellation rate—say 50 percent. Even at that level, the marketing cost per actual attendee will still reach only $100 for seminars with a price tag hovering around $500—still a healthy return on investment (ROI)—and very profitable phone marketing.

List Building   A tried-and-true method of building a list of receptive prospects for phone contact is using newspaper and magazine advertising, or even a toll-free "800" number, to generate inquiries. Many companies find it profitable to simply send out a literature package in response to inquiries with an order form enclosed. However, in most cases, if you take those names and follow up your mailing pieces with a phone call, you increase your response rate tremendously.

For the association, an inquiry follow-up call was especially appropriate, since schedules for the courses being offered were not included in the brochures mailed out—they are too complex and changeable to be handled that way. This need to provide time-and-place information gives the communicators entrée to the prospect. A similar situation would pertain if your products involved a relatively complex pricing structure that can be handled most effectively in a live conversation.

For the association, a typical call program might involve over 15,000 completed calls and produce nearly 2,000 registrations. Even after a reasonable allowance for later cancellations, the marketing expense still comes in at well below 15 percent of the revenue. It would appear that the convenience offered by a personal follow-up call provides a return at a very reasonable expense.

Summary   At this writing, the seminar marketing program on behalf of the association continues on three fronts—through an "in-house" call operation, through the services of an outbound telemarketing agency (CCI), and through several of the association's regional offices across the country. Different tasks are performed by each component of the overall effort, utilizing individuals well versed in the seminar programs and skilled in telephone communication.

The telemarketing effort has not been limited to the seminar field. Successful telephone campaigns have been undertaken to support marketing efforts for multimedia management-education packages and programs by generating screened and qualified sales leads and by inviting sales prospects to attend group product presentations at central locations.

Implications for the Marketer   In the process of developing telemarketing programs to produce seminar registrations, valuable lessons were learned about the techniques involved in successfully marketing to the business community by phone. To briefly recap some key points:

1. **Telephone can reach key prospects, even at upper management levels.** Two considerations are crucial here. First, the prospect should ideally have some prior relationship with the company or organization calling. Association members and past customers fit this category nicely. At the very least, the prospect should be made aware of the caller's business before the call takes place, through direct mail, advertising, trade-show exposure, and so on.

Second, the offer must have genuine relevance to the prospect's job function. In this regard, careful and even creative list selection is crucial.

2. **Telephone is incremental to other media.** In the programs undertaken for the association, direct mail "creams the list"—brings in the eager registrants at the lowest possible expense. Telephone then reaches out to the "potential buyers," the prospects who need to be reminded, to ask questions, to have their enthusiasm reinforced through personal sales contact.

3. **Telephone is particularly suited to marketing products and services with long customer buying lives.** This pertains to "continuity sales" but also to marketing products that are not on a specifically timed receipt schedule but rather where a strong, continuing relationship between customer and supplier is actively sought and frequently achieved.

4. **Telephone can produce higher response levels within a limited list.** When a million-piece mailing is "dropped," the response of each individual is less important than the cumulative response. However, as list segments and mailings become more selective, each prospect takes on greater significance to the success of the effort—and additional attempts at converting a prospect into a customer become more practical.

In the association's case, many of their seminars appeal to a fairly exclusive group of specialists. The focused material provided in the program is a plus for those who attend, but at the same time it limits the target market significantly—especially when you remember that the best prospects are those within a given specialty that are already on the association's house list. By calling these very select individuals, the number of registrations is increased dramatically. And the cost of soliciting registrations in this way can be built into the pricing structure for these business programs, which are sold more on the basis of their potential value than on their present cost.

5. Telephone tape message presentations utilizing "peer group" personalities can significantly improve call results in the hands of a trained communicator. More contacts with the targeted decision makers mean more sales. A professionally constructed tape message can provide the extra leverage needed to open the door and reach the specific executive at his or her desk—with his or her secretary's help! The tape message structures the call, cuts communicator training time, and allows any intelligent personality to call business executives, "smiling as they dial."

The name of the personality, the content, the length, and the overall integration of the tape within a "live" communicator's script can prove significant in the success of business-to-business call programs. Shown in Figure 6-2 is a sample of the two-sided call-record form used to track the results of the "Top 40" program calls. A label with the name, address, and telephone number of the prospect would be attached to this form in the upper left-hand box on page 123.

Figure 6-3 is one version of the script used to introduce the "Top 40" program to executive prospects—in this case, those in the financial area.

Case History: Marginal Magic

All marketers know that an established customer is a very valuable commodity. When a business has gone to the trouble and expense of introducing its company and products, establishing credit terms, and developing an ongoing business relationship, allowing that contact to be wasted because it can't be serviced profitably is very unfortunate. Yet that is precisely the problem that more and more businesses are facing. As the costs of sales visits escalate, the definition of a "marginal account"—one that produces order volumes that barely meet (or fail to meet) the costs of securing those orders—becomes more and more stringent.

How is the book publisher to continue sending a sales representative to each of the thousands of small bookstores scattered in towns and cities throughout the country? What of the calls made by the sales staff of an auto tire company to local dealerships? Or the office supply company trying to service the thousands of small and medium-sized offices that need the products they sell but not in large quantities? Or the agricultural product manufacturer that can no longer cost justify sales visits to farmers with less than 100 acres of any one crop?

CCI **AMERICAN MANAGEMENT Associations**

ZONE

CODE

NAME/ADDRESS CHANGE:

MEETING ATTENDED: # ________ DATES: ________

TITLE: ________

COMMENTS: ________

SPECIFIC AREAS OF INTEREST:

CALL BACK DATA:

FOR REGISTRATION ☐

AFTER LIT RECEIVED ☐

FUTURE CALL BACK ☐

COMMENTS:

NI ☐ SBM ☐ X ☐

SPECIAL ATTENTION AMA ☐

COMMENTS:

COMM ________ DATE ____ / ____

Date	Time	Op	Response Code				CB Time
			NA	DA	X	RCB	
			NA	DA	X	RCB	
			NA	DA	X	RCB	
			NA	DA	X	RCB	
			NA	DA	X	RCB	

DIALING COMMENTS/REASONS FOR CALL BACKS: Heard Tape ☐

CCI CAMPAIGN COMMUNICATIONS INSTITUTE OF AMERICA, INC.

Figure 6-2. Front of the "Top 40" call card record.

LITERATURE REQUEST ☐   COMM _____ DATE ____ / ____

Date Mailed TO AMA	Date Mailed BY AMA	REQUESTS LITERATURE ON:

LITERATURE CALL BACK   COMM _____ DATE ____ / ____

NI ☐   SPECIAL ATTENTION AMA ☐   FUTURE CALL BACK ☐

SBM ☐   COMMENTS: COMMENTS:

_____   _____

_____   _____

_____   _____

DATE	TIME	COMM	CALL RECORD			CALL BACK DATE TIME
			DA	NA	RCB	/
			DA	NA	RCB	/
			DA	NA	RCB	/
			DA	NA	RCB	/

REGISTRATION(S)   COMM. _____ DATE ____ /

NAME(S) _____   _____

TITLE(S) _____   _____

MEETING # _____ DATES _____

LOCATION _____

BILLING DATA _____

Figure 6-2 (Cont.). Back of the "Top 40" call card record.

AMERICAN MANAGEMENT ASSOCIATION

TOP 40

#1 - Cash Flow/Auditing - TARGET: VP Finance,
Treasurer, Controller, Auditing Manager, Director

INTRODUCTION TO PERSON ANSWERING THE PHONE:

Hello. May I speak to Mr(s)_____ (If name on card: or VP Finance, Treasurer,
Controller, Auditing Manager/Director) please? Would you connect me with him
please? (If not available, ask when you should call back--note card.)

INTRODUCTION TO PROSPECT:

Hello, Mr(s)_____. This is Mr(s)_____ calling for Mr.(name on tape) and
the _____ Associations. Mr(s)_____, Mr.(name on tape) has prepared a
specially taped message about the important career advancement courses and
seminars the _____ has planned for financial executives.

May I play Mr_____'s message now and ask for your questions and reaction after
you've heard it? It takes about 2 minutes.

IF PROSPECT WANTS TO KNOW WHAT TAPE IS ABOUT, SAY:

Mr(s)_____, Mr (name on tape) has a special message for financial executives
on problems facing business in this period of shortages that may be helpful to
you and your company. Mr (name on tape) tells it so much better than I.
May I play his message for you now?

AFTER TAPE:

Did you hear that all right, Mr(s)_____? Thank you for listening to Mr_____
Mr(s)_____, are you familiar with the various courses offered by the _____?

IF NO, GO TO APPROACH 2

IF YES, CONTINUE:

Good, perhaps you may know about -- or even have attended -- these sessions.
Please tell me if you have a special interest in any of these five courses
the A.M.A. is offering of particular interest to financial executives.

They are: 1. Corporate Cash Management
           2. New Developments in leasing
           3. The _____ Course for Staff Auditors
           4. Operational Auditing Applications, and
           5. The Job of the Corporate Controller

Tell me, Mr(s)_____, are you interested in one or more of these subject seminars?

IF NO: NOT INTERESTED -- GO TO QUESTION #1

IF YES: PROCEED TO REGISTRATION FORM

IF NO/MUST CHECK, ETC.) ASK:

When would it be most convenient for me to call back to expedite your registration --
it is a simple process by telephone.

Figure 6-3. Script for one "Top 40" campaign.

One alternative to a personal call to low-volume accounts by a company rep is a systematic direct-marketing program that offers existing marginal accounts the service they need without the high overhead of personal visits. This requires more than just supplying the customers with order forms and telling them to mail them in when they need something or even giving them a phone number to use when calling in their orders. So-called "marginal" customers don't consider themselves to be marginal. They are accustomed to having their needs serviced personally, and if they feel that their business is no longer important enough to merit a sales call, they may well take it elsewhere. In order to place an order, these customers need more than a method—they require the services traditionally performed by a live salesperson, namely:

- Providing product information
- Answering customer questions
- Periodically prodding the customer to place an order
- Familiarity with the customer's past ordering patterns
- The "human touch," which helps make doing business with your company pleasant and fosters the development of a continuing supplier relationship

Telemarketing makes it possible to provide all these functions without traveling away from a central office, thus slashing the expense of servicing marginal accounts.

One major corporation that tackled its marginal-account problem with a nationwide telemarketing effort was A. B. Dick, a leading manufacturer of duplicating and copying machines. The sale of supplies for these machines—stencils, inks, etching solutions, and, of course, paper—is handled through a network of company salespeople operating out of local branch offices, supplemented by independent distributors and dealers. As of 1973, A. B. Dick had to a great extent retained the business of selling supplies to its office-machinery customers, and this made up a major portion of its total corporate sales picture—about 25 percent of the company's total sales revenue.

However, an in-depth analysis of the company's overall sales system revealed that 40 to 60 percent of the customers purchasing supplies through the branch offices were ordering less than $200 annually, broken up into an average of four separate orders per year. With the cost of a sales rep's visit averaging $66 at the time, the $50-per-order average sale was costing the company money. Something had to be done.

The size of this marginal customer market, both in terms of percentage of total accounts and numbers of individual customers—over 100,000 nationwide, consisting primarily of small businesses, organizations, institutions, churches, and schools—was too great to surrender without a fight. This was especially true given the fact that A. B. Dick's supplies customers are likely to be A. B. Dick's equipment customers when their present machines wear out or their needs increase. Therefore, each customer is potentially far more valuable than the current supply-sales figures would indicate.

Marketing Objectives   A. B. Dick management began planning a direct-marketing effort[1] that would eliminate the need for a sales rep's visit to low-volume accounts. However, there were serious stumbling blocks to consider. These customers were used to the attention of a personal sales call. Would they feel slighted if this service was discontinued? And would they be able to order the right supplies from over 900 choices without a salesperson on hand to guide them? These were delicate questions, particularly in a market where there are many competing firms offering supplies that can be used interchangeably.

To maintain as nearly as possible the service and attention levels expected by their customers, management planned a new direct-marketing program to include three key elements:

- A telephone sales service that would call the customer on a regularly scheduled basis to solicit supply orders and answer any questions. The program would be launched with a call to each marginal customer to introduce the service and try to take an immediate order over the phone.

- To make the program more attractive to this market, periodic special mailings would be made to the list of marginal customers, offering items for mail or phone order in conjunction with special, limited-time incentive plans.

- If the program was to be continued on a longer-term basis, a complete supplies catalog would be needed. In the past, each category of supplies had been included in separate fliers and lists, and the sales rep would steer the customer to the items that were needed. With no sales rep present, however, a clearly organized, instructive catalog would be required to describe available supplies, provide prices, and explain delivery and payment arrangements. In order to be a practical sales tool it would be a fairly expensive production, and it would not be undertaken unless the preliminary telephone testing proved the effort would be worthwhile. In any case, the catalog would not be needed for the first round of phone calls, since the customers contacted were active A. B. Dick accounts and

[1] Utilizing Stone & Adler as their direct marketing agency. For more information, see *Profitable Direct Marketing*, by James Kobs, Crain Books, Chicago, 1979, Chapter 20.

knew what they needed, based on what they had ordered in the recent past.

To emphasize the idea that the marginal accounts were not going to be treated as "second-class citizens" under the new marketing strategy, the plans were dubbed the "Preferred Customer Program." The program was conceived as a continuing effort that would be run in-house by the regional A. B. Dick sales offices. In order to maximize the chances for success, a professional telemarketing agency was enlisted to design the presentation, test and measure its effectiveness using its own trained telephone communicators, and act as planning consultants in the establishment of an in-house telemarketing operation.[2]

List Segmentation   A. B. Dick management authorized an initial test of approximately 1,200 calls to marginal customers in the Boston area. There was no problem obtaining the appropriate list of names to call, since A. B. Dick's centralized computer facilities readily produced a printout of customers whose annual supply orders totaled less than $200, complete with a record of their most recent purchase.

Telemarketing Strategy   To capture the customers' attention and add a convincing personal tone to the calls, a taped message was incorporated into the telephone presentation. The spokesperson for this test would be the Boston branch manager. The tape script developed for him gave a personalized introduction to the new Preferred Customer service to potentially skeptical customers and reassured them that they were still important to A. B. Dick. He emphasized the increased convenience to the customer of ordering by mail or phone and made no reference to the reason why the person being called was selected as a Preferred Customer.

In addition to the communicator scripts and the taped message, substantial further preparation was needed to help communicators function as effective customer representatives. Long hours were spent, well in advance of the first test call, creating a quick-reference product guide listing the most frequently ordered supply items, complete with model numbers, sales quantities, and prices. A special Preferred Customer record form was developed, to maintain an up-to-date summary of the type and age of duplicating equipment (both A. B. Dick and that of competitive manufacturers) that the customer used, the volume of paper impressions made per month, and the name of the person who was currently in charge of ordering supplies.

---

[2] Campaign Communications Institute of America (CCI) was A. B. Dick's telemarketing agency.

Creative Strategy Once all the initial scripting and preparation was complete, an initial panel of 50 low-volume customers was randomly selected from the total list for an advance test. This pretesting was done to get the flavor of the responses, to be sure that the questions and answers that had been prepared in advance were indeed adequate to handle customer queries, and to uncover any unexpected bugs in the system.

An A. B. Dick representative who reviewed tapes of these 50 calls evaluated them as follows:

"The initial script was working very smoothly and only required a little fine-tuning. All A. B. Dick customers contacted were very cooperative and quite pleased with the A. B. Dick products. Most of them spent an average of 10 minutes on the phone with the communicator, listening to the branch manager's tape and answering questions. . . .

"One reason the script seemed to be working so well was that it had a customer-service approach, in terms of gathering information for A. B. Dick Company. There was no high-pressure selling, and this helped greatly."

In addition to suggesting a few minor word changes in the script (for instance, the name was changed from "Preferred Customer Service" to "Preferred Customer Program," since the original version made some listeners think the call was about servicing equipment), these 50 calls pointed out the need for some additional preparatory steps before beginning full-scale testing:

▪ An answer to questions about the shelf life of A. B. Dick supplies was added to the script.

▪ The price lists were reorganized by category, for example, mimeo, fluid, and so on, to speed communicator response to inquiries. A procedure was also established for handling questions about supplies that were not on the list of most frequently ordered items (details on all 900 individual supply items were just too numerous to be kept ready for instant reference). The communicator would tell the customer that the information was not handy but that the customer would be called back in a few minutes with a response. This allowed the communicator to take the time to check more detailed, complete price lists without inconveniencing the customer with prolonged waiting on the line. Since this program was instituted, many companies have handled similar problems of information access by installing computer terminals for each communicator, entering the appropriate product information in the memory banks and allowing communicators to instantly punch up the product specifications they need on their own CRT video screens.

▪ A list of A. B. Dick dealers was prepared, so that, if an account was currently buying from a specific supplier and it turned out to be an independent A. B. Dick dealer, the communicator could finish gathering the information for company records but not try to solicit an order, to avoid conflict with established dealer relationships.

With these minor changes accomplished, the calls were made to the full 1,200-name testing universe in the Boston area. The following is a transcript of an actual call in this program:

COMMUNICATOR (to a person answering the phone): Hello, this is Michael Graham. I'm calling for A. B. Dick Company. May I speak to the person who buys supplies for your duplicating equipment? (Notes name on record card.) That's Mrs. Smith? Thank you.
(To prospect): Hello, Mrs. Smith. I'm calling for A. B. Dick Company. Are you responsible for the purchase of supplies for your duplicating equipment?

MRS. SMITH: Yes, that's right.

COMMUNICATOR: Well, Mrs. Smith, I'm calling with our first announcement of the A. B. Dick Preferred Customer Program. Mr. Walter Whalen, our Boston branch manager, has made a special taped message describing this new service. I'd like to play that for you now—it's a little less than two minutes long—and then get your reactions after you've heard it.

MRS. SMITH: Okay.

COMMUNICATOR: Thank you very much. It'll be coming right on the line.

HELLO, THIS IS WALTER WHALEN. I'M USING THIS SPECIALLY TAPED MESSAGE APPROACH AS THE BEST POSSIBLE WAY TO SPEAK TO YOU DIRECTLY, TO TELL YOU ABOUT A NEW A. B. DICK CUSTOMER SERVICE THAT WE STARTED WITH YOU IN MIND. NOW THE REASON I FEEL IT'S IMPORTANT TO YOU IS THAT OUR NEW SERVICE WILL BE MAKING ORDERING SUPPLIES MORE SIMPLE. IT WILL ASSIST YOU IN GETTING THE BEST POSSIBLE COPIES AT THE LOWEST COST AND LET US BE OF SERVICE TO YOU IN ANY WAY WE CAN. A. B. DICK HAS ORGANIZED A PREFERRED CUSTOMER PROGRAM THAT WE FEEL IS GOING TO MAKE REORDERING AN AWFUL LOT MORE CONVENIENT FOR YOU. UNDER THIS PLAN YOU'LL BE ABLE TO ORDER SUPPLIES BY MAIL OR PHONE. WE'LL EVEN CALL YOU PERIODICALLY AS A REMINDER AND TAKE YOUR ORDER, IF THAT'S CONVENIENT.

NOW AT THE SAME TIME, A. B. DICK WILL BE CONSTANTLY SEEKING WAYS TO PROVIDE CUSTOMERS WITH THE BEST POSSIBLE SERVICE AND SUPPLIES. FOR EXAMPLE, RECENTLY OUR CENTRAL OFFICE SOLIDIFIED ARRANGEMENTS WITH A LARGE NUMBER OF PAPER MILLS. WE'RE BREATHING A LITTLE EASIER NOW, AND WE'VE BEEN ASSURED OF A

STEADY SUPPLY OF PAPER FOR OUR CUSTOMERS. IN A PERIOD OF CRIT-ICAL SHORTAGES, WE'VE GOT PAPER SUPPLIES, AND YOU CAN HAVE THEM.

IN SHORT, WE'D LIKE TO ANTICIPATE YOUR SUPPLY NEEDS AND IN-VITE YOU TO RELY ON US FOR A REMINDER. STENCILS, INKS, SPIRIT MASTERS, FLUID, OFFSET MASTERS, AND, OF COURSE, PAPER. LET US WORRY ABOUT THEM FOR YOU. WHEN WE CALL, WE'D LIKE TO RUN DOWN A LIST OF YOUR SUPPLIES TO ENSURE NOTHING GETS OVER-LOOKED, TELL YOU ABOUT ANY NEW PRODUCTS SO THAT YOU CAN TAKE ADVANTAGE OF THEM, JOT DOWN YOUR ORDER OVER THE PHONE, AND TAKE CARE OF EVERYTHING.

OUR CUSTOMER SERVICE REPRESENTATIVE WILL BE COMING BACK ON THE LINE NOW TO ANSWER ANY QUESTIONS THAT YOU MIGHT HAVE, AND SINCE THIS IS REALLY OUR FIRST CUSTOMER/SERVICE CALL, WE'LL TAKE AN ORDER FROM YOU IF YOU LIKE.

I KNOW THAT YOU'LL FIND OUR NEW A. B. DICK CUSTOMER SERVICE A CONVENIENCE, AND I HOPE THAT YOU'LL TAKE ADVANTAGE OF IT. THANK YOU FOR BEING AN A. B. DICK CUSTOMER.

COMMUNICATOR: Did you hear the tape all right, Mrs. Smith? Fine. Now may I just ask you a few questions to update our customer records?

MRS. SMITH: All right.

COMMUNICATOR: Do you presently have any A. B. Dick equipment?

MRS. SMITH: Yes.

COMMUNICATOR: O.K., and what kind of equipment would that be?

MRS. SMITH: The 460 mimeograph machine.

COMMUNICATOR: And you have one of those?

MRS. SMITH: One.

COMMUNICATOR: How long have you had this machine, Mrs. Smith?

MRS. SMITH: Oh, about three years now.

COMMUNICATOR: And can you tell me, please, approximately how many copies you make per month?

MRS. SMITH: I suppose it's around 1,000 copies, or a little over that.

COMMUNICATOR: I see. Do you have any other duplicating equipment, Mrs. Smith—not necessarily A. B. Dick?

MRS. SMITH: No, we don't.

COMMUNICATOR: All right. Now the purchase record I have before me runs through December 31. Can you tell me if you've purchased any A. B. Dick supplies or equipment since that time?

MRS. SMITH: No, I don't think so. I tried to order everything I would need at that time. But I do have another order for you when you get ready to take it.

COMMUNICATOR: O.K., fine.

MRS. SMITH: Are you ready now, or . . . ?

COMMUNICATOR: Sure.

MRS. SMITH: I need 10 reams of 8½-by-14 mimeotone paper in assorted colors, 10 reams of mimeotone in 8½ by 11. Let's see, I also need 2 bottles of mimeograph correction fluid 368 in blue. And 2 bottles of the mimeograph cement 268.

COMMUNICATOR: O.K., fine. Now let me check this with you: that's 2 bottles of mimeograph correction fluid 368 in blue, 2 bottles of mimeograph cement 268, 10 reams of mimeo paper 8¼ by 14 in assorted colors, and 10 reams of mimeotone 8¼ by 11—also assorted colors?

MRS. SMITH: As a matter of fact, if you could make those two of each color, that would help.

COMMUNICATOR: O.K. Let me check your address and make sure we don't have any problems with shipment. (Checks address.) O.K., fine, Mrs. Smith, thank you very much. Now since this is your first introduction to our new telephone service, we're anxious to make it work best for you. And our plan is to call you about once a month to give you information about special products and to see how we may best serve you. Generally, what's the best day and time to call?

MRS. SMITH: Ordinarily either Mondays or Thursdays are good.

COMMUNICATOR: Mondays or Thursdays.

MRS. SMITH: I'm only here in the morning.

COMMUNICATOR: Morning. O.K. In the meantime, Mrs. Smith, if you should have any needs or questions I'd like to suggest that you call our branch in Waltham. Do you have the number there?

MRS. SMITH: Yes, I do.

COMMUNICATOR: O.K., good. And ask for Mr. John Hutchinson; he'll be happy to serve you.

MRS. SMITH: O.K., thank you.

COMMUNICATOR: Thank you, Mrs. Smith.

Results The 1,200 calls in the Boston area were completed in about two weeks, and the results are shown in Table 6-2. Of all those called, only 5 percent were not willing to listen to Mr. Whalen's recorded message. And, as the figures in Table 6-2 show, more than 70 percent responded favorably, with a request for some specific action or for a future sales contact.

And it is in those future sales contacts that a major dividend materialized. These requests revealed that the Preferred Customer Program would serve as more than a method for handling marginal accounts—it

TABLE 6-2.   Boston Test

Result	Percentage of total
Immediate orders	10.1
Future calls requested	46.2
Asked for salesperson's visit	8.8
Required special handling	6.6
Not interested	28.3

was also an effective means for producing well-screened and qualified leads for personal sales calls. These leads quickly proved their value. The salespeople who followed up on that 8.8 percent of the phone respondents produced some $10,000 in equipment sales within three weeks of the completion of the calling program!

Further Testing   The results of the Boston test were very encouraging, but A. B. Dick management wanted to reconfirm the effectiveness of the presentation developed so far and test another significant variable before launching a nationwide "roll-out."

The Atlanta region was chosen for a follow-up test, using basically the same procedure as the Boston calls but with one notable alteration. The call universe was evenly split, with one half listening to a taped message from the Atlanta branch manager, and the other half listening to an identically worded message recorded by a professional announcer.

The results of this Atlanta test were nearly the same as the Boston test results, bolstering A. B. Dick's determination to roll-out the program across the country. As to the two halves of the test panel that heard differently recorded taped messages, their responses were virtually equal, which simplified the national plans considerably—a single prerecorded message could be taped and copies sent to each branch, instead of having 60 separate branch managers make individually recorded taped messages for local use.

Program Expansion   Initially A. B. Dick management chose to allow each local branch office to implement the phone program itself, rather than establish regional distribution centers or undertake building a single national phone center using long-distance WATS lines. However, they did want each of these satellite operations to be conducted according to the successful specifications they had worked out in their test programs. To train branch managers in the use of the phone, a comprehensive Telephone Direct-Response Program manual was prepared. This document covered all the steps needed to implement the program in detail, including:

- How to identify and segregate accounts that should be called
- How to recruit, train, and supervise telephone communicators
- An explanation of the type of telephone equipment needed to make the calls
- A step-by-step timetable for preparing and launching the calling operation

The manual spelled out the expected frequency of calls to customers (quarterly), the average number of completed outgoing calls to be expected per communicator per day, in addition to the number of incoming phone orders to be handled (about 35), and the expected revenues produced per communicator (as much as $200,000 each in annual supplies sales volume).

Along with the manual, each branch received a prerecorded message to be played in the calls and samples of the forms needed for record keeping. With this complete instructional package in hand, each branch could get its calling program off the ground with just a month of preparation.

Within a few months of the initial tests, the Preferred Customer Program was under way nationwide, and it took only a few months longer to demonstrate the success of the operation. Every local program was paying off handsomely, with substantial increases in supply sales the general rule, and at least one branch reporting that they had doubled their sales volume thanks to the phone program. And those important sales leads for equipment were produced just as they were in the test markets.

What About the Sales Force?   By now you are probably asking yourself a key question—how did A. B. Dick management secure the cooperation of its field sales force? After all, the phone program was replacing the individual salesperson in servicing a large number of accounts, and losing commissions on those accounts could easily lead to rebellion in the ranks.

The expensive answer is that the salespeople were paid full commission on the supply sales made over the phone or by mail to their established customers. That way, the new system offered the salespeople only benefits—more time to service their bigger-ticket customers and establish new accounts, a large number of strong leads to follow up for equipment sales, and their usual commission from smaller, marginal accounts.

Even when the sales force commissions were added to the cost of the direct-marketing operation itself, though, the increased sales volume for supplies still made the program profitable at the time.

Print Media Support   The original Preferred Customer Program plan called for mailings with special offers to increase customer interest in the program. Thanks to the enthusiastic response to the initial phone contact, these mailings were shelved indefinitely. However, the other major print aspect of the plan—a complete supply catalog—was still required for an ongoing program.

The catalog was produced with ordering convenience in mind, in an attractive format that would reinforce the impression that marginal customers would not be treated as "second-class citizens" in the Preferred Customer Program. It was done in 24 pages, full color throughout, and divided into color-coded product sections (offset, mimeograph, and so on) for easy reference. It featured those items that accounted for major sales volume—about 20 percent of the products offered accounted for some 85 percent of the total sales volume for supplies. The better the item sold, the more catalog space it was allocated.

The catalog included a series of helpful hints scattered throughout, aimed at improving customers' duplicating operation results. Not only did this feature encourage the customer to read the catalog and hold onto it; it also served some of the functions formerly provided by a salesperson—the tips provided chatty, helpful advice that, without being a directly sales-related message, promoted a positive attitude toward the Preferred Customer Program and the company as a whole.

The catalog design offered several special features that made it a simple tool for the customer to use and identified it clearly with the local branch office:

■ While the basic 24-page catalog remained the same for each branch, there was an overwrap letter stressing the benefits of the new Preferred Customer plan that carried the signature of the local branch manager and gave the local phone number and address.

■ A fold-out price list was also designed into the overwrap letter section. This let the customer refer to the price list without interruption, even while turning the pages of the basic catalog. This arrangement was beneficial for A. B. Dick as well—price changes could be introduced when necessary by reprinting just the overwrap, instead of the entire, fairly expensive four-color catalog.

- The catalog included a convenient full-page checklist of items not featured in the catalog that could be ordered by phone as well as a run-down of the most popular A. B. Dick equipment available.

With the initial mailing of 150,000 catalogs, the Preferred Customer Program offered a complete marketing package for low-volume accounts, providing sales information and ordering convenience without a salesperson's visit and continued profitable supplies sales to a large number of valued customers.

Summary The A. B. Dick marginal accounts experience illustrates the critical role that telemarketing plays in the growing movement toward substituting direct marketing for face-to-face selling. Due to drastic increases in the cost of serving prospective customers personally, businesses have cut down on human involvement in the marketing process by employing direct-response techniques, concentrating primarily on catalogs and direct-mail offerings.

The object of this approach to selling is clear—to cut the expense and increase the efficiency of the marketing effort. Because these worthwhile goals will not be achieved if personal service is eliminated, the human factor must be incorporated into the selling process, hence the "person-to-person" telephone contact. There are programs in which the human presence appears to have *been* dispensed with entirely. On closer examination, though, we find human interaction incorporated into even seemingly impersonal computerized marketing vehicles.

Take catalog marketing as an example. The catalog shopper selects merchandise from the printed page, without personal assistance from a salesperson. However, there's a distinctly human side to the transaction. Catalogs increasingly have a "personality" all their own. Through selective merchandise fitting special life-styles, distinctive writing, graphic approaches, and seasonal offerings, successful catalogs involve the reader in a personal relationship with the nonstore "store." L. L. Bean does this one way, Neiman Marcus quite another; Edmund Scientific reaches out for science buffs—but in all cases, the arrival of the catalog can be an event in the household, and the contents convey a special, personalized message to the consumer. And, of course, the catalog shopper increasingly has the option of phoning in his or her order and being "waited on" by the long-distance "800" phone service—thereby establishing one-to-one contact when making the actual transaction.

In the effort to inject the crucially important "human touch" in direct-response marketing, computerized personalization of letters, clever copywriting, and ingenious designs are standard strategies used to create the illusion of personal communication. Telemarketing takes the process beyond illusion, though, providing *actual* one-to-one contact on a cost-efficient basis.

In the A. B. Dick program, the personal sales force visit was replaced in a business-to-business marketing situation with substantial positive bottom-line impact. Small companies and organizations demonstrated their willingness to order from company representatives over the telephone, as long as they received the level of advice and attention needed to make purchasing simple. In fact, the level of attention these marginal customers received actually improved with the implementation of the Preferred Customer plan, since the frequency of "sales calls" by phone was substantially greater than that offered by hard-pressed salespeople.

A. B. Dick was one of the first companies to apply telemarketing expertise to their marginal accounts problem. Many other corporations, including some of the largest in the nation,[3] have followed suit in recent years, providing both incoming order taking and outgoing account service functions through in-house operations and through telephone service bureaus. With continuing pressure to trim sales overheads in companies relying on field sales forces, we can expect the servicing of marginal accounts through appropriate print-and-telemarketing combinations to become standard practice throughout the business world.

Implications for the Marketer The A. B. Dick case history is most significant in its demonstration of the efficient handling of marginal accounts; it is also worth considering the lessons it affords regarding the opportunity to gain multiple benefits from a single telephone contact as part of a direct marketing campaign.

Once personal communication with customers or prospective customers has been established, they will readily discuss whatever they need or want from the caller's company, given half a chance. In the case of A. B. Dick, calls involving sales of supplies produced solid leads for major equipment sales. The following information also surfaces frequently in the course of a phone campaign whose primary aim is direct sales, lead generation, or other sales-related activity:

- **Feedback on salespeople's activities.** If the sales force has not

---

[3] IBM, Xerox, 3M, American Express, Sears Roebuck, ATT, et al.

been servicing their accounts frequently or well enough, this will quickly be revealed through telephone contact.

■ **Upgrading and verification of accuracy of customer files.** In the process of completing a call, the communicator will discover whether the person with buying authority has changed, if the nature of the business has changed, or if the business has moved or closed down altogether.

■ **Commentary on product quality, price, design, and so on.** A telephone campaign will often produce market research information as an added benefit. When a farmer in Idaho was called by a major manufacturer of herbicides to establish a lead for a sales call, for example (see Chapter 7), he made the suggestion that all the company's granular products should be manufactured in the same-sized granule, so that the equipment used to spread the chemicals would not require frequent recalibration.

This type of user input, passed along by the telephone communicator to the product development people in-house, can lead to worthwhile improvements and new product concepts.[4] And this market research function combines naturally with the main thrust of the phone program.

---

[4] This emphasizes the synergism of direct mail and phone—each medium supporting the other. Often mail "opens the door." Here, the telephone call came first—the catalog followed later.

chapter seven /

Maximizing Sales Force Productivity

In most businesses that market through their own sales forces, it is not the fault of the salespeople themselves that the bottom line has been steadily decreasing. They are probably working just the same way they always have, or perhaps even a bit harder. But the profitability of sales operations has been hit hard by several factors: the increased expense of keeping a salesperson on the road, the success of alternative marketing methods, and the buying resistance of business and consumer alike when economic pressures dictate the need to cut expenditures.

The rise in the cost of an average sales force visit to $200 and beyond necessitates adoption of alternative forms of marketing strategy. Two prime directions are:

 ▪ **Replacing salespeople with direct-marketing media in low-volume accounts.** We have already explored this strategy with regard to the A. B. Dick Preferred Customer Program for marginal accounts.

 ▪ **Managing the sales force for maximum efficiency.** This entails making each personal sales visit count by employing systems that screen and qualify leads for the salespeople in advance. Telemarketing has proven itself particularly well suited to finding prospects with the need and the means to buy and bringing the salesperson together with them.

In the following two case histories, we will examine some programs that have undertaken to generate high-quality leads for sales force follow-up but have also gone on to give the sales force valuable background information prior to face-to-face meetings with prospects; this allows salespeople to improve their performance on the sales call by tailoring their offer to the prospect's individual needs.

The unresolved problem in the development of any lead-prospecting program is rarely the telephone call—that contact can be scripted and delivered to provide as screened and qualified a prospect as sales managers dictate. No matter how probing the question, it can be asked—and will usually be answered. Economics may determine the calling distance, the length of the call, and the number of positive responses or appointments achieved—but if the script is professionally structured, there *will be* leads and appointments demanding follow-up.

A manager can arrange for the horse to be "led to water," but that's where the problem begins with the telephone leads provided for an American sales force! Management's attempt to provide specific time periods for sales campaigns, planned tangible incentives, measured and controlled flow of leads per day, "policing" systems to monitor flow and results—all must be established in advance as integral parts of the total sales campaign, or the "medicine will work" but the patient will surely die!

Case History: Is There a Ford in Your Future?

It is interesting that one of the most important uses of telemarketing today—producing screened, qualified leads for salespeople—was also the object of the very *first* major telemarketing campaign conducted in the modern mode, using controlled, production-line techniques. And it is particularly appropriate that the birth of mass-production telemarketing skills occurred in a campaign conducted for the company that brought the production-line concept to industry as a whole—the Ford Motor Company. Henry Ford began cranking out his Model T using an assembly line in 1913. Forty-seven years later, as president of Ford Motor Company, Lee Iacocca brought the founder's production principles to the telephone in order to canvas the nation for potential buyers of Ford automobiles.

Marketing Objectives Ford engaged in every form of advertising, of course, just as its competitors did. Ford was looking for something special, however, a tool that would let them concentrate their selling efforts on those people who were actively considering a new car purchase. Once this market was identified, they could be persuaded through mailings and personal attention to visit their local Ford dealership and, hopefully, to buy a new or used car there.

Telemarketing Strategy The mechanics of putting together a telephone program that could contact a vast number of American households, glean the required information, and pass it on quickly and efficiently was awesome. However, working with the J. Walter Thompson advertising agency and Communicator Network, Inc. (CNI[1]), Ford initiated a test program to develop a workable system. The testing began with three cities, then expanded to eight, and led finally to a nationwide campaign that eventually contacted 20 *million* automobile households.

The calls for the Ford campaign were all made by home workers. They were interviewed and hired by management personnel, given a script designed for simplicity, and set to work on their own phones and selected phonebook pages. Payment was made to them on a per-call basis.

To ensure tight control of the calling process, a hierarchical structure was developed to manage the workers and monitor their results. A supervisor was the first to be screened and hired. One key criterion for employment: she would have to recruit, hire, train, and supervise 10 to 12 communicators in her neighborhood. The closer to her home the better—neighbors and friends were first on line! Training of the supervisors was usually in groups—and was intensive. Standards for calls were set, systems of control established, and details of management organized. Each home communicator was seen, and work flow was managed daily. Each communicator called her supervisor every evening after calls were completed at 9 P.M. The supervisor compiled the results and called a city or area manager that night. The following morning, each manager called the main office with the day's tabulations.

Once the program was under way nationwide, a tremendous labor force was required. At the peak of the calling operation, there were 15,000 people working on the phones for Ford. This involved 2,000 supervisors and between 20 and 22 area managers.

One prime source of communicators was handicapped people. Shut-ins, people in wheelchairs, the legally blind, and others with disabilities that restricted their access to 9-to-5 jobs could work on the phone from their homes very successfully.

The U.S. Department of Vocational Rehabilitation was recruited to assist in the hiring process. The department sent notices to their offices

---

[1] The author was president of CNI at the time and directed the 2-year prospecting campaign.

across the country asking for applications, and those who responded were interviewed by management personnel from CNI. At one point, the Ford telephone program was the largest single private employer of handicapped people in the nation, with more than 5,000 on the payroll.

The standards used to evaluate communicator performance were determined during the early phases of the program. Such evaluations were accomplished by formulas developed during the pretest period. One person could be expected to dial the phone 40 times an hour and reach 27 households. The names to be called were drawn from the local telephone directory. Of the 27 reached, the communicator would actually talk to the decision maker regarding automobile purchases 15 to 17 times.

The responses to the survey also fell into a predictable pattern—3 percent would reply that they were planning to buy a car in the next 3 months, 7 percent in 6 months, and 11 percent in 12 months. With these response standards established, it was easy to spot home workers who were not following the system or who were trying to fudge, falsify, or fabricate calls. The daily reporting system allowed management to weed out these communicators quickly—remedial action was routinely taken within three days.

The system also promptly handled "hot leads"—those planning to buy a new or used car in the next three months. Each lead was passed on to dealers and their sales force within 24 hours after the call was made. This fast action allowed dealers to call prospects personally and invite them in for a test drive immediately. This maintained the momentum created by the initial telephone contact and, not unimportantly, conveyed a sense of urgency to the sales force itself.

Creative Strategy   Given the home-worker nature of the communicator network, the script had to be simple enough to be followed by callers without much training and with no on-the-scene guidance. These novice communicators also had to be prompted to get through the calls quickly in order to meet the production standards of the program.

Through careful monitoring of call flow during the testing process, the following script was found to fulfill these requirements while gathering all the needed information and maintaining good relations with the people who were called:

Hello, Mr. (Mrs.) _____ , this is _____ calling for the sales department of the Ford Motor Company to find out about the car-buying plans for the people in the (your city) area.

1. Are you or is anybody else in your household planning to buy a car within the next two years?
(IF NO, TERMINATE THE INTERVIEW WITH: Thank you.)
2. When do you think you'll buy? Within three months, six months, one year, or when?
3. Will you buy it new or used?
4. Will it be regular size or compact?
5. Do you or does anyone else in your household own a car?
(IF NO, SKIP TO QUESTION 8.)
6. Please tell me the make and year of each car you own.
7. (FOR EACH CAR OWNED ASK: Did you buy it new or used?)
8. (QUESTION 8 ASKED ONLY IN CITIES WITH POSTAL ZONES:) Could you tell me what your postal zone is? (IF ASKED WHY YOU NEED THEIR POSTAL ZONE, SAY:) So that I will be able to determine which Ford Motor Company dealer is closest to you. We can then send your name to him so that you can be contacted with information on his cars.
TERMINATE THE CONVERSATION WITH: Thank you very much for your help.

Each person contacted who expressed interest in buying a new car was handled according to the time frame they indicated for their shopping plans (see Figure 7-1).

The names, addresses, and phone numbers of those who expected to buy a new car within three months were passed by the communicator directly to the dealership in the prospect's neighborhood on the day the call was completed. The salespeople not only knew about the prospect's buying plans; they also had information about the car currently owned and the type of car the prospect planned to purchase in the future. This made it easier to assess the sales approach that would be most appropriate in each case.

The names of everyone who planned to purchase within six months were forwarded to Ford's main office. These prospects received a series of mailings, followed by a direct contact by a sales rep.

The one-year planners were not ignored either, with special brochures and letters designed to keep Ford uppermost in their minds when car-buying plans were considered.

Dealer enthusiasm for the program was evident in the strong follow-up record by the salespeople. Ford management had learned through experi-

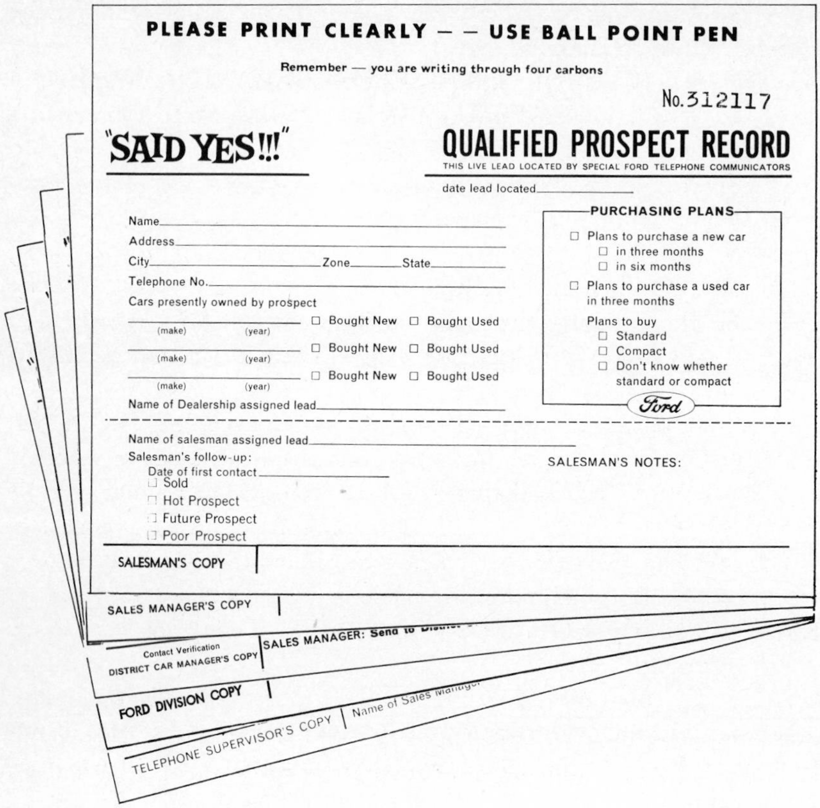

PLEASE PRINT CLEARLY — — USE BALL POINT PEN

Remember — you are writing through four carbons

No. 312117

"SAID YES!!!"

QUALIFIED PROSPECT RECORD

THIS LIVE LEAD LOCATED BY SPECIAL FORD TELEPHONE COMMUNICATORS

date lead located ________

Name ________

Address ________

City ________ Zone ________ State ________

Telephone No. ________

Cars presently owned by prospect

________ (make) (year) ☐ Bought New ☐ Bought Used

________ (make) (year) ☐ Bought New ☐ Bought Used

________ (make) (year) ☐ Bought New ☐ Bought Used

Name of Dealership assigned lead ________

PURCHASING PLANS

☐ Plans to purchase a new car
☐ in three months
☐ in six months

☐ Plans to purchase a used car in three months

Plans to buy
☐ Standard
☐ Compact
☐ Don't know whether standard or compact

Ford

Name of salesman assigned lead ________

Salesman's follow-up:

Date of first contact ________

☐ Sold
☐ Hot Prospect
☐ Future Prospect
☐ Poor Prospect

SALESMAN'S NOTES:

SALESMAN'S COPY

SALES MANAGER'S COPY

Contact Verification

DISTRICT CAR MANAGER'S COPY | SALES MANAGER: Send to

FORD DIVISION COPY

TELEPHONE SUPERVISOR'S COPY | Name of Sales Manager

Figure 7-1. The "lead" form used in the Ford campaign.

ence that salespeople usually followed up about 20 to 30 percent of their leads. For this telephone program, though, the figure jumped to 80 percent. Further testimony to this positive reaction from the people who actually do the selling is found in an opinion survey of participating dealers conducted after the first program was run. Fully 75 percent of the dealers judged the program "excellent," with a typical comment calling it "the best program the division has ever run."

Results After two years—and some 20 million calls—this longest running sales campaign was brought to a sudden halt. Ford's marketing planners decided it was time to change "image"—to shift from the family-oriented marketing program being conducted through phone and other media to a youthful image, centering around Ford-sponsored cars that had won races and similar "macho" themes. Since it was felt that phone did not fit this new concept, the telephone lead-generation campaign, which was Ford's most effective program to motivate dealers and the sales force, was dropped.

The tally of results produced by these 20 million calls reveals a remarkable record, both for lead production and eventual conversion. The communicators sent an average of two leads every day to each of 23,000 Ford salespeople throughout the program. Out of a total of 340,000 leads produced, 187,000 were valid prospects in the market for a car within a six-month period.

The sales force began turning those leads into complete sales quickly—on the first day that results were measurable, 444 cars were sold. Nine days later, car sales attributable to the phone program had reached 7,773.

The marketing cost per car sold came to $65, an incremental cost well below the level of other promotional programs run by Ford.

And in an industry where competition between manufacturers is lively and brand loyalty is a critical factor in maintaining a strong market share, it is worth noting that only 40 percent of the "hot" leads obtained during the telephone program were people who already owned Fords—60 percent were owners of competitive makers' cars.

Twenty Years Later The automobile sales picture in the 1980 to 1982 period could charitably be called dismal. In their efforts to drum up some traffic for dealer showrooms, several manufacturers experimented with factory rebate offers, providing limited-time savings off car sticker prices. As the rebate wars heated up, with competitive offers from several major manufacturers running simultaneously, Chrysler (now under a driving force—Lee Iacocca) decided to try an additional "push" to bring prospects into the dealerships. In conjunction with their offer of a 6 percent rebate, they went to the phones.

In this test program, calls were made (by CCI) in two cities, Boston and Philadelphia, to a list of prospects who had purchased a car from Chrysler in the past.

The goal here was similar to the Ford program—to put salespeople in touch with likely prospects and bring them into the showrooms for a test drive. Using trained communicators in centralized phone workshops, rather than the scattered home-caller network of the past, this campaign's calls did not follow a simple format. The communicators in this program were giving more information than they were getting.

Once the decision maker was on the line, the first item on the agenda was the key screening question: "Are you planning to buy a car in the next

3, 6, or 12 months?" If the answer was "no," the respondent was not a prospect and the communicator politely but quickly terminated the call.

A "yes" meant that the person on the phone was a valid prospect. These people were told about the rebate offer and the cutoff date for it (about a month after the call date). Prospects were then asked whether they would be interested in taking a test drive during this special-offer period. Those who said "yes" were given the name of their local dealer, the hours the dealership was open, and the name of a specific salesperson to ask for. The calls ended with a cheerful wish for a happy holiday season (the test took place in December).

In a 10-day calling period, over 20,000 people were reached, of whom over 1,300 indicated definite interest in taking a test drive; a slightly larger number said they might be interested. The follow-up results were difficult to isolate and compile, but initial feedback was promising. A month after calls were completed, a survey of a sampling of participating dealers indicated that 80 percent were actively following up on the leads produced by the phone program. Of those expressing an opinion of the campaign, nearly 85 percent said it was a worthwhile effort, and significantly, a majority of those dealers with a definite opinion said they would be willing to pay for such a program themselves, if need be.

The practical efforts of the program are clear. Through the telephone contact, a substantial group of valid prospects were pinpointed and made aware of a special promotional offer on a one-to-one basis, ensuring the manufacturer that the message got across and was delivered with the impact of personal communication. Unlike most forms of advertising, the telephone message could include detailed information about the most convenient dealership available to the prospect, its business hours, and even a name to ask for upon arrival.

In addition to delivering its distinctive advertising message, the call served a further function, since the names of the presold prospects were then passed on to individual local dealers for further targeted, personalized sales attention. And as noted earlier—and critically important—the leads were valid: screened, qualified, and often highly motivated! When's the last time (if ever!) you can remember being called by an auto sales rep? Have you ever been offered a personal test drive, a salesperson saying, "I'll be right over, demonstrate it, and let you drive it yourself"? It won't and doesn't happen, because dealers and salespeople depend on TV and print media to drive traffic into the showroom. The competitive edge usually means getting to the "walk-in" prospect first, not leaving the showroom floor to reach out for an already qualified phone prospect!

In the 60s it seemed that the auto sales rep was at the low end of sales force rating levels; he or she could only be motivated for the short term, with new incentives, "spiffs," and premiums almost weekly! It's even more true in the 80s—only now such sales-to-cost and sales-to-productivity ratios characterize most corporations that sell "eyeball-to-eyeball." The need to motivate, control, and "police" telephone lead-generation programs still constitutes a critical managerial problem in search of a solution.

Case History: Leading the Horse to Water

In the Ford program, the solution to sales force inadequacy was to bring potential buyers to the dealer's doorstep. In business-to-business telemarketing, though, the object is usually not to bring the ultimate consumer to your salesperson but to arrange your salesperson's costly travel plans so that he or she goes to the right prospect at the right time with the most persuasive possible offer for that individual's requirements.

One of America's largest manufacturers of herbicides and other chemical products has used telemarketing extensively in its efforts to get the most from its sales agents calling on farmers. By examining in some depth a program conducted on their behalf, we will see three key elements in a lead-generation campaign put to use in a particularly demanding situation.

Marketing Objectives   In several ways, the farm market presents challenges even more substantial than those faced when contacting busy executives. Farmers are likely to be harder for sales reps to locate and spend time with than executives, who are fairly desk-bound with secretaries waiting to route information to and from them. Telemarketing must take some of the cost and time burden off the agricultural decision maker by organizing contact with the "right" farmer and, when this contact is made, by paving the way for a structured personal sales visit only if the individual is a qualified prospect.

Furthermore, farmers are owner-operators, and their buying decisions usually involve an important expenditure of personal capital, so you can expect to find a very demanding customer. Telephone's role in tackling this challenge is preselling the product before the salesperson's visit. A well-written, well-presented telephone sales message can convey a number of appealing product features in a brief conversation. By including a taped message in the call presentation, you can have a persuasive company spokesperson speak directly to your prospect, providing credible, memorable background information prior to your salesperson's face-to-face visit.

Another telemarketing strength that had special importance in a sales campaign to the farm market is the ability to probe the prospect's business operations and isolate the specific areas in which your product can be of use. If you were selling vacuum cleaners, for example, the process of pinpointing prospect needs would be less of a problem, since you can safely assume that all houses need to be cleaned and can then concentrate on presenting the merits of your product as convincingly as possible.

In selling herbicides to farmers, though, you have to find out whether they are having problems with quack grass or Johnson grass or any of a dozen other very specific, bothersome weeds, each of which requires a different approach to chemical treatment. Because telemarketing can identify specific areas where the farmer needs help and convey this information to the salesperson in advance, the in-person sales call can get right to the point, and the salesperson can be prepared with the best available suggestions and products for the farmer's specific situation.

One of the telemarketing campaigns undertaken to reach this market was called the "Large Farmer Lead-Generation Program." Its goals fall under three basic headings:

Service—to offer information about the company's new products to all those called

Survey—to take a sales territory and identify those farmers whose herbicide needs would be large enough to justify the expense of a personal sales call

Sales—not to take an order from the prospect directly over the phone but to sell a personal sales visit

When all these goals were met, the telephone program would provide each company sales rep with complete, detailed dossiers on the qualified large farm prospects within his or her territory. This information would extend beyond simple yes-or-no judgments about whether to call on a specific farm. The in-depth profiles would enable salespeople to establish priorities in who they saw when and prepare them to meet the prospect's expressed needs when they did meet.

List Selection   As in all telephone programs, testing the Large Farmer Lead-Generation Program involved evaluating both the list of names to be called and the presentation designed for the communicators to follow. For the initial testing phase of the program, six counties located in Wisconsin, Illinois, Iowa, and Indiana were chosen. The selection was based on the relatively high degree of sales coverage in these regions. A crucial factor in the successs of any lead-generation program is the speed and efficiency of the follow-up on the leads produced. For the six test counties, the company felt that the quality and quantity of the sales force would ensure that prospects would be contacted before "hot" leads had a chance to cool.

A list of 1,111 farmers in these counties was delivered to a professional telemarketing agency. Some of these names came with phone numbers included, others without. The first step in the test was checking the telephone numbers for *all* 1,111 names on the list. Of the total, accurate phone numbers were available for 958. It is worth noting that nearly 20 percent of the numbers provided with the original list proved to be incorrect when checked, an interesting statistic when considering the problem of list "aging" and mobility even among "larger" farmers. Addresses and phone numbers change rapidly whatever list source you use, and it is always important to at least spot-check the information you receive, whether dealing with mail or telephone, before contacting the list of names.

Creative Strategy   The creative staff of the telemarketing agency developed a call format that would enable communicators calling from New York City to speak knowledgeably with farmers thousands of miles away about their agricultural problems. Although there was not time to enroll the communicators in a 4-H program to acquire a farming background, happily there was no need. The survey segment of the script they followed spelled out the weeds and herbicides they were to inquire about, and a special call-record form designed for the program (see Figure 7-2) made it quick and simple for them to record the information they gathered.

To begin the call, the communicator asked to speak with the person responsible for making herbicide usage decisions on the farm, indicating that he or she was calling for the chemical company and its technical manager. The company's name is familiar enough in the agricultural community to ensure instant recognition and promote agreement to answer the survey questions (see Figure 7-3).

Once the farmer had agreed to respond to some questions, the first step was to determine whether this "large" farmer had property large enough to merit further attention. The respondents were asked how many acres of corn they planted and how many acres of soybeans (the herbicides being promoted in this sales campaign were formulated to deal with weeds endangering these two crops). Based on prior company experience, it had been determined that with regard to the costs of following up on a lead (1)

Monsanto	MONSANTO AGRICULTURAL PRODUCTS COMPANY ZONE _____
	LEAD GENERATION PROGRAM CODE _____

CROP	# ACRES
CORN	
SOYBEANS	
TOTAL	

(If less than 400 Acres of one crop or less than 600 acres of both:) COMMENTS/SEND PRODUCT INFO:
_____
_____
_____

(TERMINATE:) ☐

	HERBICIDE NOW IN USE	# YRS.	SATISFIED: VERY	YES	NO	DK	WILL USE AGAIN: YES	NO	DK
On CORN ☐	_____								
On SOYBEANS ☐	_____								

TESTS HERBICIDES	YES	NO	DK
HAS USED LASSO			
HAS QUACKGRASS,JOHNSON-GRASS, CAN. THISTLE			
FAMILIAR W/ROUNDUP			
HAS USED ROUNDUP			
IS SATISFIED W/ROUNDUP			

REPRESENTATIVE INFORMATION	YES	NO
Prospect Already Knows Rep		
Prospect Feels Rep Is Helpful		
REPRESENTATIVE MAY CONTACT		
(If No, Why Not?)		

ORDER ☐   LIT ☐   NI ☐   SP ☐   SBM ☐   X ☐   COMM._____

COMMENTS: _____
_____   DATE: ___/___

Date	Time	Comm	Response Code				CB Time	DIALING COMMENTS/REASONS
			NA	DA	X	RCB		FOR CALL BACKS: Heard Tape I ☐
			NA	DA	X	RCB		Heard TapeII ☐
			NA	DA	X	RCB		
			NA	DA	X	RCB		
			NA	DA	X	RCB		

CCI CAMPAIGN COMMUNICATIONS INSTITUTE OF AMERICA, INC.

Figure 7-2.   Communicator's call-record card from Monsanto campaign.

FOLLOW-UP RECORD

MADE TELEPHONE CALL FOR APPOINTMENT: ___/___

Result: Appointment Made ☐ For ___/___

          Appointment Not Made ☐

Reason: _____

_____

MET WITH FARMER: ☐ On (Date) ___/___

Result: _____

_____

_____

       ACTION REQUIRED ☐   NO ACTION REQUIRED ☐

COMMENTS: _____

_____

RESULT OF SECOND CONTACT: Meeting Date ___/___

Result: _____

_____

_____

FINAL DISPOSITION: _____

_____

_____

_____

_____

Figure 7-2. Communicator's call-record card from Monsanto campaign. (Cont.)

CAMPAIGN COMMUNICATIONS INSTITUTE
OF AMERICA, INC.

MONSANTO AGRICULTURAL PRODUCTS CO.
LARGE FARMER PROGRAM

LEAD GENERATION/QUALIFICATION PROGRAM

(REVISED)

INTRO TO PERSON ANSWERING PHONE	1
INTRO TO PERSON ANSWERING PHONE	2
INTRO TO FARMER	3
INTRO TO FARMER	4
SCREEN TERMINATION	5
IF PLANTS ONE	6
IF PLANTS ONE	7
IF PLANTS BOTH	8
IF PLANTS BOTH	9
IF PLANTS BOTH	10
IF PLANTS BOTH	11
INTRODUCE TAPE	12
IF HESITANT ABOUT HEARING TAPE	13
IF HESITANT ABOUT HEARING TAPE	14
AFTER TAPE	15
FINAL SCREENING QUESTIONS	16
FINAL SCREENING QUESTIONS	17
REP CONTACT HELPFUL?	18
IF HESITANT/REFUSES TO ANSWER	19
CODING OF CALL-CARDS AND TALLY SHEET	20

Figure 7-3. Monsanto call script.

if the farmer did not plant at least 400 acres of one or the other (2) or 600 acres combined, further call contact could not be justified. Even if the farmer's needs did not meet this requirement, however, there was still knowledge to be gained through the telephone contact. The communicators offered to send information by mail on any product that might interest these smaller farmers. After suggesting this possibility and recording any requests for literature, the communicator politely terminated the interview with these respondents.

If the farmer was qualified, based on the size of the farm, further questions were asked about the herbicide currently used, how long it had been used, how satisfactory it was, and whether the farmer planned to use it again.

At this point in the call, the communicator asked permission to play a tape prepared by the company's technical manager. In fact, there were two tapes—one to be played for farmers who said they were satisfied with their present herbicides and another for those who were dissatisfied. In each of them the company spokesperson discussed the increasing role of science in farming and explained that the purpose of the phone call was to gather information that would help develop products and services to fit the farmer's needs. In addition, however, the tape for dissatisfied farmers emphasized the confusion that modern farming methods might be causing, offering the company's agricultural experts who might be able to help sort through the intimidating variety of herbicides on the market and help find those that would eliminate that farmer's weed problems. The purpose of the call was to survey and then offer an advertising message that was a general, institutional-style promotion of the company itself as a concerned, reputable supplier. The object here was to place the company in a "service" context in the farmer's mind, in preparation for a later personal sales call that would attempt to take an order.

After the break to play the tape, the communicator returned to the line, asking about specific products manufactured by the company, if they had not already been mentioned by the farmer in the course of answering previous questions. Eliciting information on the particular weed problems encountered and checking the farmer's familiarity with the company's line of herbicides, this marketing survey segment led finally to the offer of a sales visit by a company representative. Farmers that agreed were contacted within the week by a salesperson to arrange a specific appointment.

Results   The initial results of the test looked encouraging, at least from the telemarketing agency's vantage point. Of the 958 callable names, 659 farmers were contacted and agreed to answer the survey within the 10-day calling period. In terms of reachability, the list passed muster, and the level of cooperation on the part of the farmers was heartening. Of the 659, nearly a quarter were not qualified for sales representative contact, the great majority because they simply did not plant enough acreage. Of those who were qualified, over 60 percent agreed to have a representative visit them.

Of those who did not rank as candidates for a personal sales visit, most had chosen early in the call not to answer the survey questions. It is worth remembering that this did not mean that these farmers were definitely not prospects—only that they did not choose to be surveyed. This left the door open to future contact through other means.

Tactically, the call format quickly weeded out both those who were not qualified and those who would not cooperate, proving itself an efficient tool for its purpose. If the call had been structured differently, for instance, and the tape had been played as the first item in the call, much valuable phone time would have been wasted on farmers who would only be screened out later on.

Program Expansion   The company analyzed these results and waited for the all-important feedback from the sales force. Any decision to roll-out the telephone lead-generation campaign to a larger territory hinged not on whether the phone campaign worked well in itself but on the bottom-line question of whether the leads produced for the salespeople led to increased order volume.

The wait didn't last very long: one month after the testing was completed, communicators were back on the phones, carrying out a roll-out program to contact nearly 50,000 farmers. The names were divided into four "waves" for call sequencing, with the market segment identified as the most responsive in the testing phase receiving priority scheduling on the phones.

Only minor revisions were needed in the call presentation—for instance, the questions that specifically asked about the company's products were moved up to the first part of the script. Also, based on listening to tapes of the test calls, the decision was made to place less emphasis on getting a firm commitment to meet with a company sales representative. There was still a final general question asking whether a representative contact would be helpful, but making this into a firm appointment was left entirely to the sales force. That way, even if farmers were not comfortable committing themselves to a sales rep's visit when speaking with the communicator, the door was still open to follow-up by the sales force directly.

The call results produced in the roll-out were in line with the findings of the test phase, but the processing of the information gathered by the phone operation became more sophisticated. Now farmers with enough acreage to be considered were categorized as "priority" or "nonpriority" leads. To be classified as a priority lead, according to standards set by company management, a farmer had to meet one or more of the following criteria:

- Not satisfied with current herbicide
- Does not plan to use, or is unsure about using, current herbicide in coming year
- Has a serious perennial weed problem
- Has used, and is not satisfied with, one of the company's herbicides

Over half the farmers contacted in the program were valid leads, with nearly two-thirds of these in the priority lead category. As the "dossiers" for each salesperson's territory were completed, the forms for all farmers telephoned—whether or not they were reached or agreed to a sales visit—were photocopied for home office records. Then the originals were inserted in binders by territory, with the priority leads flagged for immediate attention. They were delivered by air express to the 160 individual field sales representatives, enabling them to devote the bulk of their time to the most promising prospects, following up on "hot" telephone leads just days after the initial contact was made by the communicator and then approaching these "quality" prospects with a knowledgeable, well-informed sales presentation tailored to the expressed needs of the farmers they were contacting.

Selling the Salespeople   While we've concentrated on the front-end process of gathering information and getting it out to the people in the field accurately and efficiently, the company had not forgotten the all-important task of creating sales force enthusiasm for the new program.

The company began with a full briefing on the upcoming phone program at their annual sales meeting and then carried the introductory program one step further. At the beginning of the roll-out, each salesperson was phoned by a communicator and given a taste of the Large Farmer Lead-Generation Program, including a taped message from the company's market research manager and actual excerpts from calls to farmers made during the testing phase of the program.

This orientation provided the sales force with a firsthand understanding of the telemarketing program and what it would do for them. The extra effort involved on the company's part in contacting the sales reps with this special program introduction also dramatically demonstrated management commitment to the phone effort, substantially reinforcing the perception on the part of the sales force that this was not just some new promotion gimmick but a major marketing effort to be taken seriously.

Implications for the Marketer   It should be clear that the telephone is an effective instrument for screening and qualifying leads for your sales force. It is possible, though, to allow a phone program to run away from you, with results that are both frustrating and counterproductive.

A case in point involved the old Railway Express Agency, which offered a nationwide shipping service to manufacturers. We put together a program to call selected businesses and, through a prospecting questionnaire, determined each respondent's current shipping needs and practices. The phone presentation included some preselling of the company's services, in order to open the door for the "field sales force" to follow up and close the lead.

Each successfully completed call would identify the appropriate decision maker in the company being called, elicit detailed information about the status of the manufacturer's shipping operation, and pave the way for a personal sales call.

After a very successful pretest and with a gung ho attitude and a full staff of communicators, we initiated some 20,000 calls to firms in New York, Chicago, Philadelphia, San Francisco, Detroit, Boston, Cleveland, St. Louis, Milwaukee, Miami, Atlanta, and Denver, because management insisted on a quick program to improve sales.

The communicators found that their presentation worked very well indeed. The businesspeople they spoke with were friendly and quite cooperative in answering questions. In fact, the response was overwhelmingly favorable—not one of the market areas produced less than 45 percent qualified leads!

Unfortunately, the key word in that last paragraph is "overwhelmingly." Suddenly the "sales force" had literally thousands of likely prospects, all expecting to hear directly from a company representative, and nowhere near enough workers to follow them all up. Only then did we discover that the sales force was nonexistent! Troubleshooters, yes; salespeople, never! Managers were swamped, and potentially valuable leads, produced at some expense through a highly effective phone operation, were wasted. Worse still, the prospects were left presold and unattended, which was bound to create ill will for the future.

The moral of this brief cautionary tale is plain—management control of the entire marketing process is vital to using the phone effectively. With controlled lead planning and distribution, this program should have been carried out in stages, allowing adequate time for follow-up by a specially trained sales force; perhaps it should have even formed the basis for enormous improvements in the way new shipping clients were acquired. As it turned out, management chose to push the accelerator to the floorboards as soon as they set out and, as a result, got nowhere. We've never found a program offering more than two leads per field salesperson per day achieving any success—and there are some old-time (REA) Railway Express Agency sales managers who still think that that's two too many!

In many lead-generation programs, the telephone communicator goes one step further and actually makes a specific appointment for the salesperson directly over the phone. This can be an efficient way of routing your salespeople, but it can also lead to problems. For instance, there will be specific times that the salesperson has already allocated for visiting new prospects, with appointments with established customers already worked into the schedule; or salespeople may have personal requirements that make it more convenient to travel to a given area on a given day. The telephone communicator making sales appointments would normally have no way of knowing any of this. Certainly prescheduling is far more likely to encounter resistance from a sales force than allowing salespeople to contact the leads unearthed and set their own appointment schedules. Salespeople pick selling as a career because they value the individualism, relative freedom, and lack of office constraints involved; too much "main office control" will only intensify its built-in pressures. As the need for a sharper balance between sales costs and profit margins increases, the pressure on sales reps and "free spirits" escalates. Tighter lead control via computer tracking systems sound great—but they, too, work only for a short time. Witness the high turnover of most sales forces. Unless a close, "interwoven" relationship is established between the individual telephone communicator and the sales representative, prescheduling may be doomed to failure. Some companies have engineered a "dependency" relationship and profit motivation, going so far as to structure a shared percentage of the commission for the communicator. Changing the names to "inside telephone sales" and "field sales" indicates another approach to solving the same old problem. Another company assigns one communicator to each sales rep: they work in tandem for a common goal—also shared!

Screening, qualifying, and "route mapping" prospects yields more sales appointments—it makes sales reps more productive and maximizes their selling time, as opposed to unproductive and prohibitively expensive travel time. Company profits go up, but the increase in personal compensation is an even more important motivator. Once a salesperson fully understands the power of the telephone, he or she may finally decide to learn how to use the new selling tool effectively!

Further Applications   Over the past 20 years, according to CCI Vice President of Health Services Rosemary Bolgar, telemarketing has evolved from an art into a science, bound by a code of ethics observed by all reputable practitioners (see Appendix D). Concurrently the escalating costs of sales visits has evoked an accelerating interest in telemarketing as a means to optimize, or substitute for, sales force activity.

Today, the spectrum of applications is remarkable. Highly qualified leads are generated for products ranging from computer software to food-service delivery systems. Telemarketing programs service marginal accounts from sporting goods stores to pharmacies, allowing salespeople to focus on high-volume accounts.

Even prospects traditionally regarded as "hard to reach," such as physicians, health care professionals, educators, or farmers are accessible through and responsive to telemarketing. Its speed of market coverage makes it an ideal substitute for the "detailer" when pharmaceutical marketers need to disseminate information rapidly on new products or expanded product indications.

Increasing mail costs have caused many companies to use the telephone to generate targeted mailing lists by identifying the name and title of *current*, appropriate decision makers, and then to screen and qualify mail inquiries to ensure rapid sales force follow-up.

Imaginative marketers are constantly discovering how telemarketing enhances sales force efficiency. The old-time door-to-door salesperson is becoming extinct. The new breed will regard telephone marketing not as a threat but as an essential support system.

chapter eight /

Building Nonprofit Associations and Fund-Raising Campaigns

Difficult economic conditions have led businesses to change their sales and marketing tactics in recent years. They are also forcing changes on the business of nonprofit institutions, organizations, and fund raising. Associations exist in every area of our lives and in our communities. Fund raising alone—whether for charitable causes or political candidates—is an enormous institution, employing perhaps 5 million people, with many times that number of volunteers involved and upwards of $40 billion raised each year for philanthropic organizations alone. With this kind of investment at stake, nonprofit professionals are developing their expertise in using the same direct-response alternatives to reach the public as other businesses. And they are finding that telemarketing is an increasingly practical, profitable means for soliciting members or contributions.

This certainly does not mean that the other media traditionally used for "nonprofits" or fund raising are obsolete. Television or radio ads are still the fastest way to reach a mass audience with information about your organization and cost less "per individual contacted" than other media— particularly when the time is donated for public service messages. Advertisements in newspapers and magazines effectively spread the word to a smaller, more select audience, offering the opportunity to print more detailed information than a broadcast message can convey and to stimulate direct response from readers through clip-out coupons.

A major mode of cost-effective solicitation is the convincing appeal directed to individual prospects, either through face-to-face meeting, direct-mail package, or telephone call. This personalized contact is more important today than ever before, as people find their pocketbooks pinched and tend to hesitate over the charitable contributions and membership dues they might once have taken for granted. It is in this area of personal appeals to individual prospects and donors that the most substantial changes in marketing procedures have taken place.

Live person-to-person contact, once a mainstay of many drives, has become a much more difficult technique to pursue successfully. Volunteers are no longer willing to knock on strangers' doors and request contributions. Even if they did, few of us would open our doors to a stranger today, especially if we live in cities. A face-to-face solicitation can still be enormously successful on a small scale, among people who know each other—a church congregation, for example. However, many groups that formerly used this procedure have switched their fund-raising tactics.

The March of Dimes was originally based on the idea of a Mother's March, with millions of women going house-to-house, ringing doorbells and asking for contributions. This worked profitably for many years—the house-to-house solicitation raised $15 million in 1955. By 1978, though, their total had plummeted to roughly half that amount. They switched their focus to direct-mail solicitation, but here too problems developed, as costs leaped upward with no end to the escalation in sight.

As a March of Dimes spokesperson told *Forbes* magazine in 1979, "With nonprofit rates it costs us $26 per thousand to do a mailing, including $7 for postage. In three years, we expect it will cost us $26 in postage alone."

We must always keep in mind that a nonprofit organization runs like a business, and the bottom-line figure is arrived at only after subtracting the costs of doing business. These costs have skyrocketed in recent years, and nowhere is this more evident than in the price of direct-mail appeals. Direct mail is now the primary fund-raising method used by nonprofits, accounting for about one-third of all dollar returns. However, the costs of postage (even at lower nonprofit rates), printing, and handling have drastically reduced the ratio of new money raised to expenses incurred in fund raising. Today direct-mail cost estimates vary from 40 to 60 percent of the amounts raised, with the average running closer to 50 percent. There is, however, a tremendous range of costs possible, from as little as 3 percent for a very successful mailing to a highly selective list of well-established donors to 100 to 150 percent for a campaign aimed at producing new donors from a fairly broad-based mailing list.

This situation has led forward-thinking nonprofit professionals to take a new look at their telephone operations. We are all familiar with the phone as a fulfillment device in a telethon situation, where the numbers to call in pledges are constantly flashed on the screen and the total pledged is immediately posted for all to see. The accent today, though, is on outbound phone operations, which reach out to high-potential donors and ask them to make a pledge directly over the telephone.

How does the phone, which is a relatively expensive medium to employ when judged on a cost-per-contact basis, work to improve the bottom line for a nonprofit organization or a fund-raising campaign? When used properly, it provides the following important advantages:

▪ **Personalized contact.** As we have discussed, it is extremely difficult to arrange a face-to-face meeting between an organization's representative and a potential member or donor in a large-scale operation today. However, the next best thing to this form of meeting is live voice-to-voice contact over the phone. No mass-produced direct-mail piece can match the one-to-one effectiveness of the phone. Making a contribution to a nonprofit organization is a very personal decision. It may involve: (1) the donor's sense of trust in the group, (2) the donor's involvement in its goals, (3) the urgency of the request, or (4) the importance of the contribution. All of these can best be inspired by a representative making a direct, personal appeal. The telephone provides this capability with a minimum of staffing and centralized control over the entire operation.

This sense of personal contact is particularly important when your organization is perceived as large and relatively faceless. Throughout Chapters 8 and 9 we will see examples of institutions working to build a sense of belonging among contributors, or building membership in an ongoing effort. The telephone has proven particularly effective when it comes to campaigns for membership organizations, tackling their three-part goals of generating new membership commitments, renewing memberships at the end of the year, and reactivating lapsed members. In the case history for this chapter we will look into the phone activities of the nonprofit American Bar Association (ABA), which brought telephone contact into its membership program at a particularly difficult period in its history. Through this means the ABA overcame troublesome doubts on the part of members of the legal community and actually increased its membership rolls despite considerable obstacles.

▪ **Prospecting for new contributors.** Prospecting operations are barely profitable in the best of times. Still, a nonprofit organization cannot hope to continue its work without a fresh supply of contributors. More and more fund raisers are finding that telephone contact produces enough new contributors per hour on the phone to match and even exceed the cost-per-dollar-raised figures of a direct-mail prospecting campaign to the same list.

It is frequently difficult to prove the cost figures relating to different media employed in a single fund-raising drive. The phone calls certainly influence the mail response, but it is hard to isolate their effect compared with the amount that mail would have brought in alone. In addition, while telephone pledges may be recorded separately, the check that fulfills the verbal commitment will come in by mail, and all too often all the receipts are lumped into a single total without differentiation by source, with the telephone donor using the previously received mail appeal envelope!

▪ **Maximum pull from limited lists.** It is axiomatic in fund raising that your strongest response will come from your previous contributor list, while finding new contributors will be a more difficult and expensive undertaking. The telephone helps to bring in the most from your list of prior contributors in two important ways: it raises the size and volume of the contributions that come in from your direct-mail appeals, and it draws additional, incremental income through pledges taken directly over the phone.

We will examine the effective use of the mail and phone combination in a case history that deals with a "hot" area of growing telephone usage—political fund raising. The case in point involves the National Republican Senatorial Committee, which picked up a lagging direct-mail fund-raising effort in 1979 by adding a telephone follow-up calling program in 1980. The results in terms of quantity of campaign dollars produced are only slightly less dramatic than the results in number of candidates elected—1980 saw the committee's most substantial financial support of its party's senatorial candidates ever and, not coincidentally, the politically surprising gain of control of the Senate by the Republican party.

In a fascinating test case undertaken on behalf of the Public Broadcasting System, systems were set up with the specific aim of maintaining a valid statistical base for comparing results of the different fund-raising vehicles employed. The findings of this study indicate that, in a high-volume fund-raising operation, telephone can actually raise more money at a lower cost per dollar raised than a direct-mail effort, even at lower nonprofit organization postage rates. The facts and figures are explored in full in Chapter 9 in the case history "Prospecting New Dollars for PBS."

The economics of telemarketing are unquestionably demanding—no one is going to successfully raise funds by calling through the phone book asking for donations. However, as Rod Smith, finance director of the National Republican Senatorial Committee has observed, "Mail gets the easy money, phone gets the tougher sells." In today's economy, more and more potential contributors fall into that "tough sell" category, and reaching those people by telephone is a key element in a successful fund-raising plan for difficult times.

Case History: Passing the Bar

Marketing Objectives   Membership in a professional association can be a very attractive proposition, providing prestige, information, the chance to meet like-minded individuals, a more powerful voice for personal interests through group lobbying efforts, and other benefits. However, association membership is rarely a necessity, on either a personal or professional basis. As business expenses escalate and every budget item is subjected to scrutiny, association membership dues become a tempting expense to eliminate. To counteract the relative vulnerability of their membership rolls in troubled financial times, associations from the smallest to the largest and most prestigious have launched more vigorous efforts to solicit new members, renew current memberships, and reactivate former members. And one of the media playing an increasing role in this membership marketing effort is the telephone.

Telemarketing Strategy   Here again we find a situation in which the personal contact made possible through telemarketing has special value in relation to the nature of the proposal being made. The feeling of belonging is a major attraction in joining a business, trade, or professional association, but this sense of personal involvement can easily be lost, despite periodic newsletters, magazines, or even occasional group meetings. A single telephone call from a representative of the association to a member effectively dramatizes the importance of that individual to the organization. This one-to-one contact not only makes the member feel important; it gives the monolithic association a recognizably human aspect in the form of the voice on the phone. Incorporating telemarketing in this way, along with the ever-present direct-mail component of a membership campaign, has produced results dramatically superior to anything accomplished by mail alone.

A particularly successful case study is the ongoing membership program conducted by the American Bar Association. In 1977, on the verge of its centennial year, the renowned 200,000-member ABA faced several major problems that threatened to cut into its membership renewal efforts severely. First the general post-Watergate climate for lawyers in the United States was less than rosy. The legal profession was also being swamped with more new, young attorneys than there were openings to fill. Competition was increasing, business was poor for many established firms (particularly in smaller practices), and many lawyers were looking for ways to cut down on their overhead.

At the same time, the ABA had found it necessary to increase its dues structure substantially—up to 100 percent in the case of one membership category. Combined with some strong stands on controversial issues taken by ABA leadership in the preceding year, the overall climate clearly called for an all-out effort to keep current members in the fold.

List Segmentation   The American Bar Association's membership department decided to test two approaches to increasing their membership-marketing impact—the telephone and the Mailgram, a Western Union service whereby a telegramlike printed document is delivered by wiring the message to a facility near the recipient's address and then delivering the transmitted data to its destination through the local mails (see Figure 8-1).

The testing of the two media took place after five direct-mail pieces had already been sent to "nonresponding" members. In pursuit of the reluctant members who had not responded to repeated mail drops, the telephone campaign outpulled the Mailgrams convincingly, by a ratio of 2.7 to 1. This paved the way for a full roll-out of the telephone program during the first two weeks of January, calling all those who had not sent in their annual dues as of December 31.

Creative Strategy   The telephone presentation included a taped message from Justin Stanley, president of the American Bar Association and one of the nation's leading attorneys. The communicator would identify himself or herself as a representative of the American Bar Association and ask to speak to the member attorney being called. The prestige of the association's name was almost universally sufficient to convince the secretary to put the call through to the individual lawyer.

Lettergram.

ABA HWAC (925080 2-024653 C337) PD 1176 1504CST TLX CHGO LTGRM

URGENT MESSAGE RE YOUR ABA MEMBERSHIP. REPLY BY RETURN MAIL ESSENTIAL TO PREVENT CANCELLATION OF YOUR MEMBERSHIP.

DUES PAYMENT NOT RECEIVED. UNLESS YOU ACT AT ONCE, YOUR MEMBERSHIP MUST BE CANCELLED FOR NON-PAYMENT ON DECEMBER 31. ABA CONSTITUTION REQUIRES DELINQUENT MEMBERS BE DROPPED.

YOU WILL LOSE ALL BENEFITS, RIGHTS AND PRIVILEGES OF MEMBERSHIP UNLESS YOU ACT. SECTION MEMBERSHIPS, YOUR SUB-SCRIPTION TO ABA JOURNAL, ABA PUBLICATIONS, RIGHT TO PARTICIPATE IN AMERICAN BAR ENDOWMENT INSURANCE, ETC., EXPIRE CONCURRENTLY WITH ABA MEMBERSHIP.

PRACTICE OF LAW CHANGING RAPIDLY. ABA IS YOUR VOICE -- VOICE OF LEGAL PROFESSION -- IN WASHINGTON, IN COMMUNICATING WITH THE PUBLIC AND THE PRESS; AIDING IMAGE OF PROFESSION. ABA ADDRESSES VITAL ISSUES -- LEGAL SERVICES, JUDICIAL REFORM, DISPUTE RESOLUTION, LAWYER ADVERTISING. ABA IS LEADER IN FIELD OF LAWYER EDUCATION, SPONSORS NATIONAL INSTITUTES AND CLE PROGRAMS, ALL FOR BENEFIT OF INDIVIDUAL LAWYER AND IMPROVEMENT OF LEGAL PROFESSION.

MAIL CHECK IN ENCLOSED ENVELOPE. HAVE NO ALTERNATIVE BUT TO DROP YOU FOR NON-PAYMENT OF DUES UNLESS RECEIVED AT ONCE. REPLY TODAY!

W. GENE MUSSELMAN, DIRECTOR OF MEMBERSHIP
AMERICAN BAR ASSOCIATION
1155 EAST 60TH STREET
CHICAGO, ILLINOIS 60637
(312) 947-3802

Figure 8-1. ABA Mailgram.

After first inquiring whether the prospect had already renewed in response to a mailgram (see Figure 8-1), the communicator immediately introduced the two-minute tape prepared by Mr. Stanley and requested permission to play it. Even those who had indicated in answer to a question about mail renewal that they had no intention of renewing their membership were generally interested in hearing what Mr. Stanley had to say. His taped message was as follows:

HELLO, THIS IS JUSTIN STANLEY. I'M UNCOMFORTABLE ABOUT USING THIS MEANS TO DISCUSS ABA MEMBERSHIP WITH YOU, BUT I CAN'T CALL EVERYONE INDIVIDUALLY, AND I DO WANT TO PERSONALLY URGE YOU TO CONTINUE YOUR MEMBERSHIP.

OUR PROFESSION HAS BEEN UNDER SEVERE ATTACK FOR A LONG TIME NOW, AND SO HAS THE MANNER IN WHICH OUR SYSTEM OF JUSTICE IS FUNCTIONING. WHILE SOME OF THE CRITICISM MAY WELL BE JUSTIFIED, LAWYERS THEMSELVES ARE AWARE OF OUR PROFESSIONAL SHORTCOMINGS; AND LAWYERS THEMSELVES, CERTAINLY THROUGH THE ABA, HAVE BEEN DOING SOMETHING ABOUT THEM. YOU KNOW OF THE WORK WE'VE DONE TO IMPROVE THE QUALITY OF PROFESSIONAL DISCIPLINE, TO IMPROVE THE LITIGATION PROCESS, AND TO DELIVER LEGAL SERVICES TO THOSE WHO NEED THEM. BUT THE FACT IS THAT MUCH OF THE PUBLIC UNDERSTANDING OF THE LAW, AND OF OUR SYSTEM OF JUSTICE, AND INDEED OF LAWYERS, IS SHAPED BY THE NATIONAL MEDIA AND BY WHAT GOES ON IN WASHINGTON.

WHAT I HOPE WE CAN ACCOMPLISH IS TO HAVE THE ABA ACHIEVE A NATIONAL IMPACT WHERE IT IS NEEDED AND, AT THE SAME TIME, SERVE THE PRACTICING LAWYER. WE ARE, I THINK, MAKING PROGRESS AT THE NATIONAL LEVEL, AND OF COURSE WE'RE WORKING HARD ON SUCH MATTERS AS LEGAL MALPRACTICE AND INSURANCE, COMPUTER RESEARCH, AND CONTINUING LEGAL EDUCATION. AND, AS YOU KNOW, WE ARE ENGAGED IN LITIGATION ABOUT THE CONTROL OF LAWYER ADVERTISING.

WE HAVE A DIVERSE GROUP, AND PERHAPS THAT IS OUR GREATEST STRENGTH. SO WHILE I DON'T EXPECT YOU TO APPROVE ALL THAT WE ARE DOING, I DO URGE YOUR SYMPATHETIC UNDERSTANDING. AND IN THE CONTINUING STRUGGLE WHICH WE AS A PROFESSION ARE FACING, I HOPE WE CAN COUNT ON YOUR HELP—WE NEED IT.

THANK YOU FOR LISTENING TO ME. YOU'LL HAVE—WHATEVER YOUR DECISION—MY BEST WISHES FOR A HAPPY AND SUCCESSFUL YEAR AHEAD.

When the tape ended, the communicator would get back on the line, make sure the message had been heard clearly, and offer to renew the prospect's membership over the phone, ensuring all membership benefits and professional privileges for another year despite the fact that the official deadline had already passed.

If the member appeared hesitant about renewing, the communicator's script included a brief recap of some of the major points in Mr. Stanley's presentation to serve as further persuasion. If the member definitely did not choose to renew, the communicator asked, "Can you tell me any special reason why you'd prefer to let your membership lapse at this time?" and recorded the response.

Of particular importance in this script were the answers to questions and objections that might arise (see Figure 8-2). Remember, the prospects in this program were lawyers, and they made their living asking questions and evaluating the answers they received. They would not only be likely to ask some tough questions before agreeing to renew but would expect the answers to these questions to be up to their professional standards when it came to clarity, accuracy, logical presentation, and concision.

Working closely with the ABA membership department, the telemarketing agency that conducted the calling program developed answers to 13 commonly asked questions, each covered with the proper response in the communicator's script. The following are excerpts from those responses.

The line in capital letters is the heading that appears on the script card in front of the communicator, allowing quick access to the appropriate response based on the prospect's statements.

CAMPAIGN COMMUNICATIONS

INSTITUTE OF AMERICA, INC.

ABA MEMBERSHIP RENEWAL TEST

COMMUNICATOR SCRIPT

INTRODUCTION TO PERSON ANSWERING PHONE		1
NOT IN OFFICE	(1 of 2)	2
NOT IN OFFICE	(2 of 2)	3
INTRODUCTION TO MEMBER	(1 of 2)	4
INTRODUCTION TO MEMBER	(2 of 2)	5
INTRODUCTION TO TAPE		6
HESITANT ABOUT HEARING TAPE		7
AFTER TAPE - RENEWAL OFFER		8
HESITANT ABOUT RENEWAL	(1 of 2)	9
HESITANT ABOUT RENEWAL	(2 of 2)	10
DECIDES TO RENEW		11

QUESTIONS/OBJECTIONS ANSWERS

ABA

NOT INTERESTED		12
IF SAYS: "I'M INACTIVE IN ABA/SEE NO VALUE IN JOINING		13
IF ASKS: "WHO ARE YOU?/ARE YOU FROM THE ABA"		14
IF SAYS: "I NO LONGER PRACTICE LAW"		15
IF ASKS: "WHY A 60% (OR MORE) INCREASE IN DUES?"		16
IF SAYS:ABA NOT RESPONSIVE TO SOLE PRACTITIONER(1of2)		17
IF SAYS:ABA NOT RESPONSIVE TO SOLE PRACTITIONER(2of2)		18
IF ASKS: "IS THERE A SPECIAL CATEGORY OF MEMBERSHIP FOR LONGTIME/RETIRED MEMBERS?"		19
IF SAYS: "I DON'T HAVE A VOICE IN ABA MATTERS"		20
IF ASKS ABOUT CANCELLATION OF INSURANCE		21
IF SAYS: "A DISABILITY PREVENTS ME FROM PAYING DUES"		22
IF ASKS:"WHAT HAS ABA DONE FOR JUDGES?"	(1 of 2)	23
IF ASKS: "WHAT HAS ABA DONE FOR JUDGES"	(2 of 2)	24
IF WANTS TO DROP SECTION MEMBERSHIP		25
IF HAS FULFILLMENT PROBLEMS		26

Figure 8-2. Communicator's script for ABA campaign.

Card A: IF SAYS, "I'M INACTIVE IN ABA/SEE NO VALUE IN JOINING."

The ABA realizes that not every member can actively participate, so we've tailored many ABA services especially for those attorneys. One of the most important services is the publications ABA offers its members. . . .

Card B: IF ASKS, "WHO ARE YOU/ARE YOU FROM THE ABA?"

I'm from a communications agency called CCI in New York City providing this service for the American Bar Association. If there are any questions you'd like to ask, I'll be happy to answer them, or if you prefer, have the ABA contact you. . . .

Card C: IF SAYS, "I NO LONGER PRACTICE LAW."

Membership in the ABA, though, can be helpful even if you're not practicing. ABA general and section publications keep you fully informed. . . .

Card D: IF ASKS, "WHY A 60 PERCENT (OR MORE) INCREASE IN DUES?"

The dues increase was not something we wanted to go with to our membership, but a study by the Board of Governors in 1975 concluded that an increase for fiscal 1976–77 was unavoidable if we were to maintain the strength of our existing programs and meet new challenges. . . .

Card E: IF SAYS, "ABA NOT RESPONSIVE TO SOLE PRACTITIONER."

Actually, the work of the association has been having a tremendous influence on the sole practitioner. In fact, well over half the sole practitioners in the country are ABA members, but even more important is that besides the tangible work ABA is doing for lawyers and for the profession as a whole, probably the most *valuable* work being accomplished is in the expanding activities in our Washington office in terms of analyzing legislation that affects us all in our daily practice, and improving the public image of lawyers in the community. . . .

Card F: IF ASKS, "IS THERE A SPECIAL CATEGORY OF MEMBERSHIP FOR LONGTIME/RETIRED MEMBERS?"

In recognizing the contribution of our long-standing members, the association has provided for the waiver of dues for those members having reached the age of 70 and who've been ABA members for 25 years. . . .

Card G: IF SAYS, "I DON'T HAVE A VOICE IN ABA MATTERS."

It's unfortunately not possible to provide a *direct* voice to each member of an association with over 200,000 members. But ABA is organized in its main governing body—the House of Delegates—so that each member is represented through an elected officer. We'd also like you to feel you can contact ABA headquarters in Chicago at *any* time to express your thoughts or seek information.

Card H: IF ASKS ABOUT CANCELLATION OF INSURANCE.
Participation in the American Bar Endowment insurance program *is* a privilege reserved exclusively for ABA members, and cancellation of membership therefore does terminate insurance coverage at the end of the paid premium period.

Card I: IF SAYS, "A DISABILITY PREVENTS ME FROM PAYING DUES."
The bar's constitution and bylaws provide for the waiver of dues for members who are unable to maintain their membership because of disability. . . .

Cards J and K: IF ASKS, "WHAT HAS ABA DONE FOR JUDGES?"
Last year, in fact, the ABA led in the creation of the Coalition for Adequate Judicial Compensation. . . .

Card L: IF WANTS TO DROP SECTION MEMBERSHIP.
Well, ABA section organization is designed so that lawyers in the same specialty can meet and exchange ideas. . . . Many members have made close personal friends and business associates through their section membership—so may I suggest you stay on as a section member? It *is* tax deductible.

Card M: IF ASKS FULFILLMENT PROBLEMS.
I'm sorry to hear that, Mr.(Mrs.) _____ , but with any group as large as ours, there are bound to be some problems with subscriptions, changes of address, and things like that. But we've taken steps to make sure that future problems will be at a minimum. If you tell me what the exact problem was, I'll have someone qualified get back to you about it.

Card N: IF SAYS, "ABA IS TOO CONSERVATIVE."
As Mr. Stanley mentioned in his message, the ABA *is* working harder for social reform. Right now some of the topics being studied by the association include prepaid legal services, legal clinics. . . .

These scripted answers to the most frequently posed questions were sufficient to handle the vast majority of problems raised during a call, but of course in any program there are always specific issues raised that are beyond the scope of the communicator's function. For example, detailed information was sometimes requested about the ABA's insurance program or the retirement plans offered or the ABA position on some specific legal matter. In that case, the communicator would carefully note the question and pass it on to the association's central office, which would call the prospect back with the answer within a few days of the initial call.

And, of course, scripted responses can be modified to include answers to further questions and objections if they begin to appear frequently in the calling process. In future script revisions, replies were added to handle objections based on a lawyer's standing membership in a local or state bar association as well as the controversial stand taken by the ABA regarding the extension of ratification time for the Equal Rights Amendment.

These carefully prepared responses accomplished the following:

- **Prospect involvement.** Drawing the prospect into a dialogue not only answers specific questions that might be raised but involves the prospect in thinking about the offer. It is also more difficult to refuse when the communicator is asking for a reason for refusal. If the question of renewing changes from "Why should I renew?" (as the prospect may see it when reading a mailing piece) to "Why shouldn't I renew?" (as heard and hopefully perceived over the phone), the number of positive responses will surely increase.

- **Caller credibility.** The fact that the association is personally contacting the individual member is a powerfully persuasive tool. By demonstrating the ability to respond intelligently to questions and problems, the communicator's phone presence is raised from simply a phone-call function to that of a true representative of the association in the eyes of the prospect. Thus, the effectiveness of the person-to-person contact is enhanced.

- **Targeted responses.** The lead paragraph of a direct-mail piece or the opening words of a phone presentation must define the benefit and must involve the recipient—and usually will, if the marketer includes the most universally appealing aspects of the offer. Segmenting the calling audience into several discrete units for the campaign and tailoring the phone script to fit the needs of each of these market segments is another unique advantage of such targeting by phone. Providing specific information in response to the prospect's particular interests and questions increases the validity of the phone contact. The prospect's response, in effect, sorts the prospect into the appropriate category—judge, for instance, or no longer actively practicing, or sole practitioner. Then the appropriate sales presentation can be made in response to questions from each interest category.

This approach also allows questions that relate to difficult issues to be answered when they arise. It was certainly preferable not to mention the dues increase early in the presentation, thereby offering it to the prospect as a potential reason not to renew, when this may not otherwise have been a major issue in the prospect's mind. Similarly, there is nothing gained by asking a young trial lawyer to wade through detailed information about the ABA's work on behalf of judges, which doesn't apply to his situation and might make it seem that the association is too busy to deal with his "lowly" concerns. The ability to present a tight, convincing message up front and follow up immediately with further information in specific areas of personal interest is a powerful persuader.

- **Uncovering hidden problems.** It is unlikely that a member who is annoyed with minor difficulties experienced with fulfillment of mailed materials or other perceived slights on the part of the association will go to the trouble of writing to ask for assistance or explanation. It is quite likely, though, that this will influence a decision when renewal time arrives. A generic mail package can't address individual members' difficulties. By providing a human ear to listen and offer to take steps to clear up problems, however, the phone can often defuse them and clear the way for a positive decision.

By recording both the reasons for not renewing and the problems that must be dealt with, the initial phone test program provided the association with a clear picture of the degree of reaction to the recent membership dues increase and further information on the types of activities and fields of interest that the attorneys contacted felt were appropriate for the ABA. In the first program, for instance, 53.9 percent of those who were not interested in renewing their memberships gave reasons for this decision. Of the 1,801 attorneys who gave reasons for their choice not to renew, 21.6 percent cited the expense, and another 9.4 percent said they did not use the benefits enough to warrant the expense. Membership in local or state bars was adequate for 4.0 percent, 8.3 percent said they were no longer in practice, and 2.9 percent cited policy disagreements with the ABA as their reason for not renewing.

This information had a direct effect on the way members were approached by telephone and mail programs for renewals in subsequent years.

Results Out of the 5,688 names in this group, phone number listings were found for 4,705 (82.7 percent), and of these, 3,583 were reached during the two-week calling period.

Of the 3,583 elapsing members reached, 372 individuals indicated that they had already renewed by mail, leaving a total of 3,211 qualified completed decisions contacted in the calling process. Of these 1,003 agreed to renew their memberships, a response rate of 31.2 percent. In addition, 407 of those reached were classified as "specials," requiring ABA follow-up or indicating that they might renew by mail. We can assume that some of these individuals did indeed later renew, at least partly as the result of the phone program's reminder (see Figure 8-3).

This high renewal rate is about *four times* the response rate achieved through direct mail by ABA. Of course, phone is far more costly per contact than a mailing, especially when the mailing is conducted by a nonprofit organization. Nevertheless, the economics of the phone campaign are impressive.

The calls produced revenues of approximately $112,180 at a cost of just over $20,000—a remarkable expense-to-income ratio of 5.4 to 1.

Keep in mind also that this ratio includes only the immediate income generated from dues payments. It is important to remember, when assessing the economics of any marketing medium in a membership campaign, that maintaining an association member produces potential income far greater than the immediate payment. The member is likely to purchase publications and services in the course of the year, pay fees for meetings and conferences, and, of course, pay dues in future years that would not have been forthcoming if the member had been lost.

Taking these additional factors into account, we find the total value of the membership renewals produced by the phone campaign far exceeds the bottom-line results for the year of the individual telephone campaign.

It is also worth remembering the less measurable but nonetheless real value of maintaining as large a membership as possible to increase the association's voice as a lobbying organization.

And the American Bar Association did indeed maintain those important membership figures, despite the substantial negative factors at work. In fact, in a year when all predictions pointed to considerable losses, the ABA chalked up the second highest membership increase in its history.

Summary The success of the first phone program led to similar campaigns in the years that followed. Drawing on the expressed concern with the economics of ABA membership, new scripts were developed that contained more emphasis on the "bread and butter" membership benefits—discounts on auto rentals, hotel accommodations, and so forth. And these revised presentations produced responses even more impressive than the initial campaign, going as high as a 45 percent renewal rate in later years.

AMERICAN BAR ASSOCIATION

Actiongram

January, 1978

Dear Member:

On behalf of William B. Spann, Jr., I am writing to thank you for renewing your American Bar Association membership when we spoke with you on the telephone. If you have not already done so, please forward your remittance of $ to the American Bar Association, 1155 East 60th Street, Chicago, IL 60637, Attn: Finance Dept. - Dues.

As a member of the American Bar you continue to share a unique heritage, and by your participation you enable the ABA to enhance the growth and development of our profession.

Sincerely,

W. Gene Musselman
Director of Membership

WGM/rg

Figure 8-3. Follow-up Mailgram for renewing members.

Implications for the Marketer The telephone can do more than produce membership renewals; that is only one aspect of its broader effect. Telephone contact achieves "involvement"; and that is a prerequisite if any nonprofit organization is to effectively interact with its members and contributors.

In the case history of the ABA, the telephone program was part of a direct, sales-oriented approach, with a specific membership commitment as the goal of the call. However, there are broader applications of organized telephone operations to consider as well. Providing an information hot line for members through incoming lines (toll-free or otherwise) makes the organization more accessible to its members. This could take the form of a taped message changed periodically with timely information, or individuals could be responsible for answering member questions on a one-to-one basis.

Telephone reminders of upcoming special meetings are also effective for boosting attendance and bolstering the feeling of membership commitment. Even if the individual does not, in fact, decide to attend, the demonstrated concern on the part of the association will have a strong positive effect.

These service-oriented calls can be revenue-generating as well. Reminders of upcoming conventions or trade shows conducted by a membership organization can produce incremental registration fees through telemarketing, as well as increasing the number of exhibitors, where applicable. Sales of books, booklets, pamphlets, and brochures published by the organization can also be accomplished through a service-oriented telephone presentation, positioned as part of the organization's efforts to keep members aware of current trends and up-to-date information.

Whatever form an organization's telephone contact takes, it comes down to the simple act of putting a member in direct, personal contact with a representative of his or her organization. Even when soliciting a financial commitment from the member, this personal contact has a beneficial "something added" effect on the strength of the individual's connection with the association.

chapter nine /

Expanding
Your Contributor Base with Phone

Case History: Republican Roundup

The telephone is becoming ever more involving and responsive—more than 500,000 citizens voted their preference by dialing a special "900" number during the presidential election of 1980—and willingly paid 50 cents for the privilege!

Our election process has evolved rapidly in recent years from one of face-to-face meetings between candidates and voters to an exercise in communication via the mass media, and the telephone's special characteristics, combining broad geographical reach and a large audience with one-to-one contact between individuals, has made it a key part of the political media mix.

The art of political telephone use is undergoing dramatic development with each new election campaign. Some telephone techniques have become well-established political procedures. For instance, manning the phones on and near Election Day to "get out the vote" is now standard practice for many political organizations, as is preelection telephone polling and neighborhood canvassing for volunteers by phone banks.

Other political applications of the telephone have been more experimental, such as the after-midnight polling messages to voters in New

Hampshire detailed in the Watergate testimony. Or the personalized tape messages responding to incoming callers, with questions segmented by special phone numbers, for example, call 000-0001 for the candidate's position on foreign policy or 000-0012 for his position on taxes, and so on.

Certainly, the interpersonal communication capabilities of the telephone will continue to be explored, expanded, and exploited in new and innovative ways in political campaigns to come.

In efforts like the one employed for the presidential debates or the earlier "call in" program to President Carter in the White House that generated 9 million responses, the phone campaigns represent groundbreaking applications for telephone as a mass medium serving a uniquely political purpose. We shall now discuss another area, where telephone's proven effectiveness and sophisticated techniques have been developed over the years in other endeavors and are now being adapted and refined for use in the political arena—that is, using telephone to raise the enormous sums of money needed to finance political campaigns in the 80s.

We have already seen how charitable organizations and other nonprofit institutions have brought direct-marketing techniques to bear upon the changing requirements of fund-raising efforts in today's demanding and fiercely competitive marketplace. In this chapter, we will examine the substantial impact of telephone fund-raising techniques on the 1980 election campaign, focusing on one of the most aggressive and successful fund-raising organizations on the political scene today—the National Republican Senatorial Committee.

It is nothing new to note that political campaigning has become an increasingly expensive undertaking. This was already a clear trend in 1931, when famed humorist Will Rogers remarked that "Politics has got so expensive that it takes a lot of money to even get beat with." This observation is even more apt in the present campaigning situation. With expensive media advertising the cornerstone of even local and regional races, the dollars-and-cents considerations of the political process have risen to ever greater prominence in planning election strategy.

"Politics is a game of communicating with voters, and it takes dollars to communicate. If you spend them correctly, the effect can be devastating, beyond, I think, anyone's current comprehension of how political campaigns run." The speaker is a more modern political observer, Rod Smith, who as treasurer and finance director of the National Republican Senatorial Committee (NRSC) had been largely responsible for building that organization into a potent force on the current political scene. At the same time the increasing economic demands of conducting a political campaign have put more emphasis on the financial strength of a candidate than ever before; legislative changes designed to control the sources of campaign finances have made party organizations such as the NRSC, the National Republican Congressional Committee, special interest groups, and political action committees (PACs) an extremely important source of those campaign funds.

Legal restrictions limiting the size of donations by individuals to the campaign coffers of specific candidates have given new importance to the smaller contributor. It is no longer possible to rely on a few "fat cat" donors to provide the bulk of needed campaign monies—instead, candidates must draw their financial backing from a broader-based constituency. Prospecting for a large number of contributors and reaching out to these contributors for more frequent and more generous donations is a special strength of direct-response marketing, which has been utilized increasingly for political fund-raising as a result of legislative slimming of the "fat cat" contributor.

The other, simultaneous influence toward greater use of direct response in the political arena has been the growth of the type of political committee mentioned above. While contributions to individual candidates are strictly limited, additional sizable contributions can be made to political committees and groups, which can then, in turn, lend financial support within legislated limits to individual candidates. This has led to the growth of many centralized organizations designed to raise and employ funds to support candidates of a given party or ideological outlook. This focusing of fund-raising forces into larger committees, often operating on a national rather than a regional scale, has been an important factor in the growing use of sophisticated fund-raising tactics for political purposes. The campaign organization of an individual candidate can rarely afford the expense and fund-raising talent of top experts in the field. Centralized committees, on the other hand, have brought the best minds in the business to the task of raising campaign funds for groups of candidates. At the same time, this centralization allows for the overhead involved in fund-raising operations to be borne by the larger central body, rather than any individual candidate.

All this has led to tremendously effective direct-response fund raising in the political world. This effort began, predictably, with direct mail. Today, though, more and more fund-raising organizations have discovered that just as phone and mail make an effective combination in marketing efforts in the business community, they combine in political fund raising to bring in more money—more quickly—than mail alone.

This lesson was brought home forcefully in the fund-raising drive conducted by the National Republican Senatorial Committee in support of the Republican candidates for Senate seats in the 1980 election. The committee exists to raise money for the campaign efforts of Republican aspirants to Senate seats, providing both direct financial grants and valuable practical assistance. It is one of three nationwide Republican fund-raising organizations—the other two are the Republican National Committee (RNC) and the National Republican Congressional Committee (NRCC). All three groups have made enormous strides since the dark days of Watergate in 1974. In the fund-raising campaign for the 1975–76 elections, the three committees together took in $44.7 million. For the 1979–80 campaign, the total was $111 million—nearly 2½ times the earlier figure. And of the three, the Senatorial Committee showed the most impressive rise, going from $2.1 million raised in 1975–76 to $20.5 million in 1979–80—nearly 10 times as much!

Marketing Objectives   A good deal of this improvement was made in the 1979–80 campaign. But as Rod Smith recalls, the future did not look quite so rosy as 1979 contributions began to arrive. At this point, the committee's small contributor program was relying almost entirely on direct-mail packages sent out on a monthly basis. "We came up with a budget in January of 1979 based on certain historic information," Smith explains. "And by July 1979 we were significantly off—to the point where we were getting 70 cents per piece mailed against a 40-cent cost. The costs were eating us alive—and that's just the mailing cost. Then you add your back-end costs to maintain the whole operation on top of that direct cost figure. We had to bolster our receipts and get them back up to the $1.50-per-piece-mailed range."

Flagging contribution levels in the face of a major election year gave the NRSC the impetus to undertake innovative fund-raising strategies.

"We couldn't afford to take any chances. Our fund raising had lagged coming out of 1979. Going into 1980, we could look at a calendar and see where Election Day fell—and nobody changes Election Day. When you deal in politics, it's like fighting a war. If you'll think back to Gettysburg, when Lee made the decision to charge across that wheat field and lost 17,000 men, he couldn't then pick up and say, 'Gee, wouldn't it be great to envelop Little Roundtop and change the course of history.' Life doesn't go that way.

"Politics is the same way. You make a commitment of resources you can never recover. If things go wrong, the opportunities are lost forever. In business, you make a mistake and you can recover next year. Your sales might drop 5 percent, 10 percent, or even 20 percent, but you've got next year to catch up, because the name of the game is to make money. The name of the game here is to win an election, and politically, certain opportunities crop up today that may never crop up again. So we wouldn't take a chance and had to try everything to improve our fund-raising effectiveness, with that election staring us in the face."

One factor that made telephone such a viable medium for boosting contributions to the NRSC was the opportunity it provided to single the committee out from the overwhelming number of direct-mail fund-raising appeals received by most households, especially in an election year, coming from individual candidates in local and national races and from national campaign organizations.

This problem was particularly troublesome to the NRSC, which is one of three similarly named but autonomous political committees attempting to raise funds simultaneously. As Rod Smith explains it, "I felt that the phone contact with people would help us in our marketplace, where our biggest competitors are our friends. You know, the Congressional (NRCC), Senatorial (NRSC), and Republican National (RNC) committees have duplicates and intermixed names accounting for perhaps 60 percent of our files. One of the problems we get into when we reach out to people across the country is that they view Washington as having a Republican organization—they don't remember the fine distinctions between the NRSC and the NRCC and the RNC—they see it as the Republican Party, Washington. In fact, we had a victorious candidate stand up at a meeting of our major contributors and state, 'I would have never won without the tremendous financial support from the Republican National Committee . . .' when in point of fact, about all the candidate's support had come from the National Republican Senatorial Committee. So you see, we needed to slice out our little piece of the marketplace, to make the donor aware of our identity, and we felt that phone would help."

Telemarketing Strategy Another strategic consideration for the NRSC was starting its telephone operation at the beginning of the year, instead of waiting until closer to Election Day to bring in a phone program, as several other fund-raising organizations had done. "Another basic principle in fund raising," says Rod Smith, "is that once you get somebody to contribute once, it's easier to get them to contribute the second time. So our whole effort was geared toward trying to get that single contribution early on, under the theory that we would then have a larger current-year contributor base to collect further donations from later on.

"We decided to use phone primarily to go after our known contributor base. We had a master file of 300,000 past contributors to the committee, which had not done well in 1979. What we did was to launch an all-fronts attack, hitting that list with mail, then reinforcing the mail with phone, and reinforcing the phone with a follow-up mail drop, because a basic premise in fund raising is: a phone call will get the commitment, but it takes a letter to collect the money.

"We set up a very, very tight mailing schedule, and simultaneously set up a massive phone operation, with the view that even if the phone program just broke even, it would beef up our direct-mail receipts."

The first phase of the NRSC phone operation, then, was brought in to support the initial, and most important, mailing of the year, the committee's membership mailing.

As will also be seen in the PBS campaign discussed later in the chapter, it is very important to develop a sense of membership in an organization in order to build up a continuing relationship with contributors. NRSC uses this principle in their political fund raising and, as we will discuss later on, has expanded on it to include offers of membership in special organizations within the committee for more generous donors.

List Segmentation   The basic annual NRSC membership mailing was sent out in January to all 300,000 names in the past contributor file. The handsome mailing piece included a laser-printed personalized letter from President Ronald Reagan urging the recipient to send in a membership renewal contribution (minimum $20), along with a plastic membership card, which looks like a credit card, with the recipient's name already embossed on it in raised letters (see Figures 9-1 and 9-2).

This mailing was then followed up with telephone calls to a list of 144,000 of the best past contributors from the 300,000-name master list. The committee arranged with two separate telemarketing agencies to handle the call volume quickly. Each agency followed the same scripted approach.

Creative Strategy   The ability to play a taped message to a potential contributor is especially valuable in a political fund-raising campaign. After all, most politicians are best known to their constituents through their appearances over the broadcast media. A letter from a politician can

REPUBLICAN **PRESIDENTIAL**

TASK FORCE

RONALD REAGAN
Founder

BOB PACKWOOD
Chairman

March 31, 1982

K. Kent Miller
1519 N Old Manor
Wichita, Kansas 67208

Dear Friend:

As your President, I am calling upon you to make a most unusual sacrifice.

Not the kind of sacrifice that a national emergency might require of you or your children or your grandchildren to protect our shores from invasion.

I pray that will never happen -- but today I still must ask you to volunteer.

And I must ask you to sacrifice for your country -- in order to keep our Republican majority status in the Senate.

For this reason, I am personally inviting you to become a member of the "Republican Presidential Task Force."

And you are urgently needed. Here's why:

Right now we Republicans only have a slim 4 vote majority lead in the Senate. That's all!

It took us 26 long years to gain 16 Senators to get that narrow majority. But the Democrats need only gain four seats in the November '82 elections to win it back from us!

This means that all the programs I am trying to get through on your behalf may be in jeopardy if we don't act fast.

Believe me, I'm not asking everyone to join this club -- only proud, flag waving Americans like you who I know are willing to sacrifice to keep our nation strong.

I am working with the National Republican Senatorial

<small>Paid for and authorized by the National Republican Senatorial Committee</small>

It's not for cons---
channels for that.

But Task Force members can call or write any day to get an accurate up-to-date report on issues that are being discussed in the Senate.

Sincerely,

Ronald Reagan

Ronald Reagan

P.S. If you truly share my vision of America then I urge you to join the "Republican Presidential Task Force."

Thanks so much for reading my letter, and, please, I need your answer within 10 days.

Ronald Reagan

Figure 9-1. Membership letter from President Reagan.

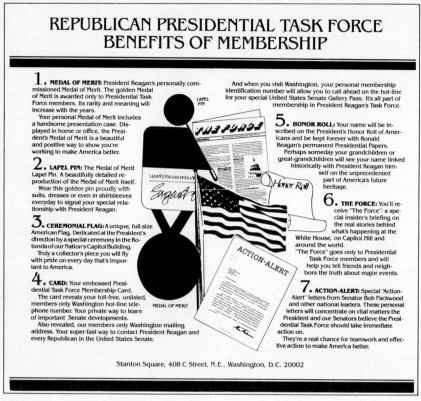

REPUBLICAN PRESIDENTIAL TASK FORCE
BENEFITS OF MEMBERSHIP

1. MEDAL OF MERIT: President Reagan's personally commissioned Medal of Merit. The golden Medal of Merit is awarded only to Presidential Task Force members. Its rarity and meaning will increase with the years.

Your personal Medal of Merit includes a handsome presentation case. Displayed in home or office, the President's Medal of Merit is a beautiful and positive way to show you're working to make America better.

2. LAPEL PIN: The Medal of Merit Lapel Pin. A beautifully detailed reproduction of the Medal of Merit itself.

Wear this golden pin proudly with suits, dresses or even in shirtsleeves everyday to signal your special relationship with President Reagan.

3. CEREMONIAL FLAG: A unique, full-size American Flag. Dedicated at the President's direction by a special ceremony in the Rotunda of our Nation's Capitol Building.

Truly a collector's piece you will fly with pride on every day that's important to America.

4. CARD: Your embossed Presidential Task Force Membership Card.

The card reveals your toll-free, unlisted, members only Washington hot-line telephone number. Your private way to learn of important Senate developments.

Also revealed, our members only Washington mailing address. Your super-fast way to contact President Reagan and every Republican in the United States Senate.

And when you visit Washington, your personal membership identification number will allow you to call ahead on the hot-line for your special United States Senate Gallery Pass. It's all part of membership in President Reagan's Task Force.

5. HONOR ROLL: Your name will be inscribed on the President's Honor Roll of Americans and be kept forever with Ronald Reagan's permanent Presidential Papers.

Perhaps someday your grandchildren or great-grandchildren will see your name linked historically with President Reagan himself on the unprecedented part of America's future heritage.

6. THE FORCE: You'll receive "The Force": a special insider's briefing on the real stories behind what's happening at the White House, on Capitol Hill and around the world.

"The Force" goes only to Presidential Task Force members and will help you tell friends and neighbors the truth about major events.

7. ACTION-ALERT: Special "Action-Alert" letters from Senator Bob Packwood and other national leaders. These personal letters will concentrate on vital matters the President and our Senators believe the Presidential Task Force should take immediate action on.

They're a real chance for teamwork and effective action to make America better.

Stanton Square, 408 C Street, N.E., Washington, D.C. 20002

Figure 9-2. Benefits-of-membership brochure.

convey a great deal of information, but it is difficult to make it come alive with the personal characteristics that voters associate with their elected officials. With a taped message, listeners receive a message from a well-known politician in the form they are accustomed to. They hear the familiar sound of the politician's voice, with all its dramatic intonation intact, and that kind of contact produces a powerful response.

The content of the message must also be carefully prepared to make a concise, focused appeal to the potential contributor, striking a particular chord and striking it hard. As Robert Strauss said when he was treasurer of the Democratic National Committee, "It doesn't make any difference whether it's ban the bomb or bomb the bastards—people contribute in response to emotional appeals."

In writing the message to be taped, it was important to be topical enough to convince listeners that there was a strong, immediate need to make a contribution to this particular committee, while maintaining a broad enough appeal to avoid alienating Republicans whose specific legislative interests might differ somewhat across the country. For the 1980 election, a strong national theme was well established for the Republican party as a whole—the need for a more powerful military and the need to fight inflation. These themes were exploited with great success in fund-raising efforts in all media.

Another ticklish question was the choice of a spokesperson. Needless to say, different political contributors will respond more strongly to different political figures. The only way to choose is to find the politicians whose appeal is most widespread within the party and then to change the spokesperson in each subsequent phone effort made to the same list, so that prospects are likely to be exposed to a political figure whose views match their own.

For the initial phone program of 1980, supporting the membership mailing, the NRSC enlisted the aid of Senator Barry Goldwater to tape a telephone message, with an introduction by Committee Chairman Senator John Heinz. The text of that taped message was as follows:

HELLO, THIS IS UNITED STATES SENATOR JOHN HEINZ, CHAIRMAN OF THE NATIONAL REPUBLICAN SENATORIAL COMMITTEE. I'M CONTACTING YOU IN THIS SPECIAL WAY BECAUSE YOU ARE AN ACTIVE REPUBLICAN SUPPORTER, AND BECAUSE I PERSONALLY WANT YOU TO KNOW HOW VITALLY CLOSE WE ARE TO BECOMING THE MAJORITY PARTY IN THE UNITED STATES SENATE IN 1980. THE ELECTION THIS YEAR OFFERS US A UNIQUE OPPORTUNITY TO RESTORE THE ECONOMIC HEALTH AND THE INTERNATIONAL STRENGTH OF OUR NATION THROUGH SUPERIOR REPUBLICAN LEADERSHIP, BY WINNING THE UNITED STATES SENATE. AND BECAUSE YOUR SUPPORT IS SO CRUCIAL TO THIS EFFORT, I'VE ASKED OUR NATIONAL FINANCE CHAIRMAN, SENATOR BARRY GOLDWATER, TO JOIN ME IN THIS MESSAGE. BARRY—

SENATOR GOLDWATER: THANK YOU, JOHN. AS A UNITED STATES SENATOR, I'VE WAITED 25 YEARS TO SEE OUR PARTY BECOME THE MAJORITY PARTY. NEVER BEFORE HAVE WE BEEN AS CLOSE TO VICTORY AS WE ARE NOW. ONLY REPUBLICAN LEADERSHIP WILL END THE TRAGIC MISMANAGEMENT OF THE DEMOCRATS. UNLESS WE PUT AN END TO THEIR BIG SPENDING IN 1980, SOARING INFLATION AND SKYROCKETING TAXES WILL REDUCE THIS NATION TO A SHADOW OF WHAT IT WAS— AND MUST BE AGAIN. THIS IS WHY YOUR SUPPORT IS SO CRUCIAL. ONLY TOGETHER CAN WE RESTORE THE GREATNESS OF AMERICA. IN ORDER TO DEFEAT THE LIBERAL DEMOCRATS IN 1980, OUR CANDIDATES NEED TO MOUNT PROFESSIONAL, HARD-HITTING CAMPAIGNS THAT WILL ENSURE A SOLID REPUBLICAN VICTORY.

YOU'VE CONTRIBUTED TO US BEFORE, AND WE'RE GRATEFUL. BUT YOUR CONTRIBUTION NOW WILL CARRY EVEN MORE INFLUENCE THAN

IT HAS IN THE PAST. SO I URGE YOU TO GIVE, GIVE AS MUCH AS YOU CAN, TO THE NATIONAL REPUBLICAN SENATORIAL COMMITTEE. I PROMISE YOU YOUR SUPPORT WILL BE A VALUABLE INVESTMENT IN BOTH THE RESTORATION OF THE SENATE AND THE RESTORATION OF THE COUNTRY.

OUR REPRESENTATIVE IS COMING BACK ON THE LINE NOW TO ACCEPT YOUR CONTRIBUTION. THANK YOU FOR LISTENING AND FOR HELPING TO MAKE THE REPUBLICAN PARTY THE MAJORITY PARTY IN 1980.

Another example of a tape script involved President Ford and then-candidate Ronald Reagan appealing, respectively, to moderate and conservative past contributors of the NRCC.

The phone operation on behalf of the NRSC to reach small contributors continued throughout 1980. It was broken into three distinct phases, returning to the same select list of 144,000 contributors each time, but with a different spokesperson on tape and a different focus of attention in each, scripted by CCI, its telemarketing agency.

The second calling phase, for instance, included a tape by Senator Howard Baker and stressed the need to raise funds for the NRSC Challenger Fund. This concept involved pinpointing for potential contributors precisely where their money would go and setting up a highly visible adversary relationship, and it was employed with strong results both in the phone presentation and through the mails.

It is worth noting in connection with the taped message strategy that, when properly carried out, the fund-raising campaign, and the phone campaign in particular, serves an additional purpose above and beyond raising money. There is enormous political importance to maintaining close ties with your supporters. The information regarding party position and policy contained in fund-raising vehicles keeps these known supporters aware of the current situation. Not only does it give them immediate encouragement to keep voting along party lines themselves but it helps maintain their level of enthusiasm as active party members. The personal attention of a phone call to their homes with a message prepared by a prominent national figure stands as further evidence of their individual importance to the party, and it can only serve to make them more involved members, both financially and electorally.

Pledge Follow-up Strategies   Of course, simply taking a pledge over the telephone is not the end of the process—the commitment must be translated into cash in hand. The basic vehicle used to accomplish this is a follow-up letter, thanking the pledger, indicating the amount of the pledge, and enclosing a business reply envelope to facilitate mailing in a check. Speed is essential in this follow-up activity. The faster the pledge letter goes out, the higher the percentage of fulfilled pledges you will receive. This led the NRSC to experiment with two means of cutting reaction time to a minimum:

■ The list of past contributors to be phoned was broken up into segments based on the dollar level of their previous contributions. For the higher-level contributors, the committee tried sending out Mailgrams to follow up on the pledges. Of course, this was more expensive than a standard letter, but they felt that the speed with which they were delivered and the sense of urgency they imparted would ensure a higher rate of response among these larger contributors.

■ One of the phone banks that handled the NRSC calling processed their pledges by forwarding the positive responses via express delivery service at the end of each calling day to a mailing service that produced the pledge letters and mailed them. This caused a delay of several days between the time the contributors said "yes" and their receipt of a pledge letter—as much as a week would elapse, in many cases. The other phone bank (and a third bank that was brought in later in the year) had on-site capability to produce pledge letters and mail them, so their letters went out within 24 hours. As the calling process progressed, a sizable discrepancy became apparent between the fulfillment processes. To make up for the gap, a tel-con linkage was arranged between the first telemarketing agency and a computer-equipped fulfillment house. During the course of the day, the pledges received were keypunched into the computer and transmitted to the fulfillment house immediately, where a computer-printed pledge letter was produced and sent out in less than 24 hours of the initial pledge commitment. When this arrangement was finally instituted, the fulfillment level rose to the point where it was essentially equal among all three phone operations.

Results For the initial phase of the year-long telephone calling operation, involving calls made from January 1 through a cut-off date in mid-March, the cumulative results are shown in Table 9-1. Actually, initial pledges arrived after that date that are not included in the table.

This operation alone raised nearly half a million dollars in pledges actually paid to the committee. This, of course, does not take into account the costs of the telephone program. One of Rod Smith's assistants has computed these costs at an average of $22.50 per telephone hour, plus an additional 90 cents per pledge to cover follow-up letters (up to three per

TABLE 9-1. *Cumulative CCI Results*

Result	Number	Percentage
Pledges	28,174	39
Will contribute by mail	6,826	9
Unsure	4,092	6
No interest/other	33,056	46
Total completed calls	72,148	100
Total pledge amount	$731,955	
Average pledge	$25.98	
Total pledges paid*	$468,326	
Pledges received*	17,520	
Average contribution	$26.73	

* Actual pledge returns attributed to telemarketing program, after all direct mail, at approximately 82 percent.

pledge), postage, and computer time. On this basis, total mail plus phone costs came to $247,319, leaving a profit of $221,007 on the pledges received directly over the phone.

It is important to remember that a basic aim of the phone program was to increase the direct-mail receipts also—a goal that met with great success, according to Rod Smith. When he decided to implement a telemarketing program, he would have been satisfied without any direct telephone profit, since he believed the effect on mail response would be significant. "In point of fact," he explains, "phone made money itself, *plus* it beefed up the mail. When I say 'beefed up,' I mean that the receipts per piece mailed were significantly higher than the previous year. Some of the 1980 mailings brought in $1.50 per piece, some $1.70, some $1.40, but without exception, the mailings in 1980, when we were using phone along with mail, did significantly better than they did in 1979, when we were not. Now some people will say, 'Well, that's just because it was an election year.' Yes, that's a part of it. The direct-mail people will say it's because of their great expertise, but then you say, 'Well, why did it go down in 1979?' There are a lot of factors which are involved, but I am satisfied that the phone program was instrumental in raising our direct-mail receipts substantially. We saw a cause-and-effect response—from the moment we launched the phone program, direct-mail receipts *did* go up. And on top of that, the phone program itself made money—it was a legitimate fund raiser in its own right."

Program Expansion While the importance of smaller contributors has grown substantially, a major factor in the National Republican Senatorial Committee's increasing economic clout has been the cultivation of larger contributors through special programs that cater to their needs.

One of their most successful efforts in this area has been the Republican Senatorial Inner Circle program. In order to enter this elite group, an individual must contribute at least $1,000. The reward for this level of contribution is more than a warm "Thank You." Membership in the Inner Circle entitles contributors to receive a regular newsletter with the "inside story" on the current political scene and to attend special meetings organized for their benefit with government and military officials.

Telephone contact plays a part in the attention paid to Inner Circle contributors. As Rod Smith observes, "Any time you're touching a contributor in a meaningful way, you are helping to draw him a little closer to your operation. And the people who give the most are the ones with whom that kind of stroking is most effective. For this reason, the Inner Circle program employs telephone contact to help build attendance at meetings held exclusively for members. One example of this personalized attention involved a Washington briefing session that would include meetings with Senators and high-ranking military officers."

The call format for this phone program included a taped message from Senator John Heinz or Barry Goldwater, thanking the individual for becoming an Inner Circle member and inviting him or her to take part in the briefing session. After the tape, the communicator returned to the line and, after recapping the particulars and answering any questions that might arise, asked for some idea of whether the member was planning to attend the session.

A formal invitation was mailed out after the phone calls, and so the member did not have to give a definite yes or no answer to the phone communicator in order to attend. However, the phone program did serve two important functions. First it gave the committee some advance information on the practical considerations involved in planning the upcoming session. With an approximate idea of the response they could expect, it was easier to reserve space and make appropriate arrangements.

More important, this was a call from a representative of the committee, providing individual attention to a contributor who is truly a VIP from a fund-raising point of view and needs to be assured of this status in order to encourage continued and perhaps expanded contributions in the future. In this case phone constitutes a part of the fulfillment of the membership, a service function on the committee's part accomplished at modest expense and with no additional staffing requirements, since the services of a professional telemarketing agency are used.

Within the committee's offices, another telephone service is maintained to further serve the needs of Inner Circle members—an "800" number is provided so that members can call the office toll-free for information or assistance.

This is just another instance of the use of telephone to court major donors. Another successful example is the annual Senate-House Dinner, a joint effort on the part of the NRSC and NRCC, which in 1980 raised $3 million from major contributors through a combined phone-mail effort.

Another idea that has been explored with some success is prospecting for new major donors by phone. Experiments in this area have been attempted on behalf of two of the NRSC's major contributor programs, with results consistently at least as cost-effective as prospecting by mail, thus opening up the possibility of expanded efforts to build the important major contributor files in upcoming years through the proven combination of phone and mail.

Another Case to Consider Formerly when you mentioned the telephone in connection with fund raising, the first and, in fact, only response you got was "telethon." In our exploration of innovative telephone fund-raising approaches, it is worth noting an interesting variation on the standard telethon format that was used to raise funds to support John Connally's bid for the Republican presidential nomination in 1980.

The Connally staff made arrangements to secure an hour of television air time on a coast-to-coast hookup that included both cable and independent stations. The telecast, which took place live on Valentine's Day, 1980, would be run in conjunction with receptions held in the homes of individual Connally supporters, where people would watch the broadcast together, hear a message from Governor Connally, and make contributions on the spot to the campaign.

Unlike the mass call-in efforts usually associated with a telethon, the contributions procedure was divided into three stages. First the hosts of the receptions would solicit contributions or pledges from those attending. These hosts would then call in their results to organizers on the state level who, in turn, would compile the tally for their area and call in these tabulated results to the central office in Atlanta, where the broadcast originated. The figures could then be presented to the viewing audience both state by state and as an overall total.

A critical factor in the success or failure of this effort was the number of supporters who could be persuaded to hold a party on Valentine's Day in their homes. These volunteer hosts would be responsible for contacting other Connally backers or potential backers and inviting them to attend, providing them with seating and refreshments, asking for and handling the contributions, and dealing with the usual preparation and cleanup chores of entertaining. This was not to be a low-income fund raiser, either—the goal for each home reception was set at $1,000. And the key to finding a substantial number of party givers and placing the necessary forms and instructions in their hands was a four-day telephone calling effort to a list of past Connally contributors.

Governor Connally *taped a brief message* to be played over the phone, providing the basic information about the upcoming telethon. After playing this message, the communicators returned to the line to ask if the respondent was willing to host a party and to answer any of the common questions that arose frequently, such as "Whom do I invite?" and "What kind of party do I give?"

There was a piggyback message in this phone campaign as well. If the listener did not want to host a home reception, the communicator moved on to a request for a contribution instead, to be counted as part of the telethon drive. This offered the respondent an opportunity to demonstrate his or her support without the bother of giving a party, and over 20 percent of those called chose this option. That figure is especially impressive when you consider that the phone presentation stressed an entirely different request, and that all the people contacted had already made substantial donations to the campaign within the year.

Of the 6,242 names of individuals who had contributed to the Connally campaign in 1979 that made up the total calling universe, 2,714 were actually reached in the four days of calling. The results of these 2,714 completed decisions are summarized in Table 9-2.

TABLE 9-2. *Results of the Connally Campaign*

Result	Number	Percentage
Agreed to host party	487	17.9
Agreed to contribute	582	21.4
(pledged specific amount)	(157)	(5.8)
Already agreed to host party	46	1.7
Already attending a party	58	2.1
Already contributed	99	3.7
Not interested	1,441	53.1
Special attention	1	0.04
Total completed decisions	2,714	100.00

It is noteworthy that the 157 people who pledged specific amounts contributed $7,130 (an average of $45.41 per pledge). Add in the pledges generated from the 425 people who agreed to contribute and consequently received envelopes and forms to do so, and the phone campaign more than paid for itself, even before the first dollar was received from its main objective, the Valentine's Day telethon parties.

Summary   As the political process has become more dependent on mass communications, the techniques employed to achieve the aims of gathering funds and swaying opinion have become increasingly sophisticated. The growing need for expertise and professionalism in making use of the public-contact media is particularly apparent in the political use of telephone.

Our traditional image of political action is still largely rooted in the idea of grass-roots activity—volunteers manning the offices, the streets, and the phones to reach out to the voting public. This basic level of involvement is still an important component of modern politics. However, these valuable human resources must be managed, controlled, and utilized with professional judgment and leadership.

In each of the cases we have examined in this section, the message conveyed through telephone was carefully crafted to create the desired impact. The program used professionally trained experts and cost-effective fund-raising management skills. Could volunteers have been used on the telephones? Absolutely. Would they have been as effective as trained telephone communicators? No, they couldn't possibly be directed, supervised, controlled via time-efficient scripts, and depended on to fill the 12-hour-per-day, 7-day-per-week production schedules! However, it is certain that unless the individuals on the phones, whether paid or unpaid, were trained and supervised in their efforts, the results would have been marginally productive at best and could possibly have become an area of expense and alienation, instead of a profitable operation utilizing friendly persuasion techniques. With its telephone fund-raising drive, the National Republican Senatorial Committee produced a massive turnaround in its financial health, as it left a disappointing 1979 and entered a triumphant 1980.

The role of centralized political committees supporting the campaigns of selected candidates across the country continues to grow. The three national Republican campaign committees mentioned in this case history—the Republican National Committee, the National Republican Congressional Committee, and the National Republican Senatorial

Committee—announced fund-raising results for the 1982 elections total-ing $173.3 million combined. This represented a record dollar level for either major political party, exceeding even presidential election cam-paigns of the past. There is no question that direct marketing was a key factor in achieving this enormous goal. And based on lessons learned in recent campaigns, telephone will continue to grow as the primary medium in the fund-raising effort.

Case History: Prospecting New Dollars for PBS

As government funding of nonprofit organizations fades in the face of budget-cutting fervor, and foundation grants become fewer and farther between, charities and philanthropic institutions are finding it more im-portant than ever to expand their contributor base. Widespread financial support insulates an organization against the potential disaster of a sudden shutoff of individual major funding sources. Prospecting for new contribu-tors, then, has taken on new prominence as a fund-raising activity, and it has become imperative that better ways to do it be found.

The standard approach to gaining additional contributors is direct-mail solicitation. Even with the increasing costs of this medium, it is still an effective method of delivering a fund-raising message to a mass audi-ence.

There is more to consider than how many people receive and open or read the fund raiser's message however; we are concerned with cost-efficient *response*. And when it comes to organizing an effective program for gaining new contributors and producing immediate income *from highly selective prospecting lists*, a modern telephone campaign can raise more money and generate more new additions to your contributor base than other, more traditional means, often at a lower cost per dollar raised!

The relative effectiveness of different fund-raising media is difficult to track. When a fund-raising drive is proceeding on several fronts, the in-termingling of influences on the audience creates a cumulative effect. Someone will often respond through the mail after having received a phone call asking for support or give a pledge on the phone after having received a mailing piece. There is also a recurring analytical problem caused by the lack of solid statistical data on the fulfillment ratio of tele-phone pledges. All too often, charities have simply taken their total re-ceipts from all forms of solicitations and banked them as soon as they arrived, without keeping accurate records of the media source that produced them.

There is, however, a "landmark" test conducted on behalf of the Ford Foundation for the Public Broadcasting Service (PBS) that will serve as a reliable documentation of telemarketing's relative fund-raising effectiveness.

Marketing Objectives   The program was called the "Station Independence Project." It was funded by the Ford Foundation, a major PBS financial supporter for many years, and designed to test the success of various media—phone, direct mail, on-air appeals, and print advertisements—in generating membership contributions for six local PBS stations. The idea behind the program was to uncover ways in which the system could rely more on individual contributors and less on major grants from corporations, foundations, and the government—to allow greater station independence.

Telemarketing Strategy   The program called for a fund-raising week to be held simultaneously at five widely scattered PBS stations—WNET in New York City, WCET in Cincinnati, KERA in Dallas, WCBB in Portland, Maine, and KQED in San Francisco. A follow-up effort was undertaken a few months later on behalf of WHYY in Philadelphia. All calling was done by a professional telemarketing agency, working with fully scripted phone presentations developed in conjunction with PBS and individual station management.

In conjunction with on-air membership drive segments, which appealed for phone-in pledges, extensive lists of high-potential membership prospects were gathered and segmented into test panels that would reveal the relative responses generated by phone alone, mail alone, and phone plus mail.

The test was structured to maintain strict segregation of results from each panel, not only by noting the amount that was originally pledged but by maintaining a separate account of the actual fulfillment of those pledges. This was accomplished through a lock box arrangement with the bank—the contributions would arrive at their number-coded box at the bank as per the code number on the business reply envelope that pledgees received. Here the money was tabulated and placed directly into the station's account. The amount of each contribution was written on the envelope as it came in, and these envelopes were immediately forwarded to the stations. This arrangement made it possible to keep an accurate record of the percentage of phone appeal pledges that were actually paid. The system also quickly identified those who had not yet sent in their money. A series of up to four follow-up letters could begin promptly if the pledged donation was not received within 10 days.

List Segmentation   It is impossible to overstress the importance of using the best possible prospect list in any direct-response effort. Happily for the Public Broadcasting Service program, there were sources of very high-potential prospects already on hand at the individual stations, and further appropriate names were readily available, based on the clearly defined demographics of the PBS audience.

The lists used broke down into four major categories as follows:

■ **Lapsed members.** As in so many consumer sales programs, these "former customers" of PBS represented hot prospects. They had demonstrated their interest with contributions in the past and often needed only a reminder to convince them to rejoin the ranks of loyal station supporters. Phone is particularly effective in this area, since a "reminder" in the form of a personal phone call can be far more thought-provoking to the lapsed member than another easily-disposed-of piece of mail advertising might be. A further benefit in using the station's lapsed member lists is the fact that all these names have already been carefully filed and organized.

■ **Viewers.** PBS programs generate viewer response. This can be in the form of a request for a program guide that accompanies a particular series, an inquiry regarding the whereabouts of a favorite show, or the frequent letters criticizing or praising an individual program offering.

These correspondents have identified themselves as PBS viewers—and involved viewers at that. Their names constitute an excellent prospecting universe. The only problem, in the case of the Station Independence Project testing, was that no systematic effort had been made to file, sort, and control these names or to sort out the duplications with the current member and lapsed member lists. When this was done relatively on the spur of the moment for this fund-raising program, the list preparation process proved both time-consuming and expensive, producing costly delays in the calling effort. However, the calls to this market segment were extremely successful, and many of those who responded positively were brand-new members, a very valuable acquisition.

To support a continuing program, the efficient handling of viewer names as they were received would be an integral part of day-to-day station procedure, and this important list could then be made available quickly and economically.

- **Local lists.** This set of names (the largest market segment used) consisted of membership rolls in local chapters of organizations such as the Audubon Society, professional rosters of educators, doctors, lawyers, and artists, and buyers of merchandise in previous station fund-raising auctions.
- **National lists.** This panel consisted of rented list segments from national organizations—political, environmental, and wildlife campaign contributors, subscribers to *Saturday Review, Psychology Today*, and *Intellectual Digest*, donors to cultural institutions, and so on—that fell within each station's broadcasting radius.

Creative Strategy For a fund-raising effort to succeed, it is important to stress the *benefits* derived by the giver as well as the cause or institution in soliciting a donation. Giving to the American Cancer Society or the local hospital, church, or scouting group may have no immediate or discernible effect on one's daily life. But there are real and desirable rewards for making such contributions—the personal satisfactions of giving, long-term improvements in health care or community conditions, and so on—that can and must be "sold" to prospective contributors.

Public television cannot draw on the emotional impact of a campaign to alleviate suffering or help the downtrodden masses for its fund-raising appeals. However, there are certain very distinct benefits to the viewer-contributor that have been capitalized on by PBS with great success.

The most apparent benefit derived from contributing, of course, is making possible the continuing offering of a special kind of programming—cultural, intellectual, controversial, educational, entertaining, and uninterrupted by commercials—that distinguishes PBS from commercial networks. There is, therefore, a direct, personal, and immediate benefit to the viewer. Often the viewer's children benefit as well, which is a very strong drawing card when it comes to motivating contributors.

The special nature of PBS programming also carries with it a sense of cultural elitism. Viewers consider themselves more involved than the average TV watcher and, as part of the central concept of a membership drive, this feeling has been a cornerstone of PBS fund-raising. Viewers are not simply asked to "send in your contribution to the station"—they are asked to become *members* of *that* station, part of an enlightened fraternity of loyal supporters who appreciate the finer aspects of television and are willing to demonstrate their enthusiasm by paying for the privilege of watching.

Some effort is expended during the course of the year to maintain the involvement of station members on a continuing basis. Members receive a monthly program guide that describes upcoming programs on the station in the weeks ahead. As the programs are introduced on the air, the fact that a particular offering was produced or purchased with member-contributed funds is prominently mentioned. Often premiums are offered with a membership pledge—a tote bag or umbrella, for instance, prominently displaying the station logo to serve as an identifying status symbol for the contributor. All this costs money, of course, but it is designed in conjunction with another basic tenet of fund-raising—it is acceptable to produce a break-even income on the contributor's initial donation, since that new contributor is very likely to become a continuing donor in future years, and those repeat contributions can be solicited at a much lower cost.

How does all this relate to a telephone presentation? First, it points out a major way in which the characteristics of phone solicitation dovetail with the contributor profile. The personalized, one-to-one contact by phone understandably appeals to the ego of the recipient far more strongly than an impersonal fund-raising letter. PBS contributors like to feel that they are very special people—the phone call fits well with that feeling.

When it comes to the call format itself, the use of a taped message—and the selection of the right taped message for the audience being reached—is critical. For the PBS program, several well-known television personalities, including Julia Child, William F. Buckley, and Alistair Cooke, were used, as well as certain local personalities important within their regions, such as former Senator Margaret Chase Smith for WCBB in Maine and newspaper columnist Arthur Hoppe for San Francisco's KQED. As an example of the sort of appeal that these celebrity spokespeople offered their listeners, here is a transcript of the taped message by Margaret Chase Smith:

I WANT TO EXPRESS TO YOU MY SUPPORT OF PUBLIC BROADCASTING FOR THE PEOPLE OF LEWISTON AND PORTLAND. AS YOU KNOW, COMMERCIAL TELEVISION HAS BEEN ATTACKED BY CHARGES OF REPORTING BIAS AND DETERIORATING QUALITY CAUSED BY THE NEED TO MAKE MONEY. WHILE I DO NOT AGREE WITH ALL OF THESE CHARGES, AND I DO THINK SOME COMMERCIAL TELEVISION PROVIDES EXCELLENT QUALITY ENTERTAINMENT AND SOME REPORTING IS TRULY OUTSTANDING IN ITS OBJECTIVITY AND RESTRAINT FROM BIAS, I FEEL THAT WE HAVE A DESPERATE NEED FOR THE PUBLIC BROADCASTING SERVICE WITH THE INNOVATION AND OBJECTIVITY ITS FREEDOM FROM COMMERCIALIZATION CAN PROVIDE. I AM INFORMED THAT WCBB-TV, THE PUBLIC BROADCASTING SERVICE IN LEWISTON/PORT-

LAND, IS IN A MOST PRECARIOUS FINANCIAL POSITION BECAUSE IT
RECEIVES NO COMMERCIAL OR ADVERTISING MONIES. FOR WCBB-
TV TO DIE WOULD BE A TRAGEDY, FOR IT WOULD MEAN THE LOSS OF
THE FINE CULTURAL, EDUCATIONAL, AND PUBLIC INTEREST PRO-
GRAMS TO YOU AND ME. WE WOULD LOSE SESAME STREET, MASTER-
PIECE THEATRE, WORLD PRESS, JULIA CHILD, AND SO MANY OTHER
QUALITY PROGRAMS FREE OF COMMERCIAL PRESSURES.

PUBLIC BROADCASTING MAKES YOU ITS PRIMARY RESPONSIBILITY—
THAT'S THE KEY AND SECRET TO ITS QUALITY SUCCESS. BUT IT'S NOT A
ONE-WAY STREET, AND YOUR FINANCIAL HELP IS DESPERATELY
NEEDED. THE MOST EFFECTIVE WAY YOU CAN HELP AND SAVE WCBB-
TV IS TO BECOME A MEMBER OF IT. THE TELEPHONE COMMUNICATOR
WILL BE HAPPY TO TAKE YOUR MEMBERSHIP PLEDGE AND ANSWER ANY
QUESTIONS YOU MAY HAVE. THANK YOU FOR TAKING THE TIME TO
LISTEN TO MY PLEA FOR WCBB-TV.

That simple, straightforward message drew membership pledges from
nearly 40 percent of those contacted in Maine. On the national level, the
best response was to a tape by Alistair Cooke, the mellifluous-voiced
British-accented host whose weekly introduction to the popular *Masterpiece Theatre* series is so strongly emblematic of what public broadcasting
means and what it offers to its viewers. The transcript of his taped appeal
appears in Figure 9-3. A spoken message from a respected celebrity figure
delivered in a one-to-one format through a telephone conversation has
proved a powerful tool for generating membership pledges.

Results Table 9-3 presents a summary of telephone pledge results and
fulfillment statistics for the five stations in the initial PBS calling campaign.

The figures show a substantial variation from station to station, but
even at the low end of the spectrum, more than one in five people reached
made a pledge, and in the best case, at WCBB, not only were the pledges
at a high of over 35 percent but the percentage of pledges fulfilled and the
percentage of pledged monies actually received were the highest in the
test as well. It is also worth noting that, without exception, the average
contribution returned was higher than the average amount initially
pledged.

Another important point to consider in evaluating these results is the
test nature of the program. The effort here was to try out a wide range of
spokespeople with a number of different list segments—selecting the *best*
taped messages and the *best* lists and targeting the calling effort even more
tightly; optimizing the overall response was the next logical step, and it
promised an even more positive level of response.

SUGGESTED TAPE MESSAGE FOR ALISTAIR COOKE ON BEHALF OF
P.B.S.

HELLO, THIS IS ALISTAIR COOKE. FOR SOME TIME, I'VE HAD THE GREAT PLEASURE TO
HOST MASTERPIECE THEATER FOR THE PUBLIC BROADCASTING SYSTEM. IN THIS TIME, I'VE
COME TO BELIEVE THAT FOR MANY AMERICAN VIEWERS, THE BEST SOURCE OF FREE FLOWING
INFORMATION AND TRULY INNOVATIVE HIGH QUALITY ENTERTAINMENT IS PUBLIC BROADCASTING.

A) AND YET, WCBB-TV, THE PUBLIC BROADCASTING STATION IN
LEWISTON IS IN TROUBLE.

B) AND YET, WQED-TV, THE PUBLIC BROADCASTING STATION IN
SAN FRANCISCO IS IN TROUBLE.

C) AND YET, KERA-TV, THE PUBLIC BROADCASTING STATION IN
DALLAS IS IN TROUBLE.

D) AND YET, WCET-TV, CHANNEL 48, THE PUBLIC BROADCASTING
STATION IN CINCINNATI, IS IN TROUBLE.

E) AND YET, WNET-TV, CHANNEL 13, THE PUBLIC BROADCASTING
STATION IN NEW YORK, IS IN TROUBLE.

LIKE ITS SISTER STATIONS ACROSS THE COUNTRY, IT'S PLACED IN THE MOST PRECARIOUS
FINANCIAL POSITION BECAUSE IT RECEIVES NO COMMERCIAL OR ADVERTISING MONIES. IF
PUBLIC BROADCASTING IS TO SURVIVE IT MUST DEPEND ON YOU - THE VIEWER. I BELIEVE
IF PUBLIC BROADCASTING IS ALLOWED TO DIE IN AMERICA, NOT ONLY WILL FINE CULTURAL,
EDUCATIONAL AND PUBLIC INTEREST PROGRAMS BE LOST AND SHOWS LIKE MASTERPIECE
THEATER NO LONGER BE POSSIBLE, BUT AN OPPORTUNITY TO ACHIEVE A NEW KIND OF AUDIENCE -

CAMPAIGN COMMUNICATIONS INSTITUTE OF AMERICA, INC.

-2-

BROADCASTER RELATIONSHIP, BASED ON MUTUAL INTEREST AND INTERACTION WILL PASS - AND
MIGHT NEVER BE ACHIEVED AGAIN. FOR ME, PUBLIC BROADCASTING HERE, LIKE THE B.B.C.
IN ENGLAND, IS A MEDIUM CONCERNED WITH BRINGING YOU QUALITY PROGRAMING -
STUNNING DRAMA - BEAUTIFUL MUSIC AND DANCE, ENCHANTING CHILDREN'S SHOWS AND A
DEEPER INSIGHT INTO OUR WORLD - FREE OF COMMERCIAL OR POLITICAL PRESSURES - WITH
YOU AS ITS PRIMARY RESPONSIBILITY. I URGE YOU TO SUPPORT PUBLIC BROADCASTING
AT THIS CRITICAL TIME. ALL OF US KNOW THAT IT'S PEOPLE LIKE YOU WHO ARE INTERESTED
IN WHAT WE HAVE TO SAY AND WHAT WE'VE BEEN DOING - BUT NOW WE NEED MORE THAN
YOUR INTEREST - - - - - -WE MUST HAVE YOUR FINANCIAL BACKING AS WELL.
WON'T YOU BECOME A MEMBER OF YOUR LOCAL PUBLIC BROADCASTING STATION? OUR
TELEPHONE COMMUNICATOR WILL BE HAPPY TO TAKE YOUR MEMBERSHIP PLEDGE AND ANSWER
ANY QUESTIONS YOU MAY HAVE. IN ANY CASE, ON BEHALF OF PUBLIC BROADCASTING AND
MYSELF, THANK YOU.

CAMPAIGN COMMUNICATIONS INSTITUTE OF AMERICA, INC.

Figure 9-3. Script for Alistair Cooke.

TABLE 9-3. *Station Independence Project—Phone Result Summary*

	Total completed calls	Pledged	Amount pledged	Average pledged	Contributions received	Return	Average contribution
WNET (New York, N.Y.)	7,575	31.5% (2,384)	$34,379	$14.42	$26,393	76.8%	$17.69
WCBB (Portland, Maine)	2,579	36.1% (930)	$10,248	$11.02	$ 9,614	93.8%	$16.52
WCET (Cincinnati, Ohio)	1,828	25.5% (466)	$ 5,417	$11.62	$ 4,219	77.9%	$14.45
KERA (Dallas, Texas)	3,232	22.7% (735)	$12,367	$16.83	$ 9,096	73.6%	$19.77
KQED (San Francisco, Calif.)	2,783	28.6% (797)	$12,724	$15.96	$10,260	80.6%	$20.56
Program total	17,997	29.5% (5,312)	$75,135	$14.14	$59,582	79.3%	$17.92

For example, the percentage of respondents who pledged overall comes to just under 29 percent. However, the lapsed member list segment responded at a 5 percent higher rate, and their average pledge was $1 more than the national average as well (see chart below). Phone achieves its greatest profitability when the approach used and the audience targeted are chosen selectively.

Type of list	Percentage pledging	Average pledge
Lapsed members	34.01%	$15.85
Viewers	30.13%	$12.62
Local lists	27.42%	$14.22
National lists	25.98%	$12.24

Phone versus Mail The direct-mail pieces sent out for the Station Independence Project were also designed by the Rapp and Collins agency, now a subsidiary of Doyle, Dane and Bernbach advertising agency, to test different approaches to the market, including varying premium offers, printed materials, and list segments. By analyzing the response levels and cost factors demonstrated for both the phone and mail segments of the test, reasonable projections of the results to be expected in a high-volume direct-marketing program were made in order to allow a direct comparison of the two media operating independently.

For a large-scale direct-mail solicitation, a 2 percent response rate was achieved, producing an average contribution of $15 at a cost per letter of 15 cents, in that less costly era.

For phone, of course, the projected cost per contact is significantly higher, plus a surcharge for invoicing and follow-up letters for each pledge taken by phone. However, the foundation's test results indicated that 30 percent of those called will pledge a donation and that 80 percent of those who pledge will have fulfilled by the time three follow-up letters have been sent after the initial invoice. At $18, the average phone-generated contribution is also higher.

In short, the cost per dollar raised works out to 50 percent with direct mail and only 40 percent with telephone—25 percent more would be raised with phone than with direct mail for the same initial investment, based on these projections. And these proportions will hold true whatever the size of the budget.

Of course, the original test was conducted in 1973, and costs have changed considerably since then. However, the cost of the actual phone calls has climbed far more slowly than postage rates and printing costs over the same period. Therefore, the effect of time has been to magnify the *difference* between mail and phone effectiveness in this type of highly select marketing program. Given the same basic response data and factoring in higher prices and inflation, we can make a rough calculation of up-to-date comparative figures as follows:

1982 cost per letter (large-scale direct-mail solicitation)	$ .30
1982 cost per completed telephone call	2.50
1982 follow-up direct-mail cost per phone pledge	.75

What does this indicate when it comes to allocating funds between the two media? The figures shown in Table 9-4 are based on the preceding projections and a budget of $50,000.

Another significant point to consider in evaluating the contrast between the mail and phone campaigns is that mail and phone work better in combination, *but* phone makes use of the available lists far more personally than the direct-mail approach. It maximizes the return from "market segments" that are highly productive but limited in number—the station viewer and lapsed member lists, for example, in this program.

TABLE 9-4. *Direct Mail versus Telephone:*
Projections of Comparative Fund
*Raising Income and Response for PBS**

Mail budget	$50,000
Appeals delivered	166,667
Response rate	2%
Total contributors	3,333
Average projected contribution	$30.00
Total raised	$100,000
Net return	$50,000
Telephone budget ($50,000)	
Appeals delivered	15,385
Response rate	30%
Total pledging	4,615
After 80% conversion	
Total contributors	3,692
Average projected contribution	$33.85
Total raised	$125,000
Net return	$75,000

* Using 1982 current direct mail and CCI tele-funding programs as a cost/expense model.

Additional Testing—Phone plus mail versus Phone Alone or Mail Alone A few months after the five-station test, a further program was conducted on behalf of WHYY, the public broadcasting station in Philadelphia. Here 5,075 calls were completed to a selection of local residents drawn from the mailing lists of *Time, Intellectual Digest,* and other appropriate magazines. The call approach was essentially the same as that developed in the earlier program, using the successful Alistair Cooke taped message. In the Philadelphia test, though, 80 percent of those called had received a fund-raising mailing piece a week before—20 percent of those called had not received the mailing. Additional market panels received only the mailing, without calls.

The overall telephone response rate for this effort was 25.81 percent, pledging a total of $16,350 for an average pledge of $12.48. The phone response by those who had not received a mailing was slightly higher than for those who had, but the difference was not statistically significant. What was extremely important was the enormous effect that the phone effort had on the mail response—the panels that received both mail and phone solicitation produced a mail response *three times* that produced by the mail-alone panel.

This is particularly revealing when it comes to the question of the fulfillment on phone pledges. The WHYY test produced a very high rate of direct fulfillment of telephone pledges—about 80 percent of the people who had pledged over the phone sent in contributions using the business reply envelopes sent to them specifically for this purpose. However, the test also offers an indication of the number of people who, after pledging by phone, send in their contributions through other PBS direct-mail return envelopes that had recently also arrived at their homes. In other words, the difference between normal mail response and *actual* mail response to the phone-plus-mail approach added nearly 10 percent to the phone-pledges finally received.

Therefore, we can project that where telephone alone will draw a healthy fulfillment level of pledges, direct mail sent in the *same* fund-raising effort will not only pay for itself but will add significantly to the actual cash total received in the integrated media effort.

Summary The Station Independence Project is still a major demonstration of telemarketing's power to motivate new contributor commitments. Under the circumstances involved in this effort, telephone proved to be even more cost-effective than direct-mail solicitation. Prospecting for new members is a difficult undertaking, and it would be inaccurate to state that telephone will *usually* be superior to mail or other media in accomplishing this goal. The relative merits of different media will depend on the specifics of the individual situation.

The key elements that distinguished the historic PBS project and helped to make it a telephone success include:

- Highly selective lists
- Strong fund-raising appeal
- Substantial average contribution level
- Availability of persuasive spokespeople

Implications for Fund Raisers   The primary lesson to be learned here for those involved in efforts to expand their organization's active contributor file is that systematic, professional-quality telephone contact will produce a significant incremental number of new donors. It is widely accepted that the costs involved in gaining new contributors are high and destined to remain so. However, the relative value of these new contributors over time justifies substantial initial expense in acquiring them.

The test program conducted for PBS indicates that telephone *did* work exceptionally well in this area, but it does not prove that telephone *will* work well in any other individual case. While it is clearly demonstrated that telephone contact with nonresponding past contributors will usually produce very profitable returns, it's probably too costly to think of telephone as a "prospecting" medium for new donors except in very special situations. It does strongly indicate that well-informed fund raisers should test the effect of including telephone contact in their multimedia efforts.

The PBS case also provides a framework for organizing and assessing the test program. Different messages and test panels should be evaluated separately. Results of the individual elements in the program should be tracked separately to allow accurate conclusions to be drawn. And keep in mind that the effect of telephone contact on mail response is a crucial factor in the overall value of the campaign—it must be carefully examined and considered.

In this chapter we have examined a range of telephone fund-raising techniques within the sphere of nonprofit campaigning. In each case, the strategy of the calling effort was tailored to the audience to which it was directed. For smaller-dollar contributors, the aim was to produce immediate contributions, with a straightforward, highly personal request. With higher-dollar contributors, the phone fulfills a more complex role as a personalized service tool, giving major donors the one-to-one attention they expect with a new, economically viable efficiency.

Whatever the audience, a key element is the frequency of the personal contact that can be achieved through telephone. It all goes back to that all-important sense of "belief" in an ongoing or current membership in the cause or organization. Establishing and maintaining this feeling can be achieved to some degree through mail. However, the difference between receiving a piece of a mass mailing—even when it is fully computer-personalized—and receiving a personal phone call from someone who shares your convictions has been demonstrated time and time again.

Note: During the period of the finance campaigns, Finance Director Wyatt Stewart III was responsible for raising over $15 million from a combination of telephone and direct mail techniques alone, according to Representative Guy Van der Jagt, Chairman of the NRCC; and Robert Perkins served as Executive Director of the Finance Committee of the RNC during this period.

chapter ten /

Establishing and Refining
In-House Telemarketing
Facilities

By the late 1970s, escalating business costs and the need for an alternative marketing system converged and set the stage for the growth of telemarketing as we know it today. Concurrently, professional telemarketing had sufficiently matured to be recognized as an effective, cost-saving supplement or alternative to traditional methods. With such recognition at the boardroom level, many of the Fortune 500 were prepared to make serious commitments to the development of dedicated in-house facilities, just as they had years before when corporate marketing and corporate advertising departments were being established.

By this time, some telemarketing professionals were well into their second decade of industry development. As this book illustrates, the viability of myriad applications for both business and consumer markets had been tested. Operational systems and controls were well defined. The most efficient equipment and line-usage configurations were understood.

Given this situation, it was unnecessary for companies that had little or no experience with the medium to "reinvent the wheel." By using the expertise of agencies in a consulting capacity, these corporations could very quickly develop an effective in-house operation, avoiding many of the pitfalls of the learning experience.

In this chapter we will look at two case histories of major United States corporations that established in-house operations in that manner.

Case History: Company X and the High Cost of Selling

Company X, an international reprographic equipment manufacturer, had developed its business very profitably in the past by concentrating field sales efforts against the higher end of the market. Due to substantial average revenue per sale to this segment, intensive, specialized sales training had been cost-justified. The average cost per sales call, in 1978, was approaching $200. However, market conditions were changing rapidly. Technological advances resulting in more compact, lower-cost machines capable of performing the dry process put high-quality copying equipment within easy reach of small businesses. Foreign competitors, less encumbered by the traditional field selling and distribution network, were able to capitalize quickly on the new and expanding opportunity. Trends in market-share figures clearly illustrated the condition.

Prior to 1978, Company X had tested telephone in ways unrelated to this situation. Also, those previous tests, conducted by an agency, had been limited in scope by both their short-term objectives and their focus on client management.

Here was a situation ripe with opportunity, a fundamental problem affecting the basic business of Company X and an awareness of the availability of professional services that could provide a solution.

Marketing Objectives and Strategy   The mission was clear: to decrease the cost of selling substantially and thereby enable the low end of the market to be penetrated. Telephone was to be the kingpin in the new marketing strategy, utilized to generate, screen, and qualify leads in a systematic, "industrialized" fashion. Expensive personal selling time could then be applied to follow up leads in a controllable and efficient manner. The project was labeled "Team Selling."

While the concept was logically conceived and beautifully simple, both client and agency anticipated the difficulties of implementation. Company X's salespeople, among the best (and probably most expensive!) in the world, had been hired because of strong independent personal characteristics not easily adaptable to the Team Selling strategy. The training program and existing compensation plan also worked against the idea. If team selling was going to be successful, changes of ingrained human behavior as well as certain external forces that supported and encouraged the behavior had to be made.

Test Design and Implementation Five test markets (branches) were chosen—two in the United States, one in Canada, and two in the United Kingdom. List segments from two sources were selected, one from the in-house prospect list compiled by salespeople, the other from a major business list compiler. Preliminary creative work produced tightly structured scripted presentations that both agency and client felt would generate the quality of lead required. Additionally, scripting was designed to gather key market information to assist in any subsequent sales contact and provide market data for analysis.

Initial test calls, to the 2 United States branches, were made from the agency's telephone workshop. During this phase various approaches to the script were tested and refined.

The key to script development was to construct a presentation that would elicit from the prospect information required to "grade" the lead. At the same time, the script would have to provide for different levels of selling based on lead quality. For instance, a comprehensive telephone sales presentation to a poor potential prospect would be an economically inefficient use of telephone time, undermining the "industrialized" approach mentioned earlier. Furthermore, leads referred to the sales force for follow-up had to be sufficiently qualified and interested to increase sales conversion rates and ensure the continued cooperation and enthusiasm of the sales force. The final version of the presentation used is illustrated by this transcript of a call made from one of the facilities in the United Kingdom:

COMMUNICATOR: Good morning, Mr. Sinclair? This is Rosemary Palfrey calling for (Company X) and our Director of Operations, Mr. _____ . He's asked me to call because we've just introduced some new products and services, and we're interested to know if they might be applicable to the British Ore Society. To that end, I wonder if I might ask you a few questions?

PROSPECT: Yes, of course.

COMMUNICATOR: Do you currently have any copying equipment?

PROSPECT: Yes, we have.

COMMUNICATOR: And what brand is that?

PROSPECT: It's (competitive brand).

COMMUNICATOR: Is it your own machine, Mr. Sinclair, or is it on lease?

PROSPECT: It's on lease.

COMMUNICATOR: And about how long have you had it?

PROSPECT: Well, it expires in February next year.

COMMUNICATOR: What are the types of documents that you're copying on it, sir?

PROSPECT: Well, it's general office correspondence, mainly.

COMMUNICATOR: What about volume, would you say you did as many as 50 copies a week, or is that underestimating?

PROSPECT: Oh, more than that, I'd say about 3,000 a month.

COMMUNICATOR: Do you have any duplicating or printing equipment?

PROSPECT: Yes, we have a (brand) duplicating machine.

COMMUNICATOR: Mr. Sinclair, do you ever have the need for outside printing on company letterhead?

PROSPECT: Yes, we do on occasion.

COMMUNICATOR: And what about the need for larger volume copying work; do you ever have to have that done for you?

PROSPECT: Yes, we do. You know, we actually have looked at this quite hard. We have peaks in volume at times, where we could use one of your larger machines. But this only happens periodically.

COMMUNICATOR: I see. Thank you very much for the information, Mr. Sinclair. Because of what you've told me, I'd like you to hear a brief message recorded on tape by Mr. _____ , our Director of Operations. He talks about recent (Company X) developments in products and services for companies similar to yours. The message is about two minutes long, and I can put it over the phone for you now. Would that be all right, Mr. Sinclair?

PROSPECT: Yes, that's fine.

COMMUNICATOR: I'll put it on now, and then I'll be back on the line right after it's finished.

HELLO, MY NAME IS _____ , DIRECTOR OF OPERATIONS FOR (COMPANY X). I HAVE CHOSEN THIS SPECIAL WAY TO REACH YOU BECAUSE I WANT TO TELL YOU PERSONALLY ABOUT A VARIETY OF NEW PRODUCTS AND SERVICES THAT MANAGERS OF COMPANIES YOUR SIZE HAVE BEEN REQUESTING FOR THE PAST FEW YEARS.

WE RECOGNIZE THAT YOU WANT FROM (COMPANY X) A RANGE OF COPYING EQUIPMENT TO MATCH YOUR NEEDS. AND BECAUSE WE REALIZE THAT IT MIGHT BE IN YOUR BEST INTEREST TO OWN YOUR COPIER, WE WILL MAKE IT EASIER FOR YOU BY FINANCING YOUR PURCHASE AND GIVING YOU A TRADE-IN ALLOWANCE FOR YOUR OLD MACHINE. YOU CAN CHOOSE TO OWN OR LEASE THE (COMPANY X) (BRAND)—WHICH, BY THE WAY, WAS RECENTLY ADJUDGED BY AN INDE-

PENDENT SOURCE TO REPRESENT ONE OF THE BEST VALUES IN LOW-COST PLAIN-PAPER COPIERS—FOR AS LITTLE AS £1 PER DAY.

AND, BASED ON YOUR NEEDS, WE CAN ALSO OFFER A COMPLETE RANGE OF COMPACT COPIERS THAT PERFORM FUNCTIONS THAT YOU SPECIFICALLY REQUIRE. ARE YOU AWARE, FOR EXAMPLE, THAT (COMPANY X) CAN ACCELERATE YOUR MAILINGS BY COPYING YOUR MAILING LIST ONTO GUMMED LABELS AND YOUR LETTERS ONTO YOUR COMPANY LETTERHEAD. (COMPANY X) IS ALSO ABLE TO SAVE YOU PROCESSING TIME BY COLLATING REPORTS AS YOU COPY.

OUR EQUIPMENT CAN CUT YOUR COST BECAUSE WE USE PLAIN PAPER AND ARE ABLE TO REDUCE LARGE DOCUMENTS TO STANDARD SIZE, AND CAN EVEN COPY ONTO BOTH SIDES OF A SHEET OF PAPER. I AM CONFIDENT THAT WE HAVE A COPIER FOR YOUR COMPANY'S UNIQUE NEEDS. I WANT TO BE SURE THAT (COMPANY X) IS PAYING ATTENTION TO YOU. WE WOULD LIKE THE OPPORTUNITY TO PROVE JUST HOW MUCH (COMPANY X'S) RECENT DEVELOPMENTS CAN BENEFIT YOU AND YOUR COMPANY.

WHEN MY COLLEAGUE COMES BACK ON THE LINE, SHE WILL ANSWER ANY QUESTIONS YOU MIGHT HAVE AND, IF YOU WISH, ARRANGE A SALES VISIT BY OUR REPRESENTATIVE ASSIGNED TO YOUR COMPANY. THANK YOU FOR YOUR TIME. NOW HERE IS MY COLLEAGUE.

COMMUNICATOR: Did you hear that all right, Mr. Sinclair?

PROSPECT: Yes, thank you.

COMMUNICATOR: Obviously, from what Mr. _____ said, we realize that you require more information about how (Company X) has developed to more directly suit your requirements. We do have a sales representative, Mr. _____ , assigned to your company, and he would be happy to more fully explain our new products and services and how they could benefit your business. Would you be free next week?

PROSPECT: Yes, but not until Thursday.

COMMUNICATOR: That's fine, let me just check Mr. _____'s schedule to see what time on Thursday he would be available. Hold on just a moment please. (Pause.) Mr. Sinclair, Mr. _____ could come and see you at 2:30 on Thursday, if that's convenient for you. Would that be OK?

PROSPECT: Yes, that's OK.

COMMUNICATOR: Good, Mr. Sinclair, Mr. _____ will be in to see you on Thursday the 25th at 2:30. Now Mr. Sinclair, is there anything at all that I can tell Mr. _____ that might help him provide any special information you might need?

PROSPECT: No, actually not, I think I've given you an accurate picture, and I'll look forward to talking in depth with him on Thursday.

COMMUNICATOR: Fine, thank you for the information you've given me, and we'll look forward to seeing you on Thursday. Good-bye.

Along with script testing and refinement, the required measurement- and lead-tracking systems were developed. After the initial test, volume calling to the United States branches was continued from the agency. The modularized components of the program were then installed by agency consultants in the Canadian affiliate agency operation.

The final phase of program setup in the United Kingdom followed a different format. There, telemarketing facilities had to be established on-site, at the two branch locations participating in the program. This was done by an agency consultant, over a period of six months. The program included:

- Blueprints for facility layout
- Design of telephone equipment configurations
- Recruitment, screening, and hiring of personnel for supervisory, communicator, tabulation, and clerical positions
- Personnel training for all functions
- Development of procedures for interaction between facility and branch personnel and for information transfer from facility to branch and corporate

Results Results, of course, had to be viewed in two stages: the up-front telephone response and the back-end sales evaluation of leads generated and sales conversion rates.

Figures varied by list sources and country; the following is representative of telephone response rates by communicator hour; total dialings, 18.

	Number	Percent
Leads (immediate appointment)	0.6	10.9
Leads (future follow-up)	1.2	21.8
Not currently a viable prospect	3.7	67.3
Total completed presentations to decision makers	5.5	100.0

Total dialings   18

Prior to the phone program, the salespeople were applying their selling time to the entire prospect universe. As the above figures indicate, 67 percent of that universe was not qualified. It is important to note here that the criteria for qualification during the phone presentation had been defined by the sales force. The greatest benefit of the telephone program was that it segmented the universe, allowing salespeople to do what they had been extensively trained to do, make presentations to prospects—only where a degree of product need and therefore a predisposition to buy existed. In the main, the prospecting function of field sales, requiring as much as 60 percent of a salesperson's time, had been assumed by the much more efficient and considerably less expensive telephone.

As with any sales force lead-generation program, measuring the thoroughness of follow-up and the ultimate conversion rate was both difficult and essential. The procedures established involved a daily feedback report by salespeople to a liaison within the telephone facility. These daily verbal reports were substantiated by individual follow-up documentation for each lead. The data were compiled and issued in a weekly lead-tracking report.

On average, approximately 20 percent of first-time visits resulted in a classification referred to as "rejects," meaning no current potential existed and no additional sales follow-up was required. However 7 percent of leads resulted in an immediate order, and an additional 70 percent fell into one of several pending categories, requiring additional visits, equipment demonstrations in-branch, and so on. Fundamentally, sales conversion rates were increased dramatically, in some cases by as much as 200 percent!

In summary, the test program was considered very successful in the Canadian and United Kingdom markets and was rolled-out all over the worldwide Company X branch network. It was aborted in the United States after the test, due in large measure to the intransigence and resistance of the domestic sales force. "Large copiers mean larger commissions, so why concentrate on small ones? It just means working harder for the same return," a sales rep explained. Abroad, where the sales force traditionally had been involved with "small machines" and were more motivated, they tried harder and increased profits by 30 percent via the new telemarketing techniques.

Management recognized the need for change due to a rapidly declining market share and developed the "retail store" as one antidote to the lack of field sales motivation. "Bring the prospect to the store demonstration" is today's framework for selling photocopiers, computers, word processors, and all other electronic office equipment.

Every direct-marketing and advertising tool is synchronized into a multimedia effort to motivate "store traffic"—TV, radio, print, direct mail, billboards, car cards, and discount coupons—but *telephone invitations* by trained, skilled communicators in each store's trading area, reaching "just those prospects most likely to buy," still brings in the most cost-efficient and profitable sales.

Our experience with lack of motivation from a sales force dramatizes the problem faced by practically all the Fortune 1,000 United States companies, because telemarketing programs demand "tight controls" over leads and sales appointments for cost-efficient management. They're a threatening experience for most sales organizations. One of the solutions is to use the phone to sell directly without requiring sales force interface! Many such totally accountable successful telemarketing programs on behalf of various products and services have been developed from start-up and "turn-key." They are today fully operating workshops profitably offering thousand-dollar electronic typewriters, multi-thousand-dollar copiers, processors, microcomputers, machinery of all kinds as well as expensive software and peripheral electronic data processing hardware—directly by phone.

Case History: Telemarketing and the Remote Branch Network

A major consumer finance organization, with over 500 branches nationwide, had engaged informally in telemarketing at the branch level for a few years. Loan officers, whose primary function was making face-to-face presentations to walk-in prospects, were also charged with phoning current borrowers in an attempt to persuade them to upgrade their loans and past borrowers in order to generate new loans.

Corporate management realized the potential positive impact that a well-structured, centrally controlled effort could have on revenue. It was clear that the more successful branches had integrated a telephone effort into normal daily branch activity to a larger degree than lower-performing branches in the network. To further substantiate the relationship between the level of telemarketing activity and branch performance and to determine the feasibility of structuring a standard telephone program that could be monitored and controlled by corporate management, an agency was hired to audit 15 branches that represented a cross-section of the network.

The audit indicated that both the amount and effectiveness of telephone activity could be increased. Level of telephone usage and quality of call presentation varied significantly by branch and within the branch according to the individual. These variations were a function of branch management, training, discipline, and control as well as individual caller capability.

Marketing Objectives and Strategy The core of the problem was that, while highly accountable to corporate management in other areas, branches were allowed to conduct telephone activity in a relatively autonomous fashion. After the audit, and several visits by client management to observe an actual operational phone workshop, the practical solution resolving the need for new methods and controls became apparent.

In the course of its business development, the agency[1] had created methods that ensured high-volume, high-quality, standardized calling and systems that measured not only the volume of presentations made but qualitative results by individual, list segment, offer, or any other variable deemed important by management. Installed to support the 500 remote branches, CCI operational systems would ensure uniform high-quality telephone contact and allow corporate understanding of both volume and effectiveness of individual branch telephone activity.

Test Design and Implementation Five branches, one per regional area, were selected to participate in a three-month pilot test, prior to nationwide expansion. The branches selected represented a spectrum of differences common to the overall network, including:

- Size or number of active accounts
- Good, average, and poor performance in meeting monthly revenue targets
- General economic condition of geographic location
- Ratio of employees to number of accounts

Before any on-site installation could begin, pretesting was completed at the agency workshop. The pretest facilitated complete package development and subsequent branch implementation and measurement. Program components developed during the pretest phase included:

- Complete development and testing of modularized, scripted presentations
- Design of measurement and tracking systems
- Determination of production and response parameters to be used as "benchmarks" against which in-branch program performance could be evaluated

---

[1] Telemarketing Development and Consulting Division of CCI.

After pretesting was completed, an agency specialist directed the program, over a five-week period, in each of the pilot branches. One of the most critical development factors was determining branch production goals. If the program was to succeed, each pilot had to be given a realistic daily production requirement, based on quantity of past and current solicitable accounts.

Once the formula for determining production requirements had been established and initial installation completed, ongoing periodic visits by the consultant were necessary to ensure proper program evolution and the continued levels of response necessary to achieve the targets.

Results Among several criteria used to evaluate pilot test results, the most comprehensive method was to view pilot performance as a group. Measurements were made relative to the region's performance as a whole as well as the change that occurred during the test period in 1981 as compared with the same time frame (prior to the test) in 1980 (see Figure 10-1).

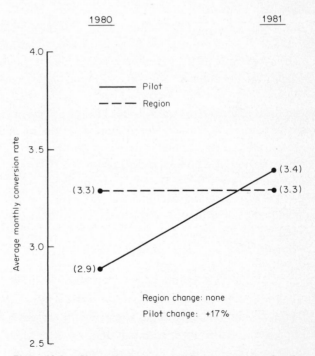

Figure 10-1. *Change in average monthly conversion rates by pilots and regions for test period 1981 versus nontest period 1980.*

The graph illustrates that while regional averages remained the same between the two time periods, pilot branch averages increased by 17 percent. Furthermore, prior to the test, average pilot branch performance was *below* average regional performance. During the test, average pilot performance increased to *above* average regional performance.

During the three-month pilot test, over $1 million in additional loan volume was generated, directly attributable to the program. Corporate management presented results to the entire branch management network at the annual conference shortly after test completion. With the aid of audio and video cassettes developed by the agency, installation of the modularized program was undertaken immediately by branch managers nationwide.

Summary With the multiplicity of telemarketing applications that have already been successfully developed by agencies and the increasing awareness by the general business community of the effectiveness and cost-efficiency of the medium, a growing number of organizations are becoming committed to building long-term, dedicated, in-house operations (see Table 10-1).

According to Michael Violanti, CCI's Development Division vice president, "Although companies in the same type of business may have similar telemarketing objectives when considering an in-house facility, each project, in our experience, has been unique. Differences in products, sales regions, customer size, ordering cycles, pricing policies, advertising and promotional programs, and so on, always call for a custom-tailored marketing plan and telephone presentation. If the telemarketing center is to operate effectively, it must be woven into the existing fabric of the organization; a thorough understanding of company structure and the "chain of command" is essential. Based on an understanding of how production-oriented telemarketing facilities function, the impact of a phone workshop on the existing structure of the company should be anticipated and provided for in the preplanning phase," he concluded.

Since in-house centers generally concentrate on only one or two products or service areas, requirements for incentive and motivation campaigns involving the telephone sales rep will quickly become apparent. There is a basic sequence of general events that should occur in establishing any in-house facility. The critical events should occur, concurrently in four areas: facility layout and design, creative development, personnel selection and training, and systems development. The foundation of the process, of course, is the definition of program objectives as we have demonstrated in our case histories and our earlier book, *Telephone Marketing*.

TABLE 10-1. *Selected Organizations and a Variety of Programs That Utilize In-House Telemarketing Workshops*

Company	Primary telemarketing objective
Domestic	
American Express	Customer service and order taking
American Management Associations	Inquiries and seminar registration
AT&T	Customer sales and service
Auerbach Publishing	Subscription acquisition and renewal for business publications
Citicorp	Direct sale of bank products and services, cross-selling, and credit card handling
Colonial Penn Insurance	Auto insurance, inquiry, and rate quotes conversion
Dreyfus Corporation	Direct-response sales, service of money funds
Fingerhut Corporation	Direct sales to mail-order customers
Foley Manufacturing	Sales and inquiry handling
GTE	Inquiry handling, customer service
Grolier	Direct sale of cookbook and other book series
Holes-Webway Co.	Credit and collection, customer service
IBM	Lead generation for computer sales, supply sales, and customer service
ITT	Consumer loan generation and customer service
Lee Wards (General Foods)	Direct sale of craft packages to consumers
McGraw-Hill	Direct sale of books, service, renewal of publications, and information handling
Minnesota Mining & Manufacturing (3M)	Direct sale of business products and services
Montgomery Ward Life Insurance	Prospecting, sales, and conversion of insurance
National Liberty Insurance	Health- and disability-insurance sales
National Republican Congressional Committee	Fund raising
The New York Times	Classified ad orders, subscriber solicitation services
Off-Track Betting Corp. (N.Y.C.)	Betting service for customers
Procter & Gamble	Solicitation of mail-order products
Signature Direct Response	Direct sale of consumer services
Time-Life Books	Direct sale of book series
TV Guide	Direct response renewals
U.S. Hospital Supply Corp.	Computerized customer and inventory service
U.S. Steel	Customer service and inquiry handling
Xerox Corporation	Lead generation, direct orders, supply sales, equipment sales

(Continued)

TABLE 10-1   *(Cont.)*

Company	Primary telemarketing objective
Foreign	
Bertelsmann (Germany, Sweden, and Switzerland)	Book sales to consumers
Euroboek (Holland)	Book sales to consumers
Guilde des Disques (France)	Direct sale of books and merchandise to consumers
La Redoute (France)	Incoming order taking, upgrading and service of mail-order customers
National Roads and Motor Association (Australia)	Sale, service, and conversions for insurance products
Quelle (Germany)	Incoming order taking, upgrading and service of mail-order customers
Rank Xerox (U.K.)	Lead generation for reprographic equipment and supply sales
Time-Life Books (Japan)	Direct sale of book series
United Magazine (Finland)	Subscription acquisition and renewal for consumer publications

chapter eleven /

Intracompany Applications

For many larger companies, communicating with executives in distant branch offices, salespeople in the field, and other far-flung staff members is a substantial problem in doing business. The limitations of transmitting information by memo or even individual letter are obvious to anyone who has ever faced a desk cluttered with too many papers to handle. Not only has written communication become a burden to deal with; it has lost much of its impact as a result of the sheer volume of paperwork received in the course of a normal business day.

When you have a message you want to deliver with immediacy, importance, and excitement, there is no more effective medium than the human voice. The telephone offers the opportunity to transmit that powerful vocal message to your business associates anywhere and to receive their response instantly. If more than two or three people have to get the word, you require more than a receiver at each end—you need a systematic program to distribute and gather information using sophisticated telephone communication skills.

A modern telephone business communications operation not only delivers information with electric speed; it makes sure that the message reaches the people it's aimed at, immediately uncovers any conflicts between your information and theirs, and takes requests for any further details that might be needed.

If an important announcement must reach a number of staff members, it can be taped by an appropriate spokesperson and combined with live communicators who get the calls through and record any feedback. This strategy will make busy executives listen and sit up and take notice.

Thanks to recent technological advances, by taking advantage of a sophisticated phone hookup known as a teleconference companies can even benefit from the interaction of their best people from across the country or around the globe—people who will not have to leave the comfort of their individual offices.

Even though the message in an internal telephone communications program will reach only company employees who are theoretically "on the same team," the program still represents a form of marketing. Each and every person contacted will have his or her own way of handling a certain task, and the telephone program will be trying to convince them to follow the requested approach. The resistance to "buying" an idea can be just as strong as that encountered when selling a product to consumers. Yet telemarketing in intracompany communications can be just as successful in allaying the doubts of a corporate vice president as it is in convincing a consumer to make a purchase by phone. In the process, the company phone program helps to unite the disparate elements of a corporation in a coordinated effort, moving smoothly forward like a deftly manipulated marionette strung together with telephone lines.

There are three basic functions a telephone operation can serve within a company—*communication, motivation,* and *education.*

Communication   Telephone is frequently used as a medium to provide product information such as price changes or inventory status to the sales force and retail outlets. If an item is temporarily out of stock, for instance, phoning salespeople with this information allows them to stop selling it immediately. This fast action prevents canceled orders that are costly both in terms of paperwork and damage to customer goodwill. The primary advantage over a written memo here is the speed of delivery, coupled with the knowledge that the information has been received and complied with—not left in a file folder on the corner of the desk.

Virtually every company already uses the telephone in some way to communicate with employees, but many could gain substantially by setting up *systematic* telephone information systems, involving incoming and/or outgoing calls. Business executives often make the erroneous assumption that if a question arises that requires a prompt answer, the person who needs the information will call the main office as a matter of course. That sometimes works, but it is often difficult to get answers by phone in the absence of established channels of communication to rely on. This is especially true if the person with the answers has a heavy workload of his or her own to handle and is often unavailable when called.

Often this situation can be avoided by setting up another level in the communications process—an individual or group of individuals with the designated responsibility of taking calls and having the answers ready at hand or knowing where they can be found and getting back to the caller quickly with the information.

Examples of tasks that can be handled by an established telephone service of this kind include the following:

- A telephone worker with access to a video terminal can supply up-to-the-minute price quotations and accurate estimates of delivery time for specific items, trace the whereabouts of orders currently being processed, report on a client's credit status, and handle other matters that could be crucial in handling a customer properly.

- For businesses involving products with technical specifications requiring more in-depth knowledge than even a trained salesperson could be expected to master, a hot-line number to staff members with expertise in these areas will help a salesperson respond to a prospective customer's questions quickly and authoritatively.

- Literature requests can be handled with maximum efficiency by having field personnel call a designated main office number, where the required materials can be gathered and mailed out immediately from a centralized facility.

- Telephone also allows the main office to monitor sales activities with up-to-date reports taken by phone with whatever frequency is practical, instead of waiting for written reports to arrive through the none-too-reliable mails. This reporting function can take the form of either an incoming operation ready to record results submitted over the phone or scheduled outbound calls from a central office to distant branches and sales offices.

Cost factors used to favor mail communication heavily over phone calls, but that balance has changed substantially in phone's favor, as the costs of postage, stationery, and the labor to take a letter and/or type it up brought the cost of the average business letter to over $6.

Motivation   Anyone who has ever tried to launch a new program, whether it's a special sales promotion, a new product, or some other change in the status quo, is well aware of the difficulties involved in selling it to the field sales force and other personnel who will be responsible for carrying it out. No amount of ingenuity, preparation, or careful planning on the management level will guarantee a successful program unless there is enthusiastic cooperation across the board. However, the natural human resistance to change is a difficult barrier to overcome. That's where telephone can be used with dramatic results, giving the personalized push needed to produce commitment to a new program.

We will examine two kickoff efforts on behalf of new products and programs, each of which used the phone to deliver the main office message with considerable clout—and impressive results.

Education   One of the most exciting areas for potential growth in business use of the telephone is in the training and workshop applications of phone technology. The general public has already been exposed to telephone as a learning aid in several ways. There are, of course, a wide selection of dial-in services offering 60-second prerecorded messages with beauty tips, horoscopes, weather and traffic information (yes, and jokes) that have become extremely popular under telephone company sponsorship.

As a community service, several hospitals provide the public with advice and information through telephone call-in programs. One popular approach offers a catalog of taped messages prepared by qualified physicians dealing with a variety of health-related topics. Callers indicate their area of interest to the hospital operator, who plays the appropriate tape for them right over the phone.

Business use of the telephone as an educational tool generally accents the two-way communication capability of the medium. A long-distance telephone link allows a company to introduce an expert offering important business information to staff members who may be scattered all over the globe. Your people learn the facts "straight from the horse's mouth," without shuttling the speaker back and forth, a time-consuming and expensive proposition. Listeners can ask questions as the presentation proceeds, a considerable advantage over printed educational materials.

Case History: Sparking Sales Force Enthusiasm with Phone

The introduction of telemarketing into a sales program is itself a prime example of a new idea that must be sold to an existing sales force in order to succeed. As we have already seen, phone can be extremely successful in producing screened, qualified leads for salespeople. Yet an undertaking of this kind cannot possibly work without prompt, consistent follow-up on those leads, and the level of follow-up can be distressingly weak. Some experts tell us that, as a rule of thumb, 30 to 35 percent of all sales leads produced for field sales forces are never pursued and that the number can reach as high as 80 percent. There have even been programs that required salespeople to pay for each lead, and still about 35 percent of them were not followed up, despite the fact that each neglected prospect represented money out of the salesperson's pocket.

With this in mind, a major corporation undertook a telephone campaign to sell its new telephone lead-generation program to its sales force. At the heart of the calling program was a no-nonsense taped message from the divisional sales manager.

He first sent each salesperson a letter saying that he had prepared a phone message for the sales force, explaining that the salesperson could either call in to receive it or wait and be called. Either way, at the appointed time communicators would begin by thanking the salesperson for his or her time and then play the following message:

HI, THIS IS JOHN JOHNSON WITH THE IMPORTANT MESSAGE I WROTE YOU ABOUT. I WANT TO TELL YOU PERSONALLY ABOUT A NEW AND EXCITING PROMOTION COMMITMENT WE'VE MADE, ONE THAT WILL DIRECTLY AFFECT YOUR SALES EFFORTS OVER THE NEXT FEW WEEKS. AND I WANT A COMMITMENT FROM YOU TODAY, TOO.

WE SET SOME THOROUGH SALES GOALS FOR YOU, AND BECAUSE WE WANT TO DO EVERYTHING WE CAN TO HELP YOU, WE'VE ENGAGED A PROFESSIONAL TELEMARKETING ORGANIZATION TO SCREEN AND QUALIFY LEADS FOR YOU. YOUR IMMEDIATE FOLLOW-UP TO THESE LEADS IS CRITICAL TO THE SUCCESS OF THIS PROGRAM. NOW HERE'S WHERE I WANT THE COMMITMENT FROM YOU. BE SURE TO CONTACT EVERY LEAD YOU RECEIVE WITHIN A WEEK.

AS USUAL, WE'LL BE TRACKING YOUR FEEDBACK, AND BECAUSE I'M SO ENTHUSIASTIC ABOUT THIS NEW PROGRAM, I'M GOING TO TAKE A PERSONAL INTEREST IN THE DILIGENCE YOU DEMONSTRATE IN FOLLOWING THIS PARTICULAR CAMPAIGN.

It should be noted that the promise of "personal interest" expressed by Mr. Johnson had very real meaning to the salespeople. He was well known as a tough taskmaster, given to making unannounced visits to his salespeople to monitor their activities. This and other practices of a similar nature might not endear him to the sales force in the field, but they did tend to keep the sales force on the ball. Given this management philosophy as an established fact, the phone message left no doubt as to the importance of making the requested "commitment."

Phone to Stimulate Seminar Attendance   Another approach to both educating and involving the sales force in a new product was taken by a major insurance corporation that had a significantly new form of policy to offer the public. This new product, called variable life insurance, combined the benefits of insurance coverage with the growth potential of investment in securities. The policy represented a major undertaking for the company and carried with it certain legal responsibilities as well. Only agents holding securities licenses registered with the National Association of Securities Dealers were eligible to sell this type of coverage, and they had to be fully versed in all the details of the plan's provisions before contacting their first customers.

To provide for full and thorough familiarity with the program, the company arranged to hold a series of "kickoff meetings" in each of the areas where the variable life insurance coverage would be tested. A team of experts from the home office would be at each of these meetings to make a presentation and answer any questions.

To introduce the new product to the agents with as much excitement as possible and, at the same time, to register the greatest possible number of eligible agents for the local meetings, the company arranged with a professional telemarketing agency to conduct a phone campaign to reach each of the agents and secure registration commitments.

Calls were made in the evenings to the agents at their homes. This strategy served to dramatize the importance of the call by removing it from the clutter of everyday business; it also made it easier to reach a busy agent, who might well be off on a sales call during the day. Timing was also a consideration in terms of proximity to the date of the meeting. Calls were scheduled for the five- to seven-day period immediately preceding the session to allow sufficient time for agents to adjust their calendar but not enough time to let them forget about the meeting or allow the initial enthusiasm generated by the call to diminish.

The $3\frac{1}{2}$-minute tape message used in this presentation carried a double-barreled message from top-level corporate figures—the executive vice president for agency operations and the president and chief executive officer of the company. In addition to briefly explaining the concept of variable life insurance, their message stressed a few "hot buttons" that were sure to catch the agents' interest:

- The new product offered agents a healthy 40 percent commission.
- It was an exclusive offering, providing agents with a policy option not available through any of their competitors.

■ The CEO was introduced as "the man who undoubtedly can take the credit for variable life insurance becoming a reality in this country. He is the nation's leading spokesman on variable life. . . ." What clearer signal could there be that there was management interest and enthusiasm for the new product at the highest levels?

This program worked—out of nearly 1,200 agents to be contacted over the course of the 25-meeting schedule, nearly 90 percent were reached by phone and listened to the presentation. And of those who were contacted, 94 percent agreed to attend the kickoff meeting scheduled for their area.

Phone as a Medium for Broadcasting and Sharing Information   In a more directly educational vein, IBM recently carried out an ingenious training program for a group of its top-level sales and management staff, providing them with a wide-ranging briefing on four types of direct marketing media—direct mail, sound sheets, telemarketing, and teleconference. What made the program particularly interesting is that the media themselves were used to tell their own stories. The executives were contacted with messages specially prepared for them by experts in the use of each medium. In addition to simply conveying the needed information, this approach brought the experience of being the audience for each marketing medium to the men and women who would be making decisions on the media to be used to promote a variety of new products in the coming year.

The six-stage presentation worked according to the domino theory— each successfully complete step triggered the next one in the series. The process went like this:

Step 1: Preprogram survey. The group of executives were split into two segments. Half received a survey form in the mail, while the other half were called by a telemarketing agency. Each group was asked the same set of eight questions, designed to determine awareness, experience, and attitudes regarding the four marketing techniques to be reviewed.

Step 2: Direct-mail presentation. The participants were each sent a direct-mail piece prepared along the same lines as the now-familiar packages received by consumers to sell everything from magazine subscriptions to record sets and packages of gift cheeses. The outer envelope directed the executive's secretary: PLEASE REMOVE THE PACKAGE FROM THIS ENVELOPE AND DELIVER IT UNOPENED TO THE ADDRESSEE. The inner envelope and the cover letter of the mailing package were imprinted with the name and address of the recipient, once more following standard, modern direct-mail procedure.

The package consisted of a cover letter introducing the orientation program, a newsletter entitled "The Mass Marketing Review," which provided some background information on direct mail and direct marketing in general, and a reply card asking the participant to indicate where he or she would like to receive the next mailing. This question was relevant because that mailing would include a sound sheet, the next marketing medium on the agenda. It would require a record player to play a sound-sheet, so receiving the mailing at home might make sense.

Step 3: Sound-sheet presentation. A sound sheet is a flexible plastic record disk, light enough to mail and playable on a standard record player at 33⅓ rpm. The sound sheet prepared for this presentation contained a spoken message from the corporation's divisional vice president discussing the productivity challenges facing the company, describing the sound-sheet concept, and introducing the next stage of the orientation program, a telemarketing call. The package containing the sound sheet had a cover photo of the divisional vice president sitting at his desk, with the legend, "If we could get together today, here are a few words I'd say to you. . . ." It also included a reply card asking for a convenient time during the business day for the recipient to receive a 15-minute telemarketing call, to be scheduled during a specified 10-day period.

Step 4: Telemarketing call. The telemarketing segment of the program was similar to a calling campaign for a product or service to be sold, except that the taped message included in the presentation was longer than a typical sales tape—about 10 minutes in all—in order to present the educational materials required. The communicator would call the participant at the time requested, arrange a call-back if necessary, and play the taped message at the executive's convenience.

The voice on tape was that of the chairman of the telemarketing agency. He explained the basic principles of phone marketing in business-to-business programs and illustrated the different uses possible with this medium by incorporating taped extracts from actual calls made in previous programs.

In line with the desires of the sponsoring corporation, the presentation stressed lead generation and direct sales to marginal customers, which were perceived as high-potential areas for the listeners.

To further dramatize the interactive nature of phone contact, the call included a segment in which the communicator returned to the line and asked the participant a series of questions about his or her office needs.

These same questions had been used in an actual program by a manufacturer of dictation equipment to screen and qualify leads for their salespeople.

The concluding element in the call was an introduction to the final phase of the orientation program—an audio teleconference. The communicator returned to the line, told the participant what dates were available in his or her area for a teleconference, and took a registration for a specific session over the phone.

Step 5: Audio teleconference. The wrap-up segment of the orientation program was an audio teleconference session. A teleconference is similar in many ways to a conference call, in which several people are linked in a telephone hookup and can exchange information and ideas simultaneously. The ability to communicate in this way has been available through the telephone company for some time. Only recently, however, have private companies also entered the field and provided the technical and structural sophistication needed to turn a conference call into a teleconference, an effective tool for bringing businesspeople all over the world together. The advantages of a professionally organized teleconference include the following:

- Technology can link in excess of 200 lines simultaneously, with excellent sound clarity. The number of participants is not limited to 200, however, since each line can represent a single telephone receiver or a speakerphone arrangement allowing a number of conferees gathered in a room to join in.
- The teleconference setup allows conferees to call in from wherever they are and be included in the hookup.
- Structure and format are crucial to the success of a teleconference. With a planned agenda and moderators prepared to keep the flow of the telephone meeting going, the process of interactive communication is made smooth and effective. Visual aids such as printed materials, slides, and on-site electronic blackboards as well as computer conferencing terminals and demonstrations can also be planned to maximize the impact of the conference. Professional teleconferencing agencies also provide the expertise and personnel needed to prepare the groundwork for the meeting in advance.

Audio teleconferencing has three broad categories of application:

- To allow communication in a workshop environment among groups meeting at distant locations
- To set up impromptu meetings to deal with problems as they arise
- To convey up-to-date information to select audiences

In addition to handling business meetings, teleconferencing has been used successfully in press conferences and in a widely heralded program of continuing medical education that allows groups of health care professionals scattered across the country to hear an expert discuss the latest findings in a given area of medicine and then join in a question-and-answer session.

For the mass-marketing media-orientation program we have been describing, the teleconference format was designed to allow both the broadcasting of information and the questioning of experts in each of the media represented.

The teleconference began with a roll call to ensure that the hookup was working properly. Then executives from the sponsoring corporation were introduced to explain the importance of the productive use of direct-marketing techniques to meet corporate goals. Next, spokespeople for each of the marketing media made presentations to the audience, expanding on the information they had presented through their respective media earlier in the orientation program. Three elements made these teleconference presentations more effective:

- Taped messages from each speaker allowed a predictable, professional presentation that would be sure to cover all the bases.
- Slides keyed in to the presentation were displayed at each teleconferencing location, cued by requests from the speaker.
- A handbook of printed materials on each marketing medium was given to each conference participant to provide further information and a permanent reference source.

At the end of each speaker's taped segment, prepared questions were presented at each of the teleconference sites and submitted to the speakers, who were available on the line to answer them live. This format allowed for a valuable exchange of ideas and clarification of points made in the initial presentation. A further question-and-answer segment at the end of the teleconference brought all the experts into the discussion together to synthesize some of the key points made.

Step 6: Postprogram survey. After the teleconference was completed, the executives involved in the program were once more surveyed, with those who had filled out a mail-in questionnaire in the preprogram survey contacted by phone this time; those who hadn't previously responded were reached by mail.

Robert Blair, IBM's Manager of Direct Marketing Communications, National Accounts Division, in evaluating the survey, said: "The executives were asked for their response to the program and asked to rate the relative merits of the different marketing media covered. Among their responses, it is interesting to note that when asked if 'you think playing the role of your customers and prospects was a good way to learn about these tools,' over 90 percent answered positively. When asked if they would like to receive more information on any of these tools, direct mail, telemarketing, and teleconferencing each drew substantial positive responses.

"And one question that was asked in both the pre- and postprogram surveys provides an interesting contrast in attitudes resulting from the orientation-program experience. The question was, 'Do you think customer reaction to these tools would be favorable?' In the preprogram survey, those who responded were almost unanimously favorable to direct mail, just under 40 percent were favorable to sound sheets, over 60 percent to telemarketing, and 75 percent to teleconferencing," Blair noted.

The postprogram survey revealed only one significant shift in attitude—the favorable rating for telemarketing jumped over 20 percentage points! This proves how important professionally prepared and delivered telemarketing programs are, compared with poorly prepared and poorly presented programs.

Here now is my own teleconferencing tape script, which summarizes the "how to" disciplines for building successful telemarketing programs—it's a fitting and hopefully helpful conclusion to this book:

THE LAST TIME WE SPOKE I STRESSED *WHAT* TELEMARKETING CAN DO FOR YOU. NOW I'D LIKE TO LOOK MORE CLOSELY AT *HOW* TELEPHONE ACHIEVES THESE RESULTS.

TO UNDERSTAND THE EXCITING POSSIBILITIES OF THIS MEDIUM, YOU HAVE TO REALIZE THAT A TELEMARKETING PROGRAM IS *MUCH* MORE THAN A SERIES OF TELEPHONE CALLS. WHAT WE ARE ACTUALLY DEALING WITH IS A COMPLETE, CAREFULLY STRUCTURED *INFORMATION PROCESSING SYSTEM*, WHICH IS VERY MUCH LIKE AN ON-LINE COMPUTER SYSTEM. I'D LIKE TO DRAW SOME COMPARISONS BETWEEN COMPUTERS AND THE TOOL *I* WORK WITH EVERY DAY—THE TELEPHONE.

A TELEMARKETING SYSTEM BEGINS WITH MARKETING INPUT—THIS INITIAL INPUT COMES FROM OUR CLIENTS, WHO TELL US THAT PRODUCTS OR SERVICES THEY HAVE TO OFFER AND WHAT GOALS THEY'RE SHOOTING FOR. THEN WE PACKAGE THAT INFORMATION IN THE MOST EFFICIENT FORMAT. THIS IS SIMILAR TO THE WAY THAT IBM PACKAGES

INSTRUCTIONS INTO SOFTWARE. WE DESIGN THE APPROPRIATE PHONE LINE REQUIREMENTS AND THEN INPUT THE PROGRAM, TRANSMITTING IT TO THE CLIENT'S CUSTOMER LIST.

THIS GENERATES FEEDBACK FROM THOSE CUSTOMERS IN THE FORM OF POSITIVE AND NEGATIVE RESPONSES—THE POSITIVE RESPONSES COULD BE APPOINTMENTS, SALES LEADS, DIRECT SALES, AND SO ON. THAT'S THE OUTPUT OF A PHONE MARKETING CAMPAIGN.

WE TABULATE AND ANALYZE THE DATA WE'VE GATHERED TO REVEAL THE MOST SIGNIFICANT RESULTS, AND WITHIN 24 HOURS WE TRANSMIT THOSE STATISTICS BACK TO THE CLIENT FOR FURTHER ACTION AND FURTHER REFINEMENT OF THE TELEMARKETING PROGRAM. THAT'S THE WAY *OUR* SYSTEM WORKS.

YOU SEE, WE ARE BOTH DEALING IN A SERVICE, AND WE BOTH OFFER THE SAME ADVANTAGES TO OUR CLIENTS—I BELIEVE YOU CALL IT "SPEED, ACCURACY, AND FLEXIBILITY." AS WITH COMPUTERS, THE TELEPHONE DOESN'T DO ANYTHING A LIVE PERSON COULDN'T DO. BUT IT REACHES YOUR CUSTOMERS QUICKLY AND EFFICIENTLY, AND IT COSTS FAR LESS THAN HAVING A MARKETING REP OR SERVICE ENGINEER MEET FACE-TO-FACE WITH EVERYONE YOU WANT TO CONTACT.

TELEMARKETING ALSO INVOLVES BOTH SOFTWARE AND HARDWARE. THE HARDWARE IS THE TELEPHONE SYSTEM. THE SOFTWARE IS THE TELEPHONE PROGRAM, WHICH INCLUDES COMMUNICATOR SCRIPTS AND CUSTOMIZED DATA MEASUREMENT SYSTEMS. OUR HARDWARE IS ALREADY IN PLACE, FOR THE MOST PART, THANKS TO THE PENETRA- TION OF THE PHONE SYSTEM INTO EVERY BUSINESS OFFICE IN THE COUNTRY.

THERE'S ANOTHER LEVEL OF HARDWARE THAT PROFESSIONAL TELE- MARKETERS OFFER. THEIR HARDWARE SYSTEM IS, IN EFFECT, HARD- WIRED IN. AND ALL THE OTHER COMPONENTS YOU'LL NEED ARE ALSO AVAILABLE—

THE COMMUNICATORS, THE BACKUP CLERICAL AND TABULATION STAFF, THE CREATIVE TEAM, THE PROFESSIONALLY DESIGNED TELE- PHONE ROOM WITH ITS WATS LINES.

AND PROGRAMMING A TELEPHONE CAMPAIGN IS NOT ALL THAT DIF- FERENT FROM PROGRAMMING A COMPUTER. IT REQUIRES HIGHLY SPECIALIZED CREATIVE SKILLS, TRAINING, AND EXPERIENCE TO TRANSLATE YOUR GOALS INTO A PROGRAM THAT PRODUCES THE NEEDED RESULTS. AND JUST AS YOU TEST A COMPUTER PROGRAM, WE TEST AND RETEST OUR TELEPHONE PRESENTATIONS AND CONTROL AND MEASUREMENT SYSTEMS UNTIL THEY PRODUCE SOLID RESULTS. AND BECAUSE OF THE FAST RESPONSE RATE THAT TELEPHONE PRO- VIDES, YOU CAN QUICKLY FINE-TUNE YOUR TESTS, WITH MINOR PRO- GRAM VARIATIONS.

OF COURSE, WE SUFFER FROM THE "GARBAGE-IN–GARBAGE-OUT" PROBLEM AS WELL. IF THE LIST OF CUSTOMERS USED IN THE MARKET-

ING SYSTEM IS NOT RIGHT, THERE'S NO WAY THE BEST-WRITTEN PRO-GRAM IN THE WORLD WILL PRODUCE ACCEPTABLE RESULTS.

BOTTOM LINE, WE'RE BOTH DEALING WITH A QUALITY PRODUCT. THAT'S WHERE CAREFUL CONTROL AND MEASUREMENT SYSTEMS COME INTO PLAY. FOR EXAMPLE, THE RESULT OF EACH AND EVERY CALL IS RECORDED, WHETHER THE COMMUNICATOR GETS AN ORDER OR A BUSY SIGNAL.

AND SINCE WE KNOW THAT EACH CALL IS A STANDARDIZED PRESENTA-TION, WE CAN DRAW FIRM CONCLUSIONS ABOUT THE TELEMARKETING CAMPAIGN.

IN THE TELEMARKETING SEGMENT OF THIS MASS-MARKETING ORIEN-TATION PROGRAM YOU'LL RECALL WE ASKED YOU SOME QUESTIONS ABOUT YOUR OFFICE NEEDS. MANY OF YOU COULD BE HOT LEADS FOR SALESPEOPLE SPECIALIZING IN DICTATION EQUIPMENT. AND THE DE-TAILED INFORMATION YOU GAVE COULD ALSO HELP THOSE SALES-PEOPLE TO DEFINE *OTHER* POTENTIAL AREAS WHERE THEIR PRODUCTS COULD FIT FOR YOU. IN A REAL LEAD-GENERATION PROGRAM, THOSE LEADS COULD HAVE BEEN IN A CLIENT'S HANDS THE DAY AFTER WE SPOKE WITH YOU.

THERE'S ONE MORE IMPORTANT ISSUE OF MUTUAL CONCERN TO COM-PUTER PEOPLE AND TELEMARKETERS THAT I'D LIKE YOU TO CON-SIDER. AND THAT'S SYSTEM COMPATIBILITY.

IT'S VERY IMPORTANT FOR YOUR CUSTOMERS TO KNOW THAT ANY NEW SYSTEM COMPONENT THEY BUY WILL BE COMPATIBLE WITH THE COM-PONENTS IN THEIR CURRENT SYSTEM. WELL, A TELEMARKETING PRO-GRAM WILL NOT ONLY INTERFACE WELL WITH OTHER MARKETING TOOLS: IT WILL ACTUALLY *MULTIPLY* THE POSITIVE RESPONSE YOU GET FROM OTHER MEDIA.

FOR EXAMPLE, WHEN CCI CALLS PEOPLE WHO DIDN'T RESPOND TO A MAIL PIECE, WE GENERATE $2\frac{1}{2}$ TO 7 TIMES THE RESPONSE RATE ACHIEVED BY THE INITIAL MAILING. TELEPHONE CAN ALSO COMPLE-MENT AND INCREASE THE RESULTS OF SOUND SHEETS AND TELECON-FERENCING, AND IT CERTAINLY ADDS TO YOUR SALES FORCE'S EFFEC-TIVENESS.

I HOPE THIS BRIEF PRESENTATION HAS MADE THE WORKING OF CCI'S TELEMARKETING SYSTEM CLEAR TO YOU AND SPARKED SOME FUR-THER QUESTIONS IN YOUR MIND.

HERE ARE A FEW COMMONLY ASKED QUESTIONS ABOUT TELEMARKET-ING. YOU PROBABLY HAVE OTHERS. PLEASE SPEND THE NEXT THREE MINUTES DISCUSSING WHICH QUESTIONS YOUR GROUP WOULD LIKE TO SUBMIT AND WHY.

WE WILL COME BACK ON THE LINE IN THREE MINUTES TO TAKE YOUR QUESTIONS. THANK YOU FOR LISTENING.

A Few of the Questions from IBM Executives, and Our Answers

1. Q: What are the product economics that affect the viability of a telemarketing campaign?
   A: In general, achieve a profitable expense-to-income ratio, ideally beyond break-even for each sale or contact. Know what the available margin is for an incremental telemarketing order. In new customer acquisition, look at the income stream for the life of the customer—as well as cross-selling potential—in judging profitability.

2. Q: What level of decision maker can I get through to?
   A: Anyone with a telephone—everybody from CEO to order clerk, to physician, to farmer, to consumers.

3. Q: How quickly could you reach an audience of 10,000 customers?
   A: As quickly as you can add phones and trained people, plus the readiness of a follow-up system via direct mail or sales force.

4. Q: What determines the cost of the telemarketing program?
   A: Consistency and level of volume over time; day, night, or weekend calling hours; completed calls per hour; geographic distance; quality of the creative effort; but most important, response rates!

5. Q: Since telemarketing is fairly new, where can I find experienced managers?
   A: It's very difficult—you'll probably have to train them or, perhaps more effective, hire a consultant to train them. The lack of competent telemarketing management is likely to exist for at least 5 more years.

6. Q: Should I try to organize the program in-house, or utilize the services of a telemarketing agency?
   A: If it's speed you want, use an agency. If you do want an in-house operation, test first, possibly via an agency, before you invest heavily in phones and people. Avoid reinventing the wheel (see Appendix J for more information).

7. Q: Is it more cost-efficient to test first to determine response rates before undertaking your own internal operation?
   A: Certainly. Testing and retesting to determine the many variables—such as product/service/creative offers, price/list/market (all of which impact on response rates)—can only make your "roll-out" program more profitable.

8. Q: How do I get started in telemarketing? Whom do I contact?
   A: The key to the telemarketing discipline is experience and successful results in a variety of business and consumer programs. We hope that our case histories have demonstrated how it works. So reach out and call an expert! It's the proven way of increasing your odds for a telemarketing success story. Again, thanks for listening, and we'll be glad to hear from you!

appendix A / The Range of Telemarketing Applications

The telephone is an extremely versatile marketing medium. Appendix A is a graphic representation of its vast range of potential applications. A marketer contemplating telephone might use such a chart to pinpoint the program and marketing target (i.e., select lists!) to which it will be applied.

Outgoing Calls

Applications	Customers — Present Major	Customers — Present Minor or Marginal	Customers — Past Major	Customers — Past Minor or Marginal	Inquiries New	Inquiries Old	Prospects — Referrals New	Prospects — Referrals Old	Prospects — Cold Calls Profiled	Prospects — Cold Calls Suspect
New sales										
Reactivations										
Renewals										
Conversions										
Trial sales										
On-approval sales										
Order taking										
Ticket upgrading										
Cross-selling										
Appointments for sales										
Information requests										
Sales to contact										
Previews										
Market research										
Update of records										
Prospect data										
Screening/qualifying										
Tie-in sales										
Price data										
Product information										
Complaints										
Screening for credit										
Solicitation of applications										
Collections										
New products/services										
Traffic building										
Validations										

Incoming Calls

Applications	Customers — Present Major	Customers — Present Minor or Marginal	Customers — Past Major	Customers — Past Minor or Marginal	Inquiries New	Inquiries Old	Prospects — Referrals New	Prospects — Referrals Old	Prospects — Cold Calls Profiled	Prospects — Cold Calls Suspect
New sales										
Reactivations										
Renewals										
Conversions										
Trial sales										
On-approval sales										
Order taking										
Ticket upgrading										
Cross-selling										
Appointments for sales										
Information requests										
Sales to contact										
Previews										
Market research										
Update of records										
Prospect data										
Screening/qualifying										
Tie-in sales										
Price data										
Product information										
Complaints										
Screening for credit										
Solicitation of applications										
Collections										
New products/services										
Traffic building										
Validations										

appendix B / **FCC Memorandum Opinion and Order in the Matter of Unsolicited Telephone Calls**

In the late 1970s the Federal Communications Commission undertook to examine the validity of complaints regarding telemarketing. After extensive hearings and investigations the commission released the following conclusions.

Before the

Federal Communications Commission
Washington, D.C. 20554

MEMORANDUM OPINION AND ORDER)   CC DOCKET NO. 78-100

In the Matter of Unsolicited Telephone Calls

ADOPTED: APRIL 24, 1980;   RELEASED: May 22, 1980

BY THE COMMISSION:

1. On March 30, 1978, the Commission instituted an Inquiry concerning unsolicited telephone calls in response to a petition filed by Walter Baer and the Citizens Communication Center. *Unsolicited Telephone Calls*, CC Docket No. 78-100, 67 F.C.C. 2d 1384 (1978). The Commission's Notice of Inquiry requested information and views concerning the constitutional, jurisdictional, and policy issues involved in regulation of both automatically and manually dialed unsolicited telephone calls. To assist in focusing the responses of interested parties, the Notice set out a number of specific questions concerning (1) various aspects of the constitutional issues; (2) the jurisdiction of the Commission to regulate intrastate unsolicited telephone calls; (3) the extent and impact of unsolicited telephone calling; and (4) the feasibility of technological solutions.[1] Formal comments were filed in response to the Commission's Notice of Inquiry by more than 45 businesses, industry associations, telephone companies, and public interest groups as well as state and federal governmental entities.[2] Approximately 4,300 informal comments were also filed.[3]

2. Unsolicited telephone calls and the automatic dialer recorded message player, or ADRMP, have recently received attention in other regulatory forums as well, although they are not new phenomena.[4] Both the American Telephone and Telegraph Company and GTE Service Corporation state that ADRMPs have been available for over 15 years. Legislation known as the "Telephone Privacy Act" aimed at restricting unsolicited calls was introduced during the 1st Session of the 96th Congress by the Honorable Representatives Guyer and Aspin, H.R. 377 and H.R. 6047, but no hearings have been scheduled.[5] Many of the states have also considered the questions posed by such calls. Regulations for unsolicited telephone calling, in most cases designed to restrict use of the ADRMP, are in effect in a number of states including Alaska, California, Florida, Illinois, Hawaii, Maryland, Missouri, Nebraska, North Carolina, Oregon, Texas, Washington and Wisconsin.[6]

3. Despite the attention which these questions have received, the Commission believes—for the reasons explained below—that it should refrain from regulating unsolicited telephone calls and ADRMP equipment at this time. In the present factual context, our jurisdiction is limited to regulation of interstate unsolicited telephone calls. Since it appears that only about three percent of all unsolicited telephone calls are interstate, regulatory action on our part would very likely affect only a small proportion of all unsolicited calls. Accordingly, we believe that

---

[1] The Commission's Notice did not specifically seek information concerning intentional telephone harassment or fraud.

[2] Formal comments which were not filed in a timely fashion will be considered by the Commission since the delays involved were not substantial.

[3] This figure includes informal comments received in response to the Public Notice concerning Walter Baer's petition, letters received during the comment period set out in the Notice of Inquiry as well as material received thereafter.

[4] The California Public Utilities Commission investigated the question of unsolicited telephone calls over 15 years ago, rejecting the idea of a telephone directory symbol which would indicate whether the subscriber wished to receive commercial and charitable solicitations. *McDaniel v. Pacific Telephone and Telegraph Co.*, 60 PUR 3d 47 (1965).

[5] Legislation concerning unsolicited telephone calls was also introduced during the 95th Congress. H.R. 9505; H.R. 9506; H.R. 10032; H.R. 10033; H.R. 10904; H.R. 12218; H.R. 12219 and S. 2193. No action was taken on any of those bills.

[6] Debt collection calls by collection agencies are regulated by the Fair Debt Collection Practices Act, 15 U.S.C. §1692c (a) and §1692d (Supp. I 1977), as well as allowing consumers to direct collection agencies to refrain from further communications with them subject to certain limited exceptions, 15 U.S.C. §1692c (c) (Supp. I 1977).

these matters can best be dealt with by the individual states should they have problems in this regard. An outright ban on unsolicited telephone calls would also appear to violate constitutional requirements. The Commission considered, but ultimately rejected, less comprehensive regulatory approaches. Thus, a regulatory scheme permitting telephone subscribers to request that they not be contacted by a particular organization was rejected because of the jurisdictional limitations mentioned above, the cost of such regulation, and the difficulty of effective enforcement. We decided against time, place and manner restrictions on unsolicited telephone calls because of jurisdictional limitations and because there do not appear to be any widespread abuses at the interstate level which would be remedied by such restrictions. Finally, we decided not to appear to be in widespread interstate use and are not causing network congestion or other substantial problems at the present time.

I. COMMENTS
A. Public Interest Groups, Governmental Organizations and Private Individuals

4. A number of private individuals, public interest groups, and government organizations supported federal regulation of unsolicited telephone calls. Walter Baer filed comments advocating (1) a prohibition on commercial advertising to subscribers who have indicated that they do not wish to be disturbed; (2) a requirement that automated calls be preceded by an announcement identifying themselves as such; and (3) special tariffs for telephone sales solicitations designed to fully reflect their costs. Mr. Baer also argued that a distinction should be made between commercial solicitations and those for political or other non-commercial purposes. The comments of the Georgetown Institute for Public Interest Representation focused on the constitutional issues. It took the position that a system prohibiting unsolicited calls to subscribers who have indicated that they do not want to receive them would be constitutional. It also argued that time-of-day or day-of-week restrictions on unsolicited calls would be lawful. The Institute suggested that the Commission avoid a regulatory scheme which distinguished between commercial and other types of unsolicited telephone calls because of the definitional problems involved, although it did not believe that differential treatment would necessarily be unconstitutional. The Institute also suggested that regulation of automated calls might be permissible even if other unsolicited calls were not restricted. The Depart-

ment of Health, Education and Welfare Office of Consumer Affairs supported restrictions on unsolicited telephone calls designed to protect the privacy interests of residential telephone subscribers. Although HEW thought that such restrictions would be constitutional, it questioned the lawfulness of distinguishing between unsolicited commercial calls and those of a nonprofit or political nature. The General Services Administration expressed concern that government agencies with blocks of contiguous telephone numbers would be particularly vulnerable to sequential dialing by ADRMPs and requested regulations designed to deal with this situation. The Federal Trade Commission (FTC) also supported regulation of unsolicited telephone calls, arguing that it was necessary to focus on the means of communication itself in order to prevent telephone fraud and harassment.[7] The Honorable Les Aspin filed comments supporting a prohibition on unsolicited calls to telephone subscribers who do not wish to receive them, but recommended an exemption for public opinion polls and other survey re search. Regulation of all unsolicited telephone calls was advocated by the Massachusetts Executive Office of Consumer Affairs. The Wisconsin Department of Justice Office of Consumer Affairs, New York City Department of Consumer Affairs and the Virginia Citizens Consumer Foundation also favored regulation. The state of California and the California Public Utilities Commission filed comments reviewing their proceedings concerning ADRMP use and unsolicited calls to residential subscribers. Morey McDaniel also provided information concerning his 1964 suit against telephone solicitation before the California PUC. *See* note 4 *supra.* In addition, most of the approximately 4,300 informal comments favored regulation.

5. Other governmental organizations questioned the desirability of federal regulation concerning unsolicited telephone calls. The National Telecommunications and Information Administration (NTIA) stated that "[i]n light of the record established so far in this inquiry, we do not believe that . . . there is any basis for restrictive FCC action." In support of its position, NTIA stated that most telephone sales organizations appear to use "carefully trained and supervised personnel, place calls chiefly to targeted customer groups and make sure that they are conducted on a pleasant and courteous basis." Although NTIA recognized that manual telephone solicitation could raise privacy issues, it concluded that this concern did not indicate a need for federal intervention when balanced

---

[7] The FTC also suggested that debt collection calls be covered by any regulations concerning unsolicited telephone calls.

The American Collectors Association opposed this idea.

against the long established use of such telephone solicitation. NTIA also argued that restrictions on the ADRMP were not warranted since very few of them are presently in use. However, it suggested that the Commission continue to monitor these areas. Both the National Association of Regulatory Utility Commissioners and the Missouri Public Service Commission opposed unilater federal action on jurisdictional grounds, stating that the Commission has no authority over local or intrastate unsolicited telephone calls. They also requested the convocation of a Federal-State Joint Board pursuant to Section 410 of the Communications Act to investigate these matters.

B. Telephone Sales Organizations

6. A large number of organizations involved in making unsolicited sales calls filed comments. Among these groups were the Magazine Publishers Association Inc., American Bankers Association, American Movers Conference, National Association of Life Underwriters, National Retail Merchants Association, American Newspaper Publishers Association, Army Times Publishing Company, American Council of Life Insurance, Health Insurance Association of America, **Campaign Communications Institute of America, Inc.**, Olan Mills, Inc., Time Inc., Chamber of Commerce of the United States, American Retail Federation, National Association of Personnel Consultants, Independent Insurance Agents of America, Inc., American Automobile Association, The Trane Company, Telephone Credit Marketers Association, Direct Mail/Marketing Association, Inc., Direct Selling Association, Republic Distributors, Inc., Water Quality Association, and Pacesetter Building Systems, Inc. They generally opposed substantial restrictions on telephone solicitation.

7. These businesses and industry associations argued that government regulation was unnecessary since market incentives dictated that calls be made only to those likely to be interested, limited to reasonable hours, and conducted in an ethical and courteous fashion. Several businesses also stated that alternative advertising media were much less effective than telephone solicitation. Many of these organizations also questioned the constitutionality of substantial restrictions on unsolicited telephone calls. In particular, they argued that a complete ban on such calls would fail to satisfy the requirements of the First Amendment. A number of them questioned the constitutionality of a system prohibiting calls to telephone subscribers who do not wish to receive them, although several other groups thought such a system might be lawful. Many of these organizations also argued that regulations concerning unsolicited telephone calls could not lawfully distinguish between commercial calls and those made for charitable, political or survey purposes. Several groups contended that most forms of regulation would involve substantial definitional problems. In addition, a number of organizations questioned the statutory basis for Commission regulations concerning unsolicited telephone calls, arguing that Title II of the Communications Act is meant to regulate common carriers and contains only limited authority for restrictions on subscriber conduct. Despite these objections, a number of groups stated that they were not opposed to limited restrictions, such as a prohibition on calls to unlisted numbers or a requirement that ADRMPs release the line when the called party hangs up.

8. The telephone sales organizations differed somewhat in their views concerning the extent of Commission jurisdiction. Many groups took the position that the Commission's basic jurisdiction was limited to interstate and foreign communications, although several favored regulatory uniformity to eliminate confusion and the possibility of conflicting requirements. A few others argued that the Commission could pre-empt state regulations that were more restrictive than those in effect at the federal level. At least one company took the position that the Commission's jurisdiction to regulate unsolicited telephone calls was plenary and exclusive regardless of whether the call was interstate or intrastate.

C. Telephone Survey Research Organizations and Other Groups

9. The Council of American Survey Research Organizations, National Association of Broadcasters, Arbitron Company, and Control Data Corporation engage in unsolicited telephone calling for survey research purposes. These organizations took the position that such calls should be exempt from regulation since they are necessary to ensure representative population samples. They stated that prohibitions on calls to subscribers with unlisted numbers or those who have indicated a desire not to receive unsolicited calls would produce serious distortions in the information gathered.

10. Aeronautical Radio, Inc. (ARINC) and the Air Transport Association (ATA) argued that calls by airlines to individuals who have requested information or made flight reservations should not be treated as unsolicited. They also urged the Commission to avoid a complete ban on the use of ADRMPs. In addition, ARINC, ATA, and the Computer and Business Equipment Manufacturers Association argued that use of the telephone for transmission of digital data between computers and terminals should

not be covered by any regulations concerning unsolicited telephone calls.

D. ADRMP Equipment Manufacturers

11. A number of ADRMP equipment manufacturers—Dycon International, Inc., Dictaphone Corporation and Trans World Telephone Contact Limited—filed comments in this proceeding. Dycon and Trans World Telephone Contact stated that the extent of unsolicited telephone calling and associated problems have been greatly exaggerated. Dycon also argued that reasonable use of ADRMP equipment could be beneficial to society. These companies opposed a ban on reasonable telephone solicitation but in most cases did not object to limited forms of regulation such as a prohibition on calls to unlisted numbers, a requirement that the calling party release the line as soon as the called party hangs up, or a limitation on the number of times a caller can ring the subscriber's telephone. Both Dycon and Dictaphone took the position that restricting only unsolicited sales calls would be unconstitutional.

E. Telephone Companies

12. Comments were also filed by the American Telephone and Telegraph Company (AT&T), GTE Service Corporation (GTE) and the United States Independent Telephone Association (USITA). AT&T expressed concern with the subscriber's right of privacy but argued that reasonable business use of the telephone should not be impaired. It took the position that a complete ban on unsolicited telephone calls would be unconstitutional and expressed doubts concerning the lawfulness of a prohibition on unsolicited calls to telephone subscribers who have not affirmatively indicated a desire to receive them. AT&T also questioned the lawfulness of treating unsolicited commercial telephone calls differently from those made for charitable, political or survey research purposes. It expressed the opinion that present controls had proved adequate so far, and urged that potential problems be dealt with by limited restrictions developed through meetings of Commission staff members, representatives of the telephone industry, consumer organizations, and telephone solicitation groups.[7]

13. The GTE Service Corporation suggested that the record in this proceeding did not demonstrate a need for regulation. If regulation was necessary, GTE favored limited restrictions such as a requirement that recorded messages be preceded by an announcement concerning the nature of the message and requesting permission to play it. GTE specifically opposed a prohibition on calls to subscribers who have indicated that they do not want to be disturbed on the ground that these programs would be ineffective and difficult to administer. They were also concerned that the telephone company would have to ensure the accuracy of any such system and enforce compliance. The United States Independent Telephone Association also argued that the information available to it did not indicate a need for regulation. USITA favored Congressional action assuming restrictions were necessary. However, it objected to any form of regulation which would require the telephone company to intercede in disputes between its customers.

14. AT&T, GTE and USITA took the position that the Commission's jurisdiction was limited to regulation of interstate unsolicited telephone calls and prescription of technical specifications for terminal equipment. They distinguished prescription of equipment specifications from regulation of customer use of equipment and services, arguing that intrastate and interstate use are separable and could be subject to different regulations.

II. BACKGROUND
A. Extent and Characteristics of Unsolicited Telephone Calling

15. The information which we received in response to the Notice of Inquiry indicates that unsolicited telephone calls[9] are a limited but well established business practice. Newspapers and magazines frequently sell subscriptions by telephone. Various other products and services are offered directly to the consumer in the home. Businesses also use the telephone to contact prospective customers and arrange personal sales presentations. Political and charitable causes use the telephone to solicit contributions. Public opinion and marketing surveys are conducted by telephone. One source claims that approximately seven million unsolicited sales calls are completed each business day.[10] About 460,000 of the people called are said to respond positively, purchasing approximately 28 million dollars worth

[7] Among the restrictions AT&T proposed for consideration were (1) requirements that recorded messages be preceded by an announcement identifying the calling party and the nature of the call; (2) limitations on the time of day during which unsolicited calls could be made; (3) limitations on the number of call attempts to a given telephone number, and (4) technical specifications for ADRMPs.

[9] The term "unsolicited telephone call" does not have a precise, generally accepted definition. For the purposes of this discussion, it should be understood as referring to a business call from an organization with which the recipient has had minimal if any prior dealings. Unless otherwise indicated, this term does not refer to unwelcome personal calls or misdialed calls.

[10] Murray Roman, *Telephone Marketing* (McGraw-Hill: New York, 1976), *cited in* Comments filed by Walter Baer; Sylvia Porter, "Get the Maximum Benefit from Business Telephoning," *New York Post, cited in* Comments filed by Campaign Communications Institute of America, Inc.

of goods and services.[11] Another source claims that 12 million call attempts are made by telephone sales personnel each working day.[12] Trans World Telephone Contact Limited, however, said that these figures appeared to be unrealistically high. The Campaign Communications Institute of America, Inc. (CCI), a large telephone sales organization, stated that it makes about 100,000 telephone sales calls each week. The other telephone sales and survey groups did not indicate the precise extent of their activities. In any event, the figures cited above represent a very modest proportion of the approximately 735 million local and long distance calls which are placed over Bell System telephone facilities each business day.

16. Further information concerning the extent of unsolicited telephone calling is contained in a survey conducted by the Field Research Corporation in California.[13] The average household covered by this study received 7.9 unsolicited telephone calls, not including misdialed calls, during the three month period involved. This figure included obscene, threatening, and crank calls as well as unsolicited sales, survey, or fund raising calls. Approximately 46 percent of the households contacted had not received any telephone sales calls during this time. An average of approximately 9.2 misdialed calls were also received by each household during the same period. Less than half of the approximately 4,000 informal comments supporting regulation referred to personal experience with unsolicited telephone calls.[14]

17. Although the ADRMP[15] has received a substantial amount of public attention, it does not appear to be in widespread use. NTIA estimated that fewer than one thousand ADRMPs were in operation.[16] Only 8.6 percent of the California households covered by the Field Research survey had received ADRMP calls. Many of the telephone sales and survey organizations participating in this proceeding also stated that they do not use ADRMPs at present and have no intention of doing so. Several specifically said that the

ADRMP is not an effective means of telephone solicitation because it does not allow the interaction possible with a live presentation. A few organizations, however, indicated that they were using ADRMPs or considering them.

B. Subscriber Reaction to Unsolicited Telephone Calls

18. It is clear that certain subscribers find unsolicited telephone calls inconvenient and annoying.[17] As previously stated, the Commission received approximately 4,000 informal comments supporting regulation. The Bell System operating companies have also received about 2,000 to 3,000 complaints concerning unsolicited telephone calls each year.[18] A certain number of complaints were also filed with the state commissions. In a 1977 survey conducted by NARUC, the Maryland Commission said that it received 10 to 15 complaints per month. Minnesota reported receiving from 12 to 16 complaints each month. Three additional states reported receiving three to four complaints per month.

19. Other telephone subscribers do not react adversely to unsolicited calls, however. As previously indicated, a substantial number of people purchase the goods or services offered. One of the survey research organizations also stated that it is not unusual for political opinion poll calls to last as long as forty minutes, indicating that recipients are willing to cooperate in such efforts. Two surveys taken by Campaign Communications Institute clients also indicated a fairly positive response to telephone sales solicitation.[19] Many of the organizations involved in telephone solicitation also stated that they received few complaints. CCI stated that it averages only about one or two complaints per 100,000 calls. In addition, eight of the states responding to the NARUC survey said that they received one complaint or less each month. Sixteen states had not received any complaints.

C. Special Concerns Related To ADRMP Use

20. There is also some concern that unsolicit-

[11] Sylvia Porter, "Get the Maximum Benefit from Business Telephoning," *New York Post, cited in* Comments filed by Campaign Communications Institute of America, Inc.

[12] Robert C. Steckel, *Profitable Sales Operations* (Arco: New York, 1976), *cited in* Reply Comments of National Telecommunications and Information Administration.

[13] "The California Public's Experience With and Attitude Toward Unsolicited Telephone Calls," Field Research Corporation, March 1978.

[14] The Commission's Notice of Inquiry did not specifically request that parties filing informal comments provide information on this point.

[15] An ADRMP contains two elements. The automatic dialer is programmed with telephone numbers to be contacted and the recorded message player presents a taped message when the telephone is answered. These elements can be used separately or in conjunction with one another. For the purposes of this discussion, the term "ADRMP equipment" includes recorded message players regardless of whether they are used with an automatic dialer.

[16] This estimate was based on a survey of ADRMP equipment manufacturers. However, NTIA noted that telephone answering machines can also be used to make recorded presentations over the telephone.

[17] Unsolicited telephone calls may also involve false and deceptive sales practices in certain instances.

[18] American Telephone and Telegraph Company Summary Statistics on Abusive Calling (1975, 1976, 1977, and 1978 and 1979).

[19] In a 1976 survey, 90 per cent of those interviewed stated that the method of solicitation used was good and that the communicator was very polite. The second survey, which took place in 1978, found that 97 per cent of those interviewed felt that the CCI communicator was courteous. Over 71 per cent said that the call had given them a better understanding of the service offered.

ed telephone calls, particularly those originated by ADRMPs or human telephone solicitors calling numbers within one local exchange could theoretically cause central office congestion. However, no instances of such problems due to unsolicited telephone calls have been cited in this proceeding. AT&T and GTE stated that they do not anticipate difficulty handling the increases in the general demand for telephone service and any specific increase in demand due to unsolicited calls. All three organizations said that they do not expect the ADRMP to have a significant adverse impact on the operation of the telephone network.

21. Use of ADRMPs also raises another concern which is not usually present in the case of manually dialed calls involving live presentations. An ADRMP used without a human monitor may continue to hold the called party's line until the recording has finished playing even though the called party has hung up. It does not appear that this problem occurs with a substantial degree of frequency, however. As indicated above, the ADRMP is not in widespread use. One of the ADRMP equipment manufacturers also said that virtually all ADRMPs are operated with a human monitor. In addition, it is important to recognize that this type of problem is experienced only in exchanges which are not equipped for automatic called-party disconnect. NTIA estimated that approximately 80 percent of all telephone company central offices have this feature.

III. DISCUSSION

22. Under Section 2 of the Communications Act of 1934 as amended, 47 U.S.C. §152 (1976), our jurisdiction is generally limited to interstate and foreign communication.[20] Although the Act does not "[sanction] any state regulation, formally restrictive only of intrastate communication, that in effect encroaches substantially upon the Commission's authority," we do not have jurisdiction "over local services, facilities and disputes that in their nature and effect are separable from and do not substantially affect the conduct or development of interstate communications." *North Carolina Utilities Commission* v. *Federal Communications Commission*, 537 F. 2d 787, 793 (4th Cir. 1976), *cert. denied*, 429 U.S. 1027 (1976). Unlike terminal equipment which is normally used for both interstate

and intrastate communications, interstate unsolicited telephone calls are clearly separable from those made within a single state or local exchange. Furthermore, as previously discussed, we find that neither ADRMP use nor unsolicited telephone calls in general presently have a significant impact on the use of the telephone network for interstate calling. Accordingly, in the present factual context, we must limit our consideration to regulation of unsolicited telephone calls that are interstate in nature. Should circumstances change, however, we might reach different conclusions concerning the extent of our jurisdiction.

23. It appears from the comments that a central controversy in the larger problem of telephone solicitation concerns use of the ADRMP. As already noted, however, there are relatively few such devices currently in operation. Moreover, most of the ADRMPs now in operation are very likely used for local, or at least intrastate calling. Since the obvious benefit of using an ADRMP for solicitation is the cost savings afforded, it seems logical to assume that these devices would not normally be used to make relatively expensive (as compared to local service) long distance, WATS or private line calls. Ninety-seven percent of all telephone calls are intrastate.[21] If this ratio is even approximated for ADRMP use, it would mean that only a tiny fraction of all ADRMP messages are interstate calls subject to our jurisdiction. Any action that this Commission could undertake would impact only a small fraction of the calls made by the relatively few ADRMPs now in use.

24. Under these circumstances, federal regulation would not appear to be warranted at this time. From the standpoint of our interstate jurisdiction, any problem raised by the use of ADRMPs, lies in their potential for abuse at some point in the future, if such use becomes widespread. We are certainly not there now. In our view, regulation in this area can best be handled by the individual states should they conclude that action is warranted.

25. We come then to the larger question of whether restrictions should be imposed on interstate telephone solicitation generally. A complete ban on unsolicited calling would raise serious constitutional difficulties. Plainly, any regulatory action by the Commission restricting use of the telephone to convey a particular type of message would have to satisfy the require-

---

[20] Section 2(a) states that [t]he provisions of this chapter shall apply to all interstate and foreign communication by wire or radio...." Section 2(b) provides, with certain exceptions not relevant here, that "...nothing in this chapter shall be construed to apply or to give the Commission jurisdiction with respect to...charges, classifications, practices, services, facilities or regulations for or in connection with intrastate communication service by wire or radio of any carrier...." 47 U.S.C. %152(a) & (b) (1976).

[21] *Bell System Statistical Manual* (April 1979) at pp. 803 & 805; *Telerent Leasing Corp.*, 45 FCC 2d 204, 211 (1974), *aff'd sub nom. North Carolina Utilities Commission* v. *Federal Communications Commission*, 537 F. 2d 787 (4th Cir. 1976), *cert. denied*, 429 U.S. 1027 (1976).

ments of the First Amendment.[22] Although privately owned, the telephone network is devoted to public use. In contemporary American society, telephones are clearly the primary means of private communications between individuals who are not in proximity to one another. The ability to speak with others over the telephone would thus appear to be entitled to substantial protection.

[In paragraphs 26-30, the F.C.C. reviews several court cases related to the matter of unsolicited telephone calls.]

31. In our view, [recent legal] cases stand for the general principle that the government may not broadly prohibit unrequested contacts with individuals in the privacy of the home absent an appropriate indication that the householder does not want to be disturbed. Thus, a complete ban on unsolicited calls or a prohibition on such calls to subscribers who have not affirmatively indicated a desire to receive them would probably be unlawful. *See* paragraph 35, *infra*.

32. Exempting calls made for political and charitable solicitation or survey research purposes from regulations applicable to commercial sales calls would also appear to raise serious constitutional questions in the absence of significant practical differences between unsolicited commercial and non-commercial calls. All solicitation calling—whether for charitable, political or business purposes—involves similar privacy implications. We have no information that subscribers would find an advertising message more offensive than a request for a charitable contribution or a political message or solicitation. As the Court noted in *Bates* v. *State Bar of Arizona*, 433 U.S. 350, 364 (1977), "the consumers' concern for the free flow of commercial speech may often be far keener than his concern for urgent political dialogue." The importance of commercial speech has been emphasized by the Court in *Bates* and a number of other recent Court decisions. For example in *Virginia Pharmacy Board* v. *Virginia Consumer Council* the Court stated that:

> Advertising, however tasteless and excessive it sometimes may seem, is nonetheless dissemination of information as to who is producing and selling what product, for what reason, and at what price. So long as we preserve a predominantly free enterprise economy, the allocation of our resources in large measure will be made through numerous private economic decisions. It is a matter of public interest that those decisions, in the aggregate, be intelligent and well informed. To this end, the free flow of commercial information is indispensable.[23]

425 U.S. 748, 765 (1976).

Although the extent of the differences between commercial and non-commercial speech have perhaps not yet been fully delineated,[24] differential treatment of protected speech based on content is usually prohibited. *Police Department* v. *Mosley*, 408 U.S. 92 (1972); *Niemotko* v. *Maryland*, 340 U.S. 268 (1951).

33. Any ban on telephone solicitation would also have to satisfy constitutional standards for clarity and specificity. *Hynes* v. *Mayor of Oradell*, 425 U.S. 610 (1976); *Grayned* v. *Rockford*, 408 U.S. 104 (1972). This would appear to present a rather difficult problem since the term "unsolicited telephone call" must be defined based on the prior relationship between the parties. For example, should a ban against solicitation preclude a store from calling a long-time customer to inform him of a sale? Should it make any difference whether the person receiving the solicitation is acquainted with the caller? These and other similar definitional questions would accompany any ban and would no doubt embroil the Commission in difficult and perhaps unresolvable problems related to First Amendment concerns.

34. Even assuming that an outright ban on telephone solicitation would be constitutionally permissible, we would be reluctant to act in an area as sensitive as free speech absent the strongest kind of public interest showing. Such a showing has not been made in this proceeding. First, we are faced with the fact that our jurisdiction is limited. Any ban promulgated by this Commission would apply only to the small portion of unsolicited telephone calls which are interstate. Second, the comments in the proceeding reveal that although many people are annoyed by telephone solicitation, this is not a universal reaction. A substantial proportion of those receiving unsolicited telephone calls are apparently willing to cooperate in surveys or purchase the goods offered. *See* paras. 15, 18 & 19 *supra*.

35. The constitutional difficulties noted above might not apply if we merely sought to promulgate time, place or manner restrictions for unsolicited calls. We believe that such restrictions would be constitutional if they served a significant interest, left open ample alternative channels of communications, and could be justified without reference to the content of the speech involved. *Virginia Pharmacy Board* v. *Virginia Consumer Council*, 425 U.S. 748, 771 (1976). Regulation of this kind, however, ap-

---

[22] The First Amendment provides, in pertinent part, "Congress shall make no law...abridging the freedom of speech...." U.S. Const. Amend. I.

[23] *See also, Carey* v. *Population Services International*, 431 U.S. 678 (1977); *Linmark Associates, Inc.* . *Township of Willingboro*, 431 U.S. 85 (1977); *Bigelow* v. *Virginia*, 421

U.S. 809 (1975).

[24] For example, although it is clear that noncommercial speech is protected, the Court stated in *Bates* that the "overbreadth doctrine" would apply only weakly if at all in a commercial context. *Id.* at 380-81.

pears unnecessary. An organization which is trying to sell something, obtain a contribution, or elicit information has an incentive to direct calls to those likely to be interested, limit calls to reasonable hours, and conduct them in an ethical and courteous manner.

36. Moreover, unreasonable interstate telephone solicitation practices can presently be dealt with through language contained in AT&T tariffs. AT&T tariff language prohibits "use of the service in such a manner as to interfere unreasonably with the use of the service by one or more other Customers." AT&T Tariff F.C.C. No. 263, Long Distance Message Telecommunications Service, Section 2.2.2(E); AT&T Tariff F.C.C. No. 259, Wide Area Telecommunications Service, Section 2.2.2(E). *See also,* AT&T "Procedures to Improve Customer Service—Annoyance Calls" (November 1, 1968, revised August 16, 1971). Although this language is not contained in AT&T's private line tariffs, this language or similar restrictions found in the local tariffs would apply to the use of private line service to access the switched network or distant local exchanges. We believe that these tariffs (which are concurred in by the independent telephone companies) are sufficient to handle any problem of solicitation in an improper or abusive manner.[25] We further note that Bell has represented in its comments that it fosters educational efforts designed to encourage adherence to reasonable telephone solicitation practices. Also, as discussed below, enforcement of regulations applicable only to interstate unsolicited telephone calls would be difficult.

37. It might be suggested that telephone subscribers be permitted to request that the telephone company notify a particular solicitor, or solicitors generally, that such subscriber is not to be called. A regulation of this kind, however, would be difficult to enforce and expensive to implement. The person called would not ordinarily be able to determine whether the solicitor was using the interstate telephone network or placing the call locally. Even if the recipient of an unsolicited telephone call could determine that the call was interstate, that person would not generally be able to determine or, perhaps even

more important, to prove that subsequent calls were also interstate and thus violative of his instructions to the telephone company. Similarly, it might be difficult for the telephone company itself to verify whether the offending call was made over the interstate network or even whether a solicitation was made. A prior notification system would also be likely to require substantial recordkeeping.

38. Here again, such an effort would appear unwarranted. The subscriber would not be protected against intrastate calls which, for reasons already described, would presumably make up the bulk of all unsolicited telephone calls. Thus, any privacy gained by the telephone user would be quite limited and, in our view, would clearly be outweighed by the complications and burdens inherent in administering any prior notification scheme.

39. For the foregoing reasons, we find that the public interest would not be served by any Commission action at this time to subject telephone solicitation to federal regulatory constraints. In the present circumstances our jurisdiction is limited to regulation of interstate unsolicited telephone calls and ADRMP usage. Interstate use of the ADRMP is not widespread at this time and appears to pose no problem of harassment to subscribers or impairment of service subject to our jurisdiction. A general ban on telephone solicitation would raise serious constitutional difficulties, affect only the small percentage of unsolicited telephone calls which are interstate, and is, in any event, questionable as a matter of policy. Finally, it does not appear that a prior notification ban or time, place and manner restrictions at the federal level are warranted because of the small percentage of calls affected, the incentives for industry self-regulation, the present tariff language prohibiting abusive solicitation, the difficulty of effective enforcement and the cost of regulation.

40. Accordingly, IT IS ORDERED, that this proceeding BE TERMINATED.

FEDERAL COMMUNICATIONS COMMISSION
William J. Tricario
Secretary

---

[25] Any action undertaken by us in this area would have to operate through the enforcement of AT&T tariffs. Accordingly, the Commission appears to have a statutory mechanism for dealing with unsolicited telephone calls. The Commission's substantive regulatory authority is subject to jurisdictional limitations, however.

Roster of
States' Legislation

Beyond the federal regulations that might affect telemarketing, each
state has the power to enact laws that govern the practice of all forms of
commerce within its jurisdiction. Appendix C lists those states that,
according to the Direct Marketing Association, have laws specifically
regulating telemarketing operations. The would-be telemarketer is advised
to examine the restrictions and limitations of these laws carefully before
attempting to set up an operation in any of the listed states.

ARKANSAS—The 1981 amendment to Ark. Sta. Ann. Sec. 70-915
added that the definition of a "home solicitation sale" shall include "all
telephone sales in which the seller had initiated contact regardless of the
location and [in which] the consumer's agreement to purchase is made in
the consumer's home. . . ." Thus, in Arkansas your telephone sales
would clearly be subject to the restrictions set out above.

CALIFORNIA—There are two sections of the California Civil Code
that we are concerned with here. Cal. Civ. Code Sec. 1689.5 defines
"home solicitation contract or offer" in part as: "any contract or offer
which is subject to approval, for the sale, lease or rental of goods or
services or both, made *at other than appropriate trade premises* in an
amount of $25.00 or more. . . ." Since the sales are to take place in the
buyer's home, it is believed that telephone solicitations do fall within the
purview of this section.

Cal. Bus. & Prof. Code Sec. 17500.3 imposes criminal sanctions on
persons soliciting sales or orders for the sale of goods or services at the
residences of prospective buyers "in person or by means of telephone. . . ." However, the requirements imposed by this section of the
code are far less burdensome than those imposed under the civil section of
the code. The requirements imposed under Sec. 17500.3 include (1) stating the identity of the person making the solicitation; (2) stating the trade
name of the business represented by the person making the solicitation; (3)
stating the kind of goods or services being offered for sale; and (4) other
requirements in the case of "in person" contact, which will not concern
the telemarketer.

DELAWARE—The previous version of Del. Code Ann. Title 6, Sec. 4403 included in the definition of "door-to-door sales" any solicitations and consummations of sales "via any telephone." The statutory amendment of 1976, however, changed the statute so that it no longer mentioned telephone except that it says telephone sales initiated *by the buyer* are excluded. Thus, in light of the two statutes, it appears that telephone sales initiated by the seller are still subject to the act. If the legislature would have wanted to exclude seller-initiated calls, according to recent cases decided on this issue, the addition of the phrase "initiated by the buyer" would have no logical basis. The statute would simply have excluded all telephone contact, if that had been the legislative intent.

FLORIDA—The opinion of the Attorney General of Florida dated March 28, 1977, stated that "telephone solicitations" made by business concerns do not qualify as "home solicitation sales" as defined in Fl. Stat. Ann. Sec. 501.021. However, this was invalidated by the statutory amendment effective October 1, 1977, which added to the definition of a home solicitation sale "a sales transaction unsolicited by the consumer and consummated by telephone and without any other contact between the buyer and seller . . . . prior to delivery of the goods. . . ."

ILLINOIS—Under Ill. Rev. Stat. Chapter 121½ Sec. 262B, a "door-to-door sale" includes a sale of merchandise as a result of or in connection with a salesperson's direct contact with *or call* on the consumer at his or her residence without the consumer's soliciting the contact or call.

INDIANA—The 1979 amendment to Ind. Code Ann. Sec. 24-4.5-2-501 inserted the following portion in the definition of "home solicitation sales": "including the solicitation *over the telephone* at the residence of the buyer and [when the] buyer's agreement or offer to purchase is then given to the seller. . . ."

LOUISIANA—The definition of home solicitation sales was amended in 1978 to read in part: "this definition shall also include *all telephone sales* in which the seller has initiated contact regardless of his location, and [in which] the consumer's agreement to purchase is made at the consumer's home." (La. Rev. Stat. Ann. Sec. 9.3516.)

MICHIGAN—Mich. Stat. Ann. Sec. 445.111 defines "home solicitation sales" in part as "a personal *or telephonic solicitation* of the sale at a residence of the buyer and [when] the buyer's agreement or offer to purchase is there given to the seller. . . ."

MONTANA—Mont. Rev. Code Ann. Sec. 30-14-502 states: " 'Personal solicitation' means any attempt by seller who regularly engages in transactions of the same kind to sell goods or services which are primarily for personal, family, or household purposes when either the seller or a person acting for him *contacts the buyer by telephone* or in person other than at the place of business of the seller. . . ."

NORTH DAKOTA—N.D. Cent. Code Sec. 51-18-01 includes in the definition of "personal solicitation sales" *a sale made by telephone* or in person when the buyer's agreement or offer to purchase is made at a place other than the place of business of the person soliciting the sale.

OHIO—The Ohio statute does not expressly include sales by telephone; however, the recent case of *Brown v. Martinelli*, 66 Ohio St. 2d 45 (*1981*) makes it clear that sales solely by means of telephone constitute home solicitation sales within the meaning of Ohio Rev. Code Ann. Sec. 1345.21. After analyzing two sections of Ohio Rev. Code Ann. Sec. 1345.21, the court stated: "They are reconcilable if the General Assembly intended to include within the meaning of 'home solicitation sale' those sales which are accomplished solely by telephone solicitation initiated by the seller. We conclude such was the intention of the General Assembly" (66 Ohio St. 2d at 49).

WISCONSIN—Here there are two relevant regulations. Wis. Stat. Ann. Sec. 423.201 includes in its definition of "consumer approval transaction" a consumer transaction that is initiated by mail *or telephonic solicitation* directed to the particular customer.

Also, the rules of the Department of Agriculture Sec. 127.01 provide that "home solicitation selling" occurs when the sale is personally solicited by seller at the residence or place of business or employment of the buyer. The rule further provides that a personal solicitation *includes a solicitation made directly or indirectly by telephone*.

WYOMING—The 1981 amendment to Wyo. Stat. Sec. 40-14-251 added the following to the definition of "home solicitation sale": ". . . *or telephone solicitation* at a place other than the place of business of the seller and [when] the buyer's agreement or offer to purchase is there given to the seller. . . ."

The following are states that do not impose strict regulations upon door-to-door selling or have not taken a definite stand in this area to date.

ALABAMA—Here there are two separate sets of laws: those for Alabama generally and those for counties with populations of 600,000 or more (Jefferson County). As for Alabama generally, Ala. Code Sec. 5-19-1 includes in the definition of "home solicitation sales" only those sales in which the seller engages in a personal solicitation of the sale at a place other than the seller's place of business. Thus, viewing the statute alone, it appears that telephone solicitations are not included, since the solicitation must be physically personal. As for the regulations that apply to Jefferson County, "solicitation at the residence of the buyer" includes *door-to-door solicitation* and all offers to sell goods or services made as part of the solicitation plan or program in which *residence visitation by salespeople* or other representatives of the seller play a major part. There is no reference made to telephone solicitation. Since door-to-door or residence visitation by salespeople obviously requires face-to-face contact, telephone sales would not be subject to the restrictions of the act.

MINNESOTA—Minn. Stat. Ann. Sec. 325G.06 includes in its definition of "home solicitation sales" only those transactions in which the seller *personally solicits* the sale. There is no mention of telephone solicitation sales; therefore, telephone contacts are presumably not to be included under the act.

However, telephone solicitations in Minnesota would fall within the bounds of Minn. Stat. Ann. Sec. 325G.12. This states: "'Personal solicitation' means any attempt by a seller . . . to sell goods or services . . . by telephone or in person other than at the place of business of the seller. . . ." But the restrictions this would impose are far less burdensome than those imposed on home solicitation sales. The relevant regulations include clearly and expressly disclosing: (1) the individual seller's name; (2) the name of the business firm or organization the seller represents; (3) the identity or kinds of goods or services the seller wishes to demonstrate or sell; and (4) that the seller wishes to demonstrate or sell the identified goods or services.

UTAH—Utah Code Ann. Sec. 70B-2-501 applies to a personal solicitation of the sale at the residence of the buyer. No mention is made of telephone contacts. However, a comment of the Utah Commissioners on Uniform State Laws requires, for a transaction to be brought within the terms of the act, a personal solicitation at the residence of the buyer. The commissioners went on to state that because the term "personal solicitation" is used, it shall apply only to sales in which the buyer and seller engage in face-to-face confrontation at the residence of the buyer.

WASHINGTON—Washington is different from the other states in that the restrictions we are concerned with are imposed upon the classification of the transaction as a "retail installment transaction." The definition of "retail installment transaction" includes any transaction in which a retail buyer purchases goods or services from a retail seller pursuant to a retail installment contract under which the buyer agrees to pay the unpaid balance in one or more installments or that provides for no service charge unless buyer agrees to pay the unpaid balance in more than four installments.

Furthermore, the retail installment transaction must be entered into by the buyer and solicited *in person* by the seller or his or her representative at a place other than the seller's address (Wash. Rev. Code Ann. Sec. 63.14.154). Therefore, even if the sale qualifies as a retail installment transaction, since the sale was not entered into and solicited in person by the seller, the restrictions that we are concerned with should not apply.

The Direct Marketing Association Guidelines

Every professional organization sets guidelines for its members. In the case of the marketing profession such guidelines outline for the membership carefully considered courtesies designed to enhance the relationship between consumer and seller. With such an enhancement in mind the Direct Marketing Association has published the following Guidelines for Ethical Business Practices:

1. Advertisers/marketers selling products or services or raising funds for nonprofit organizations should make their telephone presentations clear and honest. There should be no attempt to mislead, to exaggerate, or to use partial truths. Telemarketers should not make calls in the guise of research or a survey when the real intent is to sell.

2. Telephone contacts should be made within the framework of federal, state, and local laws. Taping of telephone conversations is illegal without a beeping device.

3. Telephone contacts to consumers should be made during reasonable hours.

4. Telephone orders should not be accepted from minors without adult approval. (The legal definition of a minor may vary from state to state.)

5. Telemarketers should not use what is commonly referred to as "high-pressure" tactics. They should observe the normal rules of telephone courtesy.

5. Telemarketers should make conscientious efforts to remove names from their contact lists when requested to do so.

7. Telemarketers should not call unlisted or unpublished telephone numbers unless a current telephone relationship exists.

What Your Customers
Think about
Telemarketing—
ZIP *Magazine*

Public interest and concern over the impact of telemarketing has
spurred several surveys to attempt to measure consumer response to the
telephone. The response of women nationwide to telephone solicitation
was studied by Jerry Thomas of San Jose State School of Business. The
results of his study were discussed in an article in *ZIP* magazine that
is reprinted here.[1]

Study shows familiarity breeds results
What Your Customers Think
About Telephone Marketing
A nationwide study of the attitudes of female consumers in their homes toward
buying (and being solicited to buy) over the telephone reveals a probable surge
in the overall effectiveness of telephone marketing in the years just ahead.

A university researcher at San Jose State School of Business in California
selected a statistically representative sample of households in four different sections of the country. Calling them on the phone, he first determined their status
for the projectable validity of the study: they were (1) female head of household,
at least 18 years old; (2) wife of the male head of household; (3) unmarried
female living with male or (4) unmarried female responsible for making principal purchasing decisions in the dwelling unit itself.

Sampling all Bell System subscribers, the study chose 349 from the 15.3 million in the East; 324 from the 14.5 million in the North Central states; 391 from
the 17.5 million in the South; and 254 from the 11.3 million in the West.

By and large, the overwhelming majority of the women contacted were
pleased to receive telephone solicitations from retailers that they had previously
dealt with. Most were very positive toward the programs that would inform
them of special products or sale opportunities from marketers with which they
were already familiar. The study, however, did not seek to determine their
attitudes toward uninvited calls from marketers whom they did not already
know or buy from.

This nationwide study confirmed what retailers have sensed for some time:
that today's homemaker does not look forward to shopping in stores as a desirable leisure-time activity. For working women in particular, traveling to stores
and spending precious non-working time browsing is poorly regarded. Shopping
from catalogs, over TV, and through other in-the-home media is growing in

[1] Reprinted with permission from ZIP magazine, 545 Madison Avenue, New York, N.Y.
10022; from the May 1981 issue.

acceptance and favor, the study shows. And the telephone is increasingly the order-placing instrument of choice for these women.

The "Psychographics of Telephone Shopping" study was made by Jerry Thomas as part of his doctoral dissertation research at San Jose State. Working with the co-operation of AT&T, he has completed his preliminary report, and will now embark on a further, more detailed survey on the subject.

Specifically, the women contacted indicated that they would welcome the opportunity to shop at home for goods carried by retailers who were not in their immediate geographical area. This finding, reflecting the views of eight out of ten of the women contacted, should encourage retailers to "reach out" from their home bases to outlying areas, and even to neighborhoods far afield which match the demographic profiles of their heaviest-penetration customer blocs.

Several retailers at the convention of the National Retail Merchants Assn., where the study was introduced, indicated that they would now explore the possibilities of mailing into target areas in anticipation of opening branch stores there. Others showed interest in creating entirely new telephone marketing operations following up on saturation mailings of catalogs and mini-catalogs to specific test areas.

Seven out of ten of the women said that they would probably *increase* their use of the telephone to place orders after seeing a product they liked in a catalog, on television, or in another medium (including direct-mail solicitation). And eight out of ten are definitely in favor of purchasing generic items like linens, domestic goods, personal items, and small appliances (especially major national brands) over the telephone—without the necessity of inspecting the goods personally.

Ordering at Their Leisure

Proof of the flexibility of the telephone (when combined with the in-store visit) came when 87% of the women agreed that they would like to use the telephone to order products which they had actually examined and comparison-shopped in the stores, waiting until they returned home to reach a final purchasing decision, and ordering at their leisure.

Many of the shoppers even indicated that they might be willing to pay for at least part of the cost of ordering by phone from a distant source, paving the way for future applications of the '900' number.

Already, there is a trend for well-respected retailers like Neiman-Marcus in Dallas to do a substantial nationwide business with buyers from coast to coast. Specialty stores have climbed aboard the bandwagon, and a virtual flood of specialized mailing pieces and mini-catalogs is now going out to select neighborhoods across the country.

Resident mailers report an increase in pieces delivered to choice areas well away from their retail clients' home bases, with either local or '800' numbers displayed prominently on the material.

Some retailers have attempted to upgrade their own in-house telephone order centers to keep up with the surge of incoming questions and orders—and complaints. Others are contracting with leading local and Inwats services to handle the call load, which is unpredictable in volume from hour to hour, and which increasingly comes at night and on weekends.

A number of marketers in the retail field with limited telephone operations are already embarking on their own surveys, usually within range of their present delivery systems. "But with UPS so handy, and with the growing reach of TV and radio advertising, we are actively considering a much broader base," said an executive of a southern store. "We want to document the feelings of both our present customers and of several hundred potential customers who are at varying distances from our stores before proceeding," noted a western retailer, "but our gut feeling is that this will open up an entirely new profit center for us."

Many of those attending the conference felt that the telephone could certainly maximize their current newspaper advertising campaigns, which already reach thousands of potential customers too far away for convenient store shopping. And others were discussing the possibility of placing their newspaper pre-print inserts into specific small-town or regional newspapers which they had not previously considered as viable, in an effort to test the "drawing power" of incoming telephone marketing.

It was pointed out that "life-cycle" promotion is already undertaken on a local basis by many leading retailers. Sears, for instance, calls buyers of its laundry detergent and other products on a regular schedule to obtain re-orders, sometimes adding a sales pitch for a "weekly special" that would be of interest to housewives. Calls made to existing department-store customers offering rug cleaning and furniture upholstery services are also proving to be cost-effective in many localities.

Apprehension Over Guarantees

One of the problems associated with ordering over the telephone is the continuing apprehension in the minds of many consumers as to quality, guarantees, and returnability. A great many of the women surveyed stated that they still had some notion that an article bought in the store was probably of better quality than one bought via telephone, sight unseen—this despite their agreement that they would probably not receive the same exact piece that they had examined in the store when delivery was made from the warehouse.

It was generally agreed that the deciding factor in motivating both current and new customers to order by telephone was the *perceived reputation* for quality and reliability already established by the retailer in local markets, and perhaps nationally (even for retailers operating in only a few localities). Prominently displayed guarantees of returnability in printed and broadcast advertising were felt to be crucial in establishing the necessary climate of confidence that is a prerequisite to a successful telephone operation.

Expanding Use of Credit

Other retailers saw the opportunities inherent in expanding their own credit card networks. Several commented about programs conducted over the telephone to the immediate neighbors of current account-holders, noting that preliminary results (credit applications which had been approved) looked extremely encouraging. It was pointed out, however, that the ultimate success of these programs could not be determined until the stores had had the opportunity to "track" these new charge customers for a least six months to ascertain the levels of purchase on account.

"There are lots of promising new technologies developing in various parts of the country that will allow retailers to expand their operations well beyond the confines of the retail store and the shopping center," said the director of marketing of a major chain operation. "A number of us are already examining a limited catalog-type operation, whereby the customer can order from her home at any hour, and then drive in to a miniwarehouse two or three days later to pick up her purchase, all at a considerable saving over ordinary in-store purchasing. This idea is truly revolutionary to some of those who have built the department store business from scratch in this country, but it may be the wave of the future."

Whatever the final outcome of these exploratory efforts, the telephone will be a principal ingredient in speeding incoming orders, and it may play a significant role in aggressive out-calling sales programs as well. The nation's leading retailers are certainly studying this medium with renewed interest, and their convention next year may turn up a host of new programs.

appendix F / *The Inappropriateness of Longer, Literate Taped Messages*

Often when marketers consider using taped messages of known personalities they naturally want to give full play to their notables. Appendix F is a script that was tested in Norman Cousins' *World* magazine campaign. It was delivered by author James Michener. And it proved to be less effective as a telemarketing message than simpler, more direct scripts. The rule of thumb for telemarketing is that a simple and direct appeal is more effective than even the most literate of efforts.

HELLO, THIS IS NORMAN COUSINS. MY PURPOSE IN CALLING YOU IS TO SHARE WITH YOU THE EXCITING AND IMPORTANT NEWS THAT A NATIONAL SOCIETY FOR LITERATURE AND THE ARTS HAS BEEN FORMED FOR THE PURPOSE OF UPGRADING THE CONDITIONS OF THE CREATIVE ARTS IN THE UNITED STATES. AS AN ARTIST, YOU ARE ELIGI-BLE FOR MEMBERSHIP. THE CHAIRMAN IS MR. JAMES MICHENER, THE NOVELIST. HE IS SITTING ALONGSIDE ME NOW AND WOULD LIKE TO INVITE YOU TO JOIN. JAMES MICHENER.

HELLO, THIS IS JAMES MICHENER. I WANT TO SPEAK TO YOU BRIEFLY ABOUT AN EXCITING NEW DEVELOPMENT IN OUR NATIONAL CULTURE. A NUMBER OF PEOPLE WHO ARE PROMINENT IN THE ARTS, PEOPLE LIKE ANDREW WYETH, RICHARD RODGERS, LEONTYNE PRICE, AGNES DE MILLE, BUCKMINSTER FULLER, AND ROGER STEVENS, HAVE JOINED TOGETHER TO FORM THE NATIONAL SOCIETY OF LITERATURE AND THE ARTS. WE INTEND THIS SOCIETY TO PROVIDE APPROPRIATE REC-OGNITION FOR ACHIEVEMENT IN THE ARTS. JUST AS IMPORTANT, WE HOPE TO IMPROVE THE CONDITION OF CREATIVE ARTS IN AMERICA. THOSE OF US WHO ARE PROFESSIONALLY INVOLVED IN WRITING OR POETRY OR PAINTING OR MUSIC OR THE THEATER OR ARCHITECTURE OR DESIGN HAVE COME TOGETHER TO MAKE CERTAIN THAT THE ARTS WILL NOT BE SHORTCHANGED, WHETHER IN WASHINGTON OR IN THE LOCAL COMMUNITY BY OUR LEGISLATURES. WE WANT TO BE SURE THAT CREATIVE PERSONS ARE GIVEN ENCOURAGEMENT AND ASSIS-TANCE. BY BANDING TOGETHER AS AN ORGANIZATION, THE SOCIETY IS ABLE TO PROVIDE MEMBERS WITH SUBSTANTIAL BENEFITS THAT MORE THAN OFFSET THE $16 ANNUAL DUES. FOR INSTANCE, EVERY MEMBER OF THE SOCIETY RECEIVES A REGULAR YEARLY SUBSCRIPTION TO *SATURDAY REVIEW*, WHICH IN ITSELF IS ABOUT WORTH THE COST OF MEMBERSHIP. EVERY MEMBER RECEIVES A 15 PERCENT DISCOUNT FOR ALL NEW BOOKS ORDERED THROUGH THE SOCIETY. EVERY MEMBER

RECEIVES REGULAR REPORTS ON THE SOCIETY'S ACTIVITIES. EVERY MEMBER HAS THE RIGHT TO NOMINATE PROMISING WRITERS, MUSICIANS, AND ARTISTS FOR SCHOLARSHIPS. AND, OF COURSE, EVERY MEMBER RECEIVES SAVINGS ON ART REPRODUCTIONS, RECORDS, AND CASSETTES AND DISCOUNTS FOR GROUP TRAVEL. ON BEHALF OF THE BOARD OF GOVERNORS I TAKE PLEASURE IN INVITING YOU TO BECOME A MEMBER OF THE NATIONAL SOCIETY OF LITERATURE AND THE ARTS. EACH MEMBER WILL RECEIVE A MEMBERSHIP SCROLL. DUES ARE NOT PAYABLE UNTIL THE END OF THE YEAR.

THANK YOU JAMES MICHENER, AND THANK YOU FOR LISTENING. THIS IS NORMAN COUSINS AGAIN. WE THINK THAT YOU HAVE A PLACE IN THE SOCIETY FOR LITERATURE AND THE ARTS. OUR REPRESENTATIVE WILL NOW RETURN TO THE TELEPHONE AND ACCEPT YOUR MEMBERSHIP. THANK YOU.

appendix G / *Louisiana National Bank Survey of Customer Response to Telemarketing*[1]

The directors of the Louisiana National Bank had expressed some concern that soliciting by telephone might impact unfavorably on the bank's image in the community. Consequently they decided to find out exactly what impact telemarketing was having. Appendix G is a summary of the results of their survey.

During the week of February 13, a telephone survey was completed among a sample of our customers who were called by CCI during the Phase 1 test run. The Phase 1 test experimented with the use of three different taped messages to complement the interviewer's script: (1) Mr. McCoy (chairman of LNB) only; (2) Mr. McCoy plus a testimonial from a TBS (Telephone Bill System) user; and (3) J. D. Parker (actor and personality testimonial) only. The sample for the Phase 1 test was drawn from the Entree customer base. In all, 202 calls were completed, with 102 acceptors and 100 rejectors of the TBS offer.

Our objective for implementing the survey was to determine the effectiveness of the telephone solicitation with regard to bank image, the use of taped messages, the degree of motivation attributed to the call, and the overall reaction to the sales call (interviewer courtesy, assistance in understanding the TBS product, and an overall rating from the respondent). The responses received were favorable and, we think, open the door for us to continue our telemarketing efforts to the balance of our Entree and LTF customer bases. An analysis is given below for each question asked.

   1. **Bank Image:** "Do you feel that selling the Bill System over the phone changed your opinion of LNB?"
Yes—15.8 percent, or 32 of 202
No—84.1 percent, or 170 of 202
Most of the respondents indicated that the call did not affect their opinion of LNB: 82.3 percent of the acceptors and 86.0 percent of the rejectors did

---

[1] Excerpted, with no changes of substance.

not change their opinion of the bank. Comments offered by those who had changed their opinion of LNB were split down the middle—half positive and half negative. A majority of the negative comments came from those who rejected the offer, as one would expect.

2. Courtesy: "Was the telephone representative courteous?"

Yes—97.0 percent

No—3.0 percent

There is no question that the representatives came across favorably with regard to courtesy: 99 percent of the acceptors and 95 percent of the rejectors reacted positively to this question. There were no negative comments relating to courtesy. Six respondents offered miscellaneous negative comments. As expected, most of the few negative reactions that there were came from rejectors of the offer.

3. Product understanding: "Do you feel the explanation of the Bill System gave you a better understanding of how the service works?"

Yes—71.7 percent

No—27.2 percent

No response—0.9 percent

The responses are favorable here, especially when one considers the product descriptions involved and the limited time with which to work. 77.4 percent of the acceptors and 66 percent of the rejectors answered positively. The "no" group did not appreciate the use of taped messages at all. Perhaps the taped presentations turned off the "no" group to the point of interfering with their opportunity, if not desire, to understand the Bill System product more fully.

4. Effectiveness of tape: "The presentation included a taped message. Do you feel that this taped message was persuasive or effective?"

Of those responding (181 of 202):

Yes—45.3 percent

No—54.7 percent

The use of taped messages didn't seem to fare too well among the sample as a whole or among the separate acceptor and rejector groups, though a better rating was given by the acceptors. Among the acceptors, 51.6 percent of those responding indicated that the taped messages were effective, whereas, among the responding rejectors, 61.6 percent found them to be ineffective. It's interesting to note that of the comments received from both the acceptor and rejector groups, acceptors contributed more positive *and* negative comments than did the rejectors. In contrast, more rejectors either simply didn't remember the tape, were unaware of the tape, or refused to listen to the tape.

5. **Effectiveness of components of presentation:** "Which part of the presentation did you feel was most effective?"

Overall	Of those responding
Tape—10.9 percent	Tape—18.0 percent
Interviewer's comments—49.7 percent	Interviewer's comments—82.0 percent
Don't know/won't say—39.3 percent	

The response to this question was disappointing, with 39 percent not offering an opinion. Among the preferences given, the interviewer was given the nod over the tape by 86.6 percent of the acceptors and 72.5 percent of the rejectors.

6. **Overall rating:** "How would you rate the overall telephone presentation?"

Noting that a five-response scale was used to measure the responses to the question, from "very effective" on the extremely positive end to "not at all effective" on the extremely negative end, the resultant percentages were favorable. Also, by computing the weighted averages of the responses, we were able to determine the general tendencies or reactions among the groups surveyed. As a whole, the response from both acceptor and rejector groups tended to be in the "somewhat effective" category. In fact, 85.2 percent of the ratings were neutral at worse, with 68.8 percent of them above neutral. The acceptors' responses also centered in the "somewhat effective category." Among acceptors, 96 percent gave the presentation ratings a neutral at worst, with 86.2 percent of the ratings above neutral. As would be expected, rejectors centered their reactions in the neutral corner. Still, 73.6 percent of the rejectors gave the presentation a neutral or better score, with 50.4 percent of the ratings above neutral.

For acceptors only:

7. **Motivation effect:** "Would you have opened a Bill System account even if the service had not been offered to you over the phone?"

Yes—25.0 percent (but when?)

No—53.0 percent (CCI motivated—very good!)

Maybe—22.0 percent (telephone call acted as the catalyst!)

The results shown here are super. There seems to be little doubt about the motivating effect of the CCI calls among the acceptors. Assuming that the "maybe" responses were from "borderline" TBS sign-ups, up to 75 percent of the acceptors would not have opened up a TBS account without some sort of catalyst. In general, this type of specialized catalyzing sales approach for a particular product cannot be found presently in the branch system, given the many and varied services and responsibilities with which branch personnel must cope.

Summary   The results from our survey of Phase I participants indicate that telephone solicitations do not harm the image of LNB. The telephone sales technique appears to be a very effective motivating force when it comes down to signing up TBS accounts. In addition to the acceptability and effectiveness of the telephone sales technique, it seems too that CCI personnel presented themselves and their product with the necessary degree of decorum required by representatives of a financial institution.

Montgomery Ward's Survey of Customer Response to Telemarketing

As a follow-up to the CCI telephone campaign, Montgomery Ward initiated a market research survey to determine the extent of the effectiveness of the CCI campaign. Appendix H is a summary of the results of this survey.

Montgomery Ward Auto Club Surveys

Through a request initiated by Signature Agency, a marketing research company became involved in examining consumer reaction to the telemarketing campaign on behalf of Montgomery Ward Auto Club (MWAC). A survey was undertaken involving the following excerpted details.

Unconfirmed MWAC Membership Inquiry Several thousand households were contacted nationwide by Campaign Communications Institute of America, Inc. (CCI), a telephone solicitation company commissioned by MWAC. Of these, after hearing a solicitation given by the CCI representative, 499 households verbally agreed to become members of MWAC. Confirmation cards were then sent to these households. However, only 239 confirmation cards were returned. MWAC management is interested in learning why the cards were not returned and whether or not the CCI representatives were polite, informative, and truthful in their solicitation. The marketing research company designed a telephone-administered questionnaire to probe the 260 households that did not return the confirmation card, and during the first week in March, 163 interviews were completed, yielding the following results.

Findings Interviewers asked solicited households to rate overall the "method of solicitation" as presented by the CCI representative. Over

90 percent of these respondents rated the method of solicitation as "good."

CCI representatives were apparently polite during their telephone solicitations. Over 90 percent of the respondents rated them as "very polite," while the remaining respondents felt they were "reasonably polite" in their solicitation.

CCI's representatives were also informative. Over 62 percent of the households surveyed rated their representative as "very informative," while 31 percent felt the solicitations to be "reasonably informative." Some items of information about the MWAC that respondents most remember hearing from the CCI representatives are shown in Table H-1.

CCI's representatives seemed to be well informed themselves about MWAC, as 87 percent of the respondents mentioned that all the questions they had asked the representatives about MWAC were answered.

Approximately two-thirds (66 percent) of the respondents contacted indicated they had joined MWAC during the telephone solicitation. Thirty percent (30 percent), however, indicated that although they verbally committed themselves over the telephone, they did not regard this as a final affirmation.

While all these respondents were sent a confirmation card in the mail, only 63 percent remembered receiving it, while 23 percent denied having received a card. Fourteen percent (14 percent) could not remember whether or not they received a card.

Among those households that acknowledged receiving the card, 24 percent actually thought they had returned it, while 68 percent knew definitely that they had not.

TABLE H-1. *Items Best Remembered from MWAC Telemarketing Presentation*

Items of information	Number of times mentioned	Percentage of times mentioned
Describing service benefits	31	19.0
General information about the club	27	16.6
Bail bond service	17	10.4
Cost of MWAC	15	9.2
Could put MWAC on charge account	14	8.6

When asked what information the representative gave them over the phone about the auto club, they answered as follows:

Information	Number of times mentioned	Percentage of times mentioned
Towing service	31	19.0
About program	27	16.6
Bail bond service	17	10.4
Cost	15	9.2
Could put MWAC on charge accounts	14	8.6
Trip planning/maps/arrangements	10	6.1
Pay for towing	9	5.5
Would send more information	9	5.5
Recording tape was played	9	4.9
Membership good on hotel discounts	8	3.7
Emergency road service	6	3.7
Towing rate information	5	3.1
If car broke down, MWAC would pay motel room	5	3.1
Includes car/accident insurance	5	3.1
Told me it was like AAA	5	3.1
Can use services of club anywhere	4	2.5
Said it was inexpensive	3	1.8
Representative said he would send a card	3	1.8
Flat tire fixing service	3	1.8
Said program was good	3	1.8
Played a record of club's president	2	1.2
Tape told how MWAC will come to help	1	.6
Told me club covers any service on the car	1	.6
Told about recharging batteries	1	.6
Tried to talk me into joining	1	.6
Don't remember	47	28.8

Table H-2, which follows, is a statistical summary.

TABLE H-2. *Statistical Summary of*
Unconfirmed MWAC
Membership Inquiry

Subject	Raw score	Percentage of respondents
1. The CCI representative was:		
Very polite	143	87.8
Reasonably polite	14	8.6
Don't know	6	3.6
2. The conversation with the CCI representative was:		
Very informative	101	62.0
Reasonably informative	51	31.3
Not informative	3	1.8
Don't know	8	4.9
3. Was the CCI representative able to answer all your questions?		
Yes	142	87.2
No	3	1.8
Don't know	18	11.0
4. Would you rate CCI's method of solicitation as:		
Good	147	90.2
Fair	10	6.1
Poor	2	1.2
Don't know	4	2.5
5. Did you agree to join the auto club during the phone conversation with the representative?		
Yes	108	66.3
No	49	30.0
Don't know	6	3.7
6. Did you receive a confirmation card in the mail?		
Yes	103	63.2
No	37	22.7
Don't know	23	14.1
7. The households that were sent the card were asked to sign it and return it. Did you return the card?		
Yes	25	24.3
No	70	68.0
Don't know	8	7.7

appendix I / **_Sample Results of Telemarketing_**

Telemarketing has been extremely successful over a wide range of products, industries, and services. The case histories in this book are only a few of the great number of potential examples. Appendix I is a sampling of the results of telemarketing for various agricultural companies, nonprofit organizations, associations, and pharmaceutical companies.

TABLE I-1. *Results of Telemarketing Programs for Various Agricultural Companies*

Program	Objective	Strategy	Results
New product introduction: herbicide	Build retail traffic	Telephone contact with farmers to stimulate interest in purchasing products from retail outlets	20%
Territory and lead management	Generate screened and qualified leads for field sales force	Telephone contact with farmers in 160 territories to screen, qualify, and prioritize for rep follow-up	33%
Membership in agricultural association	Generate membership *and* registration for the association's annual conference	Telephone follow-up to recipients of direct mail targeted to select lists	5% membership 10% registrants
New product introduction: livestock identification tags	Direct sale of tags to farmers	Telephone follow-up of direct mailings to farmers and ranches with livestock	13%
Water well drilling equipment	Direct sale of drilling rigs and drill bits	Two-step process to generate inquiries via mail, with telephone follow-up	14.5%

TABLE I-2. *Results of Telemarketing Programs for Various Nonprofit Organizations*

Program	Objective	Strategy	Response
Salvation Army	Contributions	Telephone to past contributors and prospects	Past contributors 25% Prospects 13%
Planned Parenthood	Solicit donations from nonrespondents to direct mail	Telephone to contributors in each of three years who did not respond to appeal with tape message appeal	37%, 27%, 19% respectively
National Women's Organization (NOW)	Legal and education funds	Telephone select list from women's magazine	40%
PBS—Nonprofit educational broadcasting	Test media for cost-effective fund raising	Telephone pledges sought from past contributors, local prospecting lists, national prospecting lists, and viewers utilizing key personality tape messages	34%, 28%, 25%, 30% respectively
Study center	Membership	Telephone to past contributors and past members	$25 donors—39% $50–100 donors—18% $26
Presidential campaign	Raise political funds	Telephone follow-up to select prospect list with President on tape message	+34%
National Women's Political Caucus	Campaign funds	Telephone follow-up to activist prospects	40%
Political party finance committee (Republican)	Political funds	Telephone to past contributors	40%
Catholic Church	Raise building funds	Telephone tape message from priest to church parishioners	24%

TABLE 1-3. *Results of Telemarketing Programs for Various Membership Associations**

Association program	Objective	Membership fee	Target	Response
National Restaurant Association	Membership acquisition	$150	Members of the restaurant and food service industry	8%
American Bar Association	Membership renewal	$60/100	Attorneys	20%
Bank Marketing Association	Membership renewal	$475	Directors or vice presidents of service and corporate members	24%
Presidents Association of the American Management Associations	Membership acquisition		Presidents of companies	6.3%
American Medical Association	Membership renewal and acquisition	$275†	Physicians	30%

* Peer group tape messages were key to the success of these telemarketing campaigns.
† This is a median figure.

TABLE I-4. *Results of Telemarketing Programs for Various Pharmaceutical Companies*

Program	Objective	Strategy	Results
New product introduction	Stimulate the use of product samples, provide information	Telephone to physicians to determine if they have used product samples, provide information highlighting product features	56.0% had used product 92.0% said they would use in the future
Lead generation for diagnostic testing services	Generate qualified leads for sales force	Telephone to physicians segmented by medical specialty to: Relay information on new tests Expand/upgrade current accounts Reactivate accounts	58.0% expressed interest in using new tests 43.9% expressed interest in additional tests 38.0% expressed interest in reactivating their accounts

Direct product sales to pharmacies	Telephone contact with pharmacist re special offer of drug product after TV/Radio awareness program (communicator then placed order with preferred wholesaler)	25% purchased product 14% accepted counter display unit
Restock inventory and/or open new accounts		
Product update program	Brief physicians with update by telephone on results of clinical research, through taped messages	60% listened to tapes
Maintain product awareness while sales force involved in new product introduction		
Provide details on expanded indication	Data provided by telephoned tape message, pharmascripts offered	87.0% listened to tapes 71.0% accepted pharmascripts
Announcement of expanded indication for a dermatological product		
Generate registrations	Telephone to physicians after mail to generate registrants to attend broadcast symposium (confirmation calls made shortly before symposium to ensure presence)	30% registered
Symposium at annual conference of physicians		

appendix J / *Criteria for Selecting an In-House or Agency Workshop*

HOW TO CHOOSE BETWEEN IN-HOUSE OR OUT-OF-HOUSE TELEMARKETING[1]

Since we began publication of this newsletter the one question which our readers have asked us most consistently is, "Should I set up an in-house telemarketing operation, or go to an outside service bureau?"

The decision to go in-house or out-of-house is never a simple one. Unfortunately, there are those within the industry who would have us believe that it is. On the one hand there is the overzealous service bureau salesperson who claims that almost everything should be and can be handled by a vendor. On the other hand there is the consultant who advises that programs should be handled in-house so that fat consulting fees can be collected. Finally there are revenue-hungry telephone company account executives who exaggerate the "simplicity" of setting up in-house operations.

It is wise to remember from the beginning that service bureau personnel, consultants, and telco account execs may put their own self-interest ahead of your best interests when helping you make your decision. One good way to gauge the trustworthiness of such advice is to find out if the opposite advice has ever been offered. When service bureau representatives tell you that your program should be handled by a vendor, ask them if they have ever advised anyone to set up in-house and, if so, who. Likewise, ask the consultants and telco account execs if they have ever advised clients to use a vendor. Whatever advice you are receiving, you should know that each case is different. By better understanding the specific advantages offered by both options, you will be better able to make the right decision.

[1] Excerpts from v. 3, no. 15, of *AIS* "800" Report, which is published twice monthly by Advertising Information Services, Inc., New York, New York.

Advantages of Out-of-House Service Bureaus

LOWER COSTS. By combining your volume with that of other clients, a service center can generate sufficient volume to reduce dramatically labor and telephone costs, which make up as much as 80 percent of total costs. Most of these companies charge minimal set-up fees and have low minimum charges per month. The cost factor is especially important in start-up situations where you may be unwilling to make large-scale capital investments.

QUICKER, EASIER START-UP. A service center can set up a program faster, cheaper, and with fewer problems than is usually possible in-house, because experienced telephone representatives and the necessary lines and equipment are usually already in place.

ROUND-THE-CLOCK OPERATION. For inbound telemarketers it is often important to answer calls 24 hours a day 365 days a year. Most out-of-house centers provide this service. It is very seldom economically feasible for an in-house operation to do so unless the call volume is substantial.

KNOWLEDGE AND EXPERIENCE. Service centers are often run by the most capable and experienced managers in the telephone marketing field. Their operations know-how allows them to avoid mistakes you might make on your own. They may even have handled programs similar to yours and have access to hard data which can be helpful in planning.

TESTING SIMPLIFIED. A service center is often the best place to conduct a test of a new program. You can determine the program's viability very quickly and with very little initial capital outlay.

GREATER ABILITY TO HANDLE PEAKS. Inbound calls, particularly in response to broadcast advertising, come in patterns showing pronounced peaks and valleys. A large service center with dozens of lines will usually be better equipped to handle such peaks than would the typical in-house operation with ten or fewer lines. For this reason calls in response to broadcast ads are usually handled out-of-house.

Drawbacks to Working with Outside Service Centers

FREQUENT BUSIES. Inbound service bureaus are able to provide economical service only maintaining call patterns that result in many callers' receiving busy signals. If you use a service center, you know that some of your potential customers will not be able to get through. In addition, if you share the service with a broadcast advertiser whose response rates are underestimated, your customers may experience increased busy signals as a result. Several marketers had that experience when Elvis Presley died suddenly at a time when his records were being marketed on TV.

BANKRUPTCY. The telephone service center business is not an easy one. The past five years have seen the sudden bankruptcies of several major services—both inbound and outbound. In some cases the phone company simply shut off the center's phone lines with no warnings to the center's clients. The clients then had to scramble to find new centers. This can be particularly damaging in inbound telemarketing if advertising has been placed before the center is shut down.

Advantages of In-House Operations

CONTROL. The number one advantage of the in-house operation is control. You hire the telephone representatives, train them, and write their scripts. In inbound operations, you control how many lines are installed, how many phone reps are working, and how much advertising is generating calls.

ACCESSIBILITY OF DATA BASE. In an in-house operation, your phone reps can have access to your company's data base, including customer records and inventory. They can thus confirm delivery, authorize credit, suggest alternatives to out-of-stock items, and ask for up-sells and add-ons.

ABILITY TO HANDLE COMPLEX CALLS. In-house programs can handle highly technical calls and customer service calls . . . . most customer service operations and many complex industrial sales programs are handled in-house. The ability to handle difficult or complicated calls is a function of the hiring and training programs for the phone reps.

EMPLOYEE COMMITMENT. Answering telephones involves people, and it is easier to get good performance from people who are committed to you and your company.

In addition you can train them in the total scope of the company and its products. You can, in short, make their employment more rewarding and a possible avenue for further advancement within your organization.

EXPERIENCE ACCUMULATION. With your own internal telemarketing department you will be able to accumulate a variety of experience from your operation in a much greater quantity than if you use outside services. When your telephone representatives are physically close to you, you will be able to spend a great deal more time observing and listening to calls.

Drawbacks of In-House Operations

UNFAMILIAR MANAGEMENT PROBLEMS. Telephone marketing involves a range of management problems that are more familiar to factory foremen than to most marketing personnel. In particular, telemarketing is labor intensive, often employing people on a part-time basis at near minimum wage. Many companies do not have the management capabilities and commitment necessary to run such an operation.

LARGE CAPITAL OUTLAY. An in-house operation requires tremendous initial expenditures for real estate, desks, phone lines, telephone sets, CRTs, hiring, training, etc. Often it is difficult to justify gambling such expenses on an untested program.

Assess Your Situation

Before making your decision, assess your situation. Ask yourself what type of campaign you are contemplating and what you expect to accomplish. Make an honest appraisal of your company's resources, its management capabilities, and its commitment to the program. If your needs involve handling response to broadcast ads, you will probably want to go out-of-house. If you anticipate calls of a highly technical nature and are convinced that you have the necessary resources and commitment, take the program in-house. If you would like calls to be handled by people committed to your company but are unable to justify the upfront expenditures on an untried program, test it first out-of-house and bring it in-house if it proves viable.

HOW TO CHOOSE
AN OUT-OF-HOUSE TELEMARKETING CENTER[2]

Once you have decided to place your business out-of-house, how do you go about choosing which center to use?

Criteria for Making the Choice

The first step in choosing a telemarketing service center is putting together a list of the criteria to be used in making the decision. Following are the most important characteristics for which to look.

[2] Excerpts from v. 3, no. 16, of *AIS* "800" Report.

FINANCIAL STABILITY. Financial stability is listed first because it may well be the most important criterion. The telemarketing industry has seen over a dozen service centers go bankrupt with little or no advance notice to clients.

The problem of service center bankruptcies has been particularly severe on the inbound 800 number side of the business.

Check into the company's history and credit rating. If possible, pull a Dun and Bradstreet report on the company.

EXPERIENCE. Recently the telephone has become the hottest medium in direct marketing. As a result, quite a few "Johnny Come Lately's" have entered the service center business. It is important that you place your business with a firm that has been in existence long enough (at least 2 years) to have worked out any bugs. The managers of the operation should be people with several years of telemarketing management experience. Also make certain that the service center has experience in handling your type of program. If you are a fund-raiser, make certain the company you choose has handled fund-raisers. If you are a broadcast advertiser, be sure the company has handled broadcast response.

MANAGEMENT. In addition to checking on the experience of the company's managers, make sure that they are people with whom you can work. Inquire what their management philosophies are. It is important to have good personal relations with the managers of your telemarketing service because you will be working extremely closely with them.

CAPABILITIES. How many lines and phone representatives does the service center maintain? Is this enough to fulfill your needs? For outbound programs, it is important that enough reps and lines are available to complete your program within the specified time frame. For inbound programs, it is essential that there be enough lines to handle the response generated. Most centers have busy reports, either generated by their own equipment or by the local telephone company. Ask to see these reports; they can tell you how good a job the company does in staffing for peaks.

CLIENTS. Find out who the company's past and current clients are. Particularly for inbound telemarketing, it is important to be certain that the center has no clients that might be objectionable to your target audience.

COMMITMENT. How committed is the company to telephone marketing? Is telemarketing the major business of the organization or simply an adjunct to another business? A few service centers have gotten into the business because they had WATS lines that were not being fully utilized.

CONTROLS. Make certain that the service you choose has adequate systems to provide for the monitoring of telephone reps and for checking that orders are taken and delivered accurately. Monitoring is of particular importance in outbound programs or inbound programs involving upselling. Telephone reps will probably be compensated in part by commissions.[3] Monitoring is essential to ensure that your offer is delivered as you intended. If reps are allowed to chalk up orders by stressing free trial offers or (as has happened in some instances) enter bogus orders to collect commissions, your back end will suffer.

COST. The cost of service is an important consideration, but it should not be paramount. In inbound programs a service that charges a higher per call rate may in the end be more economical. Remember that your biggest expense will probably be your advertising. A service that is more expensive because it maintains more lines may give you a lower cost per order because it will capture more orders to cover the cost of advertising.

In outbound programs cost comparisons should be based on back end results. A service that offers extensive monitoring and controls may be more expensive on an hourly basis or even on the basis of the number of orders obtained on the front end. When back end results are read, however, the service that seemed more expensive may provide more *paid* orders and thus be more economical on the basis of the cost per paid order.

TELEPHONE REPS. What is the general quality of the telephone reps who staff the service center? How extensively are they trained? Remember the service center will be your company's voice to your customers.

EQUIPMENT. Does the service center have the telecommunications and data processing equipment necessary to do the job? Will the software allow your orders to be entered the way you want? Has all equipment been in operation for at least six months?

LOCATION. You may need to visit the center frequently; it will be helpful if it is reasonably close and easy to get to. Is the center located in an area where there is enough labor available to handle your program? Is the center located in a city that has sufficient excess network capacity so that you are not shut down by an "all circuits busy" situation?

FULFILLMENT CAPACITY. Is the company set up to handle your order processing equipment? How will orders be delivered to you? Is direct computer link available? Does the company provide its own letter shop?

[3] This is more often true for direct sales programs.

MEDIA. For inbound programs, it is crucial that your center be able to handle response to the media you use. If you are generating response from print media, make certain you are not going to be crowded out by broadcast advertisers. For print response you should look for a company that specializes only in print response or that maintains a group of lines at the head of its rotor group exclusively for print response. For broadcast response, make certain the center has the necessary capacity and know-how.

How to Proceed

Once you have a clear idea of which criteria are most important for your program and what capabilities you will require, it is time to begin the selection process. PLAN. It is vital that the steps in your selection process be planned and that you allow sufficient time to carry them out. Know that information you need to capture during the call and know the form in which you will want your data . . . . INVESTIGATE. Assemble a list of all the possible service centers . . . QUESTION. Draw up a list of questions for the centers you are considering . . . COMPARE . . . MONITOR . . . . CHECK REFERENCES . . . VISIT. Make on-site inspections of the centers . . . MAKE THE CHOICE.

Index